Brave, Not Perfect

Brave, Not Perfect

Fear Less, Fail More, and Live Bolder

Reshma Saujani

Currency
New York

CURRENCY and its colophon are trademarks of
Penguin Random House LLC.

Currency books are available at special discounts for bulk purchases for
sales promotions or corporate use. Special editions, including personalized
covers, excerpts of existing books, or books with corporate logos, can
be created in large quantities for special needs. For more information,
contact Premium Sales at (212) 572–2232 or e-mail specialmarkets@
penguinrandomhouse.com.

Library of Congress Cataloging-in-Publication Data
Names: Saujani, Reshma, author.
Title: Brave, not perfect : fear less, fail more, and live bolder /
Reshma Saujani.
Description: 1 Edition. | New York : Currency, 2019. |
Includes bibliographical references and index.
Identifiers: LCCN 2018017150 | ISBN 9781524762339 (hardback)
Subjects: LCSH: Women—Psychology. | Girls—Psychology. |
Self-esteem in women. | Leadership in women. | BISAC: SELF-HELP /
Personal Growth / Success. | SOCIAL SCIENCE / Women's Studies.
Classification: LCC HQ1206 .S278 2019 | DDC 155.3/33—dc23
LC record available at https://lccn.loc.gov/2018017150

ISBN 978-1-5247-6233-9
Ebook ISBN 978-1-5247-6234-6
International Edition 978-1-9848-2491-2

Printed in the United States of America

Book design by Lauren Dong
Jacket design by Zak Tebbal

1 3 5 7 9 10 8 6 4 2

First Edition

To every "perfect" girl and woman:
You are braver than you know.

Contents

Introduction

Daring the Unthinkable

*I*n 2010, I did the unthinkable. At the age of thirty-three, never having held an elected position, I ran for US Congress.

Up until then, even though it had been my dream from the time I was thirteen years old to run for public office and effect real change, I had stayed safely tucked behind the scenes of politics. By day, I worked long, grueling hours in a big-name investment firm—a high-paying, glamorous job that I hated but stayed in because it was what I thought I was supposed to be doing. At night and in every spare moment on weekends, I worked as a fund-raiser and organizer; these were all valuable contributions that had impact, but in my heart, I wanted to play big and do big things.

With every passing day, I became more and more miserable in my job, until I reached a moment of deep despair when I knew something needed to change. That was when I heard a whisper in the New York political community that the sitting congresswoman in my district was going to vacate her seat after eighteen years to run for Senate. I knew this was my opening. I met with a few key people to ask what they thought, and everyone said enthusiastically that I should go for it. I knew how to raise money, I had good policy ideas, I had a good background story; although I had no experience personally running for office, the rest was there. For the first time in as long as I could remember, I felt fired up. I was finally heading toward the life of public service I'd always dreamed about, and there was no stopping me.

Then it happened. The congresswoman decided not to vacate her seat, which meant I would need to run against her if I wanted it. Suddenly, all the people who'd supported me and said go for it were saying, "Oh, no, no . . . you can't run against her." She was a venerable insider, a force to be reckoned with, and they said I didn't stand a chance. Not only did I lose the enthusiastic support of the female party elite—they outright told me it wasn't my turn and demanded that I back down.

But by that point, I was in too deep to give up. Here was my dream, just inches within reach. I *wanted* this—way too much to turn and run away. Believe me, there were plenty of moments that I thought to myself, *I must be nuts.* But I went for it anyway. I knew this would be my one shot and that I'd regret it for the rest of my life if I didn't take it.

To my surprise—and the surprise of a lot of other people—my race caught a lot of positive attention. Here I was, a young South Asian upstart who had never held public office, but people were listening, the campaign donations were flowing in; I was even endorsed by the *New York Observer* and the *Daily News.* I went from tentatively hopeful to confident I would win after being featured on the cover of two national newspapers, and having CNBC tout my race as one of the hottest in the country.

But when push came to shove, it turned out that voters cared a lot more about my lack of experience than anyone thought. I didn't just lose; I got clobbered, winning just 19 percent of the vote to my opponent's 81.

What's remarkable about this story isn't that I ran for Congress. Or how stunningly and spectacularly I ended up losing, or even how I picked myself back up after such a public and humiliating defeat. What makes this story worth telling is the fact that when I ran for public office at the age of thirty-three, it was the first time in my entire adult life that I had done something truly brave.

If you looked at my pedigree up until that point—Yale Law School, followed by a string of prestigious jobs in the corporate world—you probably would think I was a gutsy go-getter. But being a go-getter and being gutsy aren't necessarily the same. It was the drive to cultivate the perfect résumé that got me into Yale Law School after being rejected by them a whopping three times, not bravery. It wasn't genuine passion for the law or big business that compelled me to go after a job at a top-five law firm and then a premier financial assets management firm; it was the desire to please my immigrant father and fulfill his dreams for me. From the time I was a little girl, I had always set my sights on being the best, and every move I made was an effort to make me appear smart and competent and in turn open doors to other positions that would make me appear smart and competent. I made all these choices to build the "perfect me," because I believed that would lead to the perfect life.

Despite how things looked from the outside, none of my life choices up until that point were truly brave for one simple reason: there was nothing on the line. This was the first time I was going off-script, doing something that truly mattered to me, in a deeply personal way. It was the first time I had gone for something even though I wasn't 100 percent confident I could succeed and stood to lose far more than just the election if I failed. I could lose my dignity, my reputation, and my self-confidence. It could hurt, big-time. Could I recover from that?

I'm not alone in having spent my adult life only pursuing positions or projects I knew I'd ace. So many women stick to doing only the things at which they excel, rarely going beyond what makes them feel confident and comfortable. I hear this over and over from the thousands of women I meet around the country, regardless of their race, age, or economic circumstances. I heard it from the twenty-four-year-old dog walker I chatted with at Starbucks who had a fantastic idea for revolutionizing her service but was convinced she could never do it because she's "bad at business," and from the fifty-eight-year-old magazine editor I sat next to at a political fundraiser who told me she is miles past burned out and unhappy but won't leave her job, even though she can financially afford to. Why? Because, she says with a shrug, "It's what I'm good at." As CEO of the nonprofit Girls Who Code I see it in my young female employees who don't volunteer for projects in areas where they don't have prior experience, while the men jump hard and fast into unfamiliar territory without worrying one iota about failing or looking foolish.

There's a reason why we women feel and act this way. It has nothing to do with biology and everything to do with how we've been trained. As girls, we're taught from a very young age to play it safe. To strive to get all A's to please our parents and teachers. To be careful not to climb too high on the jungle gym so we don't fall and get hurt. To sit quietly and obediently, to look pretty, to be agreeable so we will be liked. Well-meaning parents and teachers guide us toward activities we excel at so we can shine, and they steer us away from the ones we aren't naturally good at to spare our feelings and grade point averages. Of course the intentions are good; no parent wants to see their daughter injured, disappointed, or discouraged. The bubble wrap in which we are cocooned comes with love and caring, so no one realizes how much it insulates us from taking risks and going after our dreams later in life.

Boys, on the other hand, absorb a very different message. They are taught to explore, play rough, swing high, climb to the top of the monkey bars—and fall down trying. They are encouraged to try new things, tinker with gadgets and tools, and get right back in the game if they take a hit. From a young age, boys are groomed to be adventurous. Research proves they are given freer rein to play on their own and are encouraged to attempt more daring physical activities with fewer directives and assistance from parents. By the time boys are teenagers asking someone on a date, or young adults negotiating their first raise, they are already well habituated to take risk after risk and are, for the most part, unfazed by failure. Unlike girls, they are rewarded with approval and praise for taking chances, even if things don't work out.

In other words, boys are taught to be *brave*, while girls are taught to be *perfect*.

Rewarded for perfection from the time we're young, we grow up to be women who are terrified to fail. We don't take risks in our personal and professional lives because we fear that we'll be judged, embarrassed, discredited, ostracized, or fired if we get it wrong. We hold ourselves back, consciously or unconsciously, from trying anything that we're not certain we'll ace to avoid the potential pain and humiliation. We won't take on any role or endeavor unless we are certain we can meet or exceed expectations.

Men, on the other hand, will jump into uncharted waters without hesitation or apprehension about what might happen if they don't succeed. Case in point: the now-famous corporate report that found that men apply for a job when they meet only 60 percent of the qualifications, but women apply only if they meet 100 percent of the qualifications.

We want to be perfect before we even try.

The need to be perfect holds us back in so many ways. We don't speak up for ourselves, as we know deep down we should, because we don't want to be seen as pushy, bitchy, or just straight-up unlikable. When we do speak up, we agonize and overthink how to express ourselves, trying to hit just the right note of assertiveness without seeming too "bossy" or aggressive. We obsessively analyze, consider, discuss, and weigh every angle before making a decision, no matter how small. And if we do, heaven forbid, make a mistake, we feel as though our world is falling apart.

And yet, when we hold ourselves back for fear of not being good enough, or fear of being rejected, we tamp down our dreams and narrow our world—along with our opportunities for happiness. How many offers or experiences have we passed up because we were afraid? How many brilliant ideas have we let go by, or personal goals have we backed away from, because we feared we wouldn't get it right? How many times have we begged off a position of leadership saying, "I'm just not good at that"? I believe this "perfect or bust" mentality is a big part of why women are underrepresented in C-suites, in boardrooms, in Congress, and pretty much everywhere you look.

This drive to be perfect takes a serious toll on our well-being, too, as we lose sleep ruminating over the slightest mistake or worrying that someone was offended by something we said or did. Trained to be helpful and accommodating at all costs, we run ourselves ragged trying to do it all and end up exhausted, depleted, even sick because we give away so much of our energy and time to others.

Our self-esteem takes a hit when we stay silent in moments we know we should have spoken up, or when we say yes when we really wanted to say no out of fear of not being liked. Our relationships and hearts suffer when we put up a glossy veneer of perfection; the protective layer may keep others from seeing our flaws and vulnerabilities, but it also isolates us from those we love and keeps us from forging truly meaningful and authentic connections.

Imagine if you lived without the fear of failure, without the fear of not measuring up. If you no longer felt the need to stifle your thoughts and swallow what you really want to say in order to please and appease others. If you could stop berating yourself mercilessly for human mistakes, let go of the guilt and the strangling pressure to be perfect, and just *breathe*. What if, in every decision you faced, you made the brave choice or took the bolder path. Would you be happier? Would you impact the world in the ways you dream you can? I believe the answer to both is yes.

I wrote *Brave, Not Perfect* because that pursuit of perfection caused me to hold myself back for too many years. At the age of thirty-three, I finally learned how to be brave in my professional life, which taught me how to be brave in my personal life, too. I've been exercising that bravery muscle every day since. It wasn't easy to go for in vitro fertilization after three devastating miscarriages, or to launch a tech start-up without knowing anything about coding (or about start-ups). But because I did these things, I am a deliriously happy mom to a little boy and am making a difference in the world in the way I always knew deep down I could.

When we relinquish the punishing need for perfection—or, rather, let go of the fear of *not* being perfect—we find freedom, joy, and all the other good stuff we want in life. It's time to stop giving up before we try. Because when we do give up on anything that is challenging or doesn't come to us naturally, we become trapped in a state of discontent and inertia that's soul crushing. We stay in the relationship that brings us pain, in the social circle that brings us down, in the career that makes us miserable. We let our good ideas wither and die on the vine; or, worse, we painfully watch others succeed at something we *knew* we should have pursued. Being afraid to try something new, to boldly ask for what we want, to make mistakes, and, yes, maybe even to look a little foolish leads to a lot of wasted brilliance, swallowed ambitions, and regret.

When we hold ourselves to the impossible standard of perfection, there's no such thing, really, as "success," because nothing is ever enough.

What if we just said, *Fuck it? I'm going to say what's on my mind even if they don't like it . . . or volunteer for that assignment that feels too hard . . . or make the life change I secretly dream about without worrying about the outcome.* What would our lives look like?

Letting go of the fear of being less than perfect is easier than you think. It all comes down to exercising your bravery muscles, one little bit at a time. That's what this book is about. It's a look at how we were wired way back when to pursue perfection and avoid failure at all costs, and how that girlhood wiring holds sway over us in our adult lives. Most importantly, it's about how to reset that wiring. It's never too late. By letting go of the need to be perfect and retraining ourselves to be brave, every one of us can dare her own version of the unthinkable.

Why Me?

How did I go from being a failed congressional candidate to a champion for women and bravery? Great question.

After I picked myself up off the floor—literally—in the weeks following my crushing defeat, I looked around and thought, *What's next?* As I searched inside myself for an answer, I thought about how, back when I was crisscrossing the city during my political campaign, I had visited numerous schools where I saw coding and robotics classes filled with boys, and how I couldn't stop thinking about the faces *I hadn't* seen. Where were the girls? It started to become clear to me that someone needed to take steps toward closing the gender gap in technology by reaching girls at an early age. Pretty quickly I knew that this was my next calling and how I would be of service in the big way I'd dreamed. By 2012, I'd founded Girls Who Code, which has grown into a national movement with more than ninety thousand girls in fifty states participating.

The original mission of Girls Who Code was to reverse the trend of girls' interest in STEM dropping off between the ages of thirteen and seventeen, so that by the year 2020, women will be on track to fill much more than just their current 3 percent of the 1.4 million jobs that will be available in computing-related fields. But once GWC got off the ground, I quickly realized we were doing far more than setting up these girls for future job success. By teaching them to code, we were also teaching them to be brave.

You see, coding is an endless process of trial and error with sometimes just a semicolon making all the difference between success and failure. Code breaks and falls apart, and it often takes many, many tries before you experience that magical moment when what you're trying to create comes to life. To get there requires perseverance and comfort with imperfection.

In February of 2016, I gave a TED talk based on what I'd

observed firsthand about girls, perfection, and bravery. The talk was a rallying cry to change how we were socializing our girls—and to encourage women to let go of our people-pleasing, perfectionist instincts and reclaim our voices, courage, and power.

The talk hit a deep nerve that took me by surprise. I knew the topic was profoundly meaningful to me, but it turns out that it resonated with thousands of girls and women around the country as well. Within days, emails started flooding in. Some women shared how they recognized themselves in the message. "I've been crying since I heard your talk," one wrote. "I realized how much I do this to myself," said another. I heard from countless women who shared how they had passed up opportunities because they were afraid of appearing foolish, of failing, of not living up to the impossible standards they set for themselves.

Some of the emails made me cry as I read how women and girls felt tyrannized by perfectionism: "When I make a mistake or let someone down, I beat myself up for days," one woman said. "It's all I can think about." Another wrote, "Everyone thinks I'm this person who has everything under control . . . if they only knew how hard I work to look that way and how afraid I am that someone will see the mess that I really am."

Others made me indescribably proud. One college sophomore wrote about how, after many years crying in frustration over homework, unable to ask for help, afraid of being seen as dumb, alienated in school because of her own fixation on perfection, she finally let go of her need to be perfect. "It was incredibly empowering," she wrote. "I can ask questions. So what if an ignorant person thinks I'm dumb because I need something clarified? I'm here for myself and my education."

I heard from parents of kindergartners worried about how

hyperconcerned their five-year-old girls were with doing everything exactly "right," and from educators who wanted me to know they had sent mass emails or newsletters to parents imploring them to watch my talk with their family.

The message of "brave, not perfect" continued to spread through bloggers and social media, and through interviews with major news outlets. As of the writing of this book, the TED talk has been viewed almost four million times. I've had the privilege of speaking at the Fortune Most Powerful Women Summit and with former first lady Michelle Obama at the United States of Women Summit in Washington, D.C.

That's all been exciting and gratifying, but for me, the most amazing part has been seeing firsthand how the "brave, not perfect" message is sparking personal and meaningful change. Each week, I travel to at least one or two cities to speak at conferences, schools, and corporations; and everywhere I go, I am overwhelmed and touched to learn how my talk inspired women and girls to try something new or intimidating, even if it scared the hell out of them. To ask the questions, or venture the answer, even if they worried they would look foolish or appear less than polished. To leave the "safe" career path for the one they'd always dreamed of, even if people told them they were crazy. To take that leap into the unknown, even if they knew they might stumble and fall—and trust that the world wouldn't come to an end even if they did.

I wrote this book because I believe that every single one of us can learn to be brave enough to achieve our greatest dreams. Whether that dream is to be a multimillionaire, to climb Mt. Everest, or just to live without the fear of judgment hanging over our heads all the time, it all starts to become possible when we override our perfect-girl programming and retrain ourselves to be brave.

No more silencing or holding ourselves back, or teaching

our daughters to do the same. It's time to stop this paradigm in its tracks. And just in case you're thinking that bravery is a luxury reserved for the 1 percent, let me assure you: I've spoken to women across a wide range of backgrounds and economic circumstances, and this is a problem that affects us all. My goal is to create a far-reaching movement of women that will inspire *all* women to embrace imperfection, so they can build a better life and a better world. No more letting opportunities go by, no more dimming our brilliance, no more deferring our dreams. It's time to stop pursuing perfection and start chasing bravery instead.

Anaïs Nin wrote, "Life shrinks or expands in proportion to one's courage." If this is true—and I believe that it is—then courage is the key to living the biggest life we can create for ourselves. I am writing this book because I believe every woman deserves a shot at breaking free from the perfection-or-bust chokehold and living the joyful, audacious life she was meant to lead.

Part One

How Girls Are Trained for Perfection

1

Sugar and Spice and Everything Nice

Sixteen-year-old Erica is a shining star. The daughter of two prominent professors, she is the vice president of her class with an impeccable grade point average. Her report card is peppered with praise from her teachers about her diligence and what a joy she is to have in class. She volunteers twice a month at a local hospital. At the end of sophomore year, she was voted "Best Smile" by her classmates, and her friends will tell you she's the sweetest person they know.

Beneath that bright smile, though, things aren't quite as sunny. If you open Erica's journal, you'll read about how she feels like it's her full-time job to be perfect in order to make everyone else happy. You'll learn that she works to the point of exhaustion every night and all weekend to get all A's and please her parents and teachers; disappointing them is just about the worst thing she can imagine. Once, because of an accidental scheduling mistake, she had to back out of a debate competition at school because it conflicted with a volunteer trip she'd committed to go on with her church; she was so hysterical that her teacher was going to "hate her" that she literally made herself sick.

Erica despises volunteering at the hospital (don't even get her started on emptying the bedpans . . .) but sticks with it because her guidance counselor said it would look good on her college applications. Even though she desperately wanted to try out for cheerleading team because she thought it looked like fun, she didn't, because her friends told her the jumps were really hard to learn and the last thing she wanted to do was make an idiot of herself. Truth be told, she doesn't really even like most of her friends, who can be mean and catty, but she just quietly goes along with what they say and do because it's too scary to imagine doing otherwise.

Like so many girls, Erica is hardwired to please everyone, play it safe, and avoid any hint of failure at all costs.

I know this story because today, Erica is forty-two and a good friend of mine. She is still supersweet with a dazzling smile—and still a prisoner of her own perfectionism. A successful political consultant with no kids, she works until after midnight most nights to impress her colleagues and overdeliver for her clients. Every time I see her she looks fabulously put together; she's that friend who always says just the right thing, always sends just the right gift or note, and is always on time. But just like her sixteen-year-old self, she'll only reveal privately that she still feels strangled by the constant need to please everyone. I asked her recently what she would do if she didn't care what anyone else thought. She immediately ticked off a list of goals and dreams she wished she had the guts to go after but wouldn't dare, ranging from telling her biggest client that she disagrees with his strategies to moving out of the city and having a child on her own.

Our culture has shaped generations of perfect girls like Erica who grow up to be women afraid to take a chance. Afraid of speaking their minds, of making bold choices, of owning and celebrating their achievements, and of living the life *they* want to live, without constantly seeking outside approval. In other words: afraid of being brave.

From the time they are babies, girls absorb hundreds of micromessages each day telling them that they should be nice, polite, and polished. Adoring parents and caretakers dress them impeccably in color-coordinated outfits (with matching bows) and tell them how pretty they look. They are praised mightily for being A students and for being helpful, polite, and accommodating and are chided (however lovingly) for being messy, assertive, or loud.

Well-meaning parents and educators guide girls toward activities and endeavors they are good at so they can shine, and steer them away from ones they might find frustrating, or worse, at which they could fail. It's understandable because we see girls as vulnerable and fragile, we instinctively want to protect them from harm and judgment.

Our boys, on the other hand, are given freedom to roam, explore, get dirty, fall down, and yes, fail—all in the name of teaching them to "man up" as early as possible. Even now, for all our social progress, people get a little uncomfortable if a boy is too hesitant, cautious, or vulnerable—let alone sheds a tear. I see this even with my own twenty-first-century feminist husband, who regularly roughhouses with my son to "toughen him up" and tells me to let him cry it out when he's screaming at night. I once asked him if he would do the same if Shaan were a girl and he immediately responded, "Of course not."

Of course, these beliefs don't vanish just because we grow up. If anything, the pressure on women to be perfect ramps up as life gets more complex. We go from trying to be perfect students and daughters to perfect professionals, perfect girlfriends, perfect wives, and perfect mommies, hitting the marks we're supposed to and wondering why we're overwhelmed, frustrated, and unhappy. Something is just *missing*. We did everything right, so what went wrong?

When you're writing a book about women and perfectionism,

you start to see it everywhere. In airports, at coffee shops, at conferences, at the nail salon . . . pretty much anywhere I went, I'd strike up a conversation on the topic and women would invariably sigh or roll their eyes knowingly, nod or laugh in recognition, or get sad as they shared a personal story. They'd tell me how their daily lives are ruled by a relentless inner drive to do everything flawlessly, from curating their Instagram feed to pleasing their partner (or struggling to find the "perfect" partner) to raising all-star kids who are also well adjusted (and who go straight from a year of breastfeeding to eating homemade, organic meals); from staying in shape and looking "good for their age" to striving ceaselessly to be the best in the office, in their congregation or volunteer group or community, in Soul-Cycle and CrossFit classes, and everywhere else.

So many women of all ages opened up to me about unfulfilled life dreams or ambitions they harbor because they're too afraid to act on them. Regardless of ethnicity, profession, economic circumstances, or what town they call home, I was struck by how many of their experiences were the same. You'll hear from many of them throughout this book.

But first, I want to show you all the ways the drive to be perfect got ingrained in us. What follows in this chapter is a glimpse into how our perfectionism took root as girls, how it shaped us as women, and how it colored every choice we've made along the way. We need to understand how we got here so we can thoughtfully navigate our way out. This is the beginning of the road map that leads us off a path of regret and onto one where we fully express who and what we most want to be.

The Origins of Perfectionism

Where along the way did we trade in our confidence and courage for approval and acceptance? And why?

The categorization of girls as pleasant and agreeable starts almost as soon as they're born. Instinctually, whether we realize it or not, we ascribe certain expectations to infants we see in pink or blue; babies in pink are all sugar and spice, babies in blue are tough little men. But it turns out that we even make assumptions when there are no other telltale signs of gender. One study showed that when infants are dressed in a neutral color, adults tend to identify the ones who appear upset or angry as boys, and those they described as nice and happy as girls. The training begins before we're even out of onesies.

In girls, the drive to be perfect shows up and bravery shuts down somewhere around age eight—right around the time when our inner critic shows up. You know the one I'm talking about: it's that nitpicking voice in your head that tells you every which way you aren't as good as others . . . that you blew it . . . that you should feel guilty or ashamed . . . that you *fucking suck* (I don't know about yours, but my inner critic can be a bit harsh).

Catherine Steiner-Adair is a renowned clinical psychologist, school consultant, and research associate at Harvard Medical School. She works with hundreds of girls and young women across the country and has seen firsthand how devastating perfectionism can be.

At around the age of eight, she says, kids start to see that ability and agility matter. "That's the age when girls start to develop different interests, and they want to bond with others who do what they like to do. Along with that awareness of differences comes an inner sense of who and what is better."

This is also the age in which kids begin to be graded, ranked, and told their scores—whether it's in soccer, math, or music, Steiner-Adair explains. "If you're told you're not as good, it requires a great deal of courage and self-esteem to try something. This sets the stage for getting a C means you're bad at it, and you don't like it. That feeds the lack of courage."

As girls get older, their radars sharpen. Around this age, they start to tune in when their moms compare themselves to others ("I wish I looked like that in jeans") or talk about other girls or women critically ("She should *not* be wearing that"). Suddenly they're caught up in this dynamic of comparison, and naturally redirect their radar inward to determine where they fall on the spectrum of pretty or not, bright or average, unpopular or adored.

These impulses are so deeply ingrained in us as adults and parents that we don't realize how much we inadvertently model them for our girls. Catherine shared a story from her own life that brought the point home. When her daughter was in third grade, she and some classmates overheard one mom say to another girl, "You have such pretty hair." Some of the girls stopped dead in their tracks and furrowed their brows as if to wonder, *So is my hair pretty or ugly?* And so it begins.

The Overpowering Need to Please

Like most women, I was taught from an early age to be helpful, obedient, and care for other people's needs, even to put them above my own. When my parents told me not to date until I was sixteen, I didn't. When they said no makeup, or showing cleavage, or staying out past 10 p.m., I obeyed. I complied at all times with the behavior my family expected

of me. In our Indian household, one greeted elders by touching their feet as a sign of respect; if I came home from school
with a friend and found an older auntie there having tea, I
would never dream of disrespecting my parents by not doing
it, although I was mortified in front of my friend. At family
dinners, my sister and I set and cleared the table, never questioning why our male cousins didn't have to take a turn. Even
though I would have much rather been outside playing with
my friends, I always agreed to babysit my neighbor's (bratty)
kids. That's just what helpful girls my age did.

Thus began my lifelong mission to be the perfect daughter,
the perfect girlfriend, the perfect employee, the perfect mom.
In this I know I'm not alone. We go from yes-girls to yes-
women, caught in a never-ending cycle of constantly having
to prove our worth to others—and to ourselves—by being
selfless, accommodating, and agreeable.

A great example of how powerful the people-pleasing im-
pulse can be comes from an experiment about lemonade. Yes,
lemonade. ABC News, with the help of psychologist Camp-
bell Leaper from the University of California, gave groups of
boys and girls a glass of lemonade that was objectively awful
(they added salt instead of sugar) and asked how they liked
it. The boys immediately said, "Eeech . . . this tastes disgusting!" All the girls, however, politely drank it, even choked it
down. Only when the researchers pushed and asked the girls
why they hadn't told them the lemonade was terrible did the
girls admit that they hadn't wanted to make the researchers
feel bad.

The need to please people often shows up in the way girls
scramble to give the "right" answer. Ask a girl her opinion
on a topic and she'll do a quick calculation. Should she say
what the teacher/parent/friend/boy is looking for her to say,

or should she reveal what she genuinely thinks and believes? It usually comes down to whichever she thinks will be more likely to secure approval or affection.

Girls are also far more likely than boys to say yes to requests even when they really want (and even need) to say no. Remember, being accommodating has been baked into their emotional DNA. When I ask girls what they do if a friend asks them to do her a favor they really don't want or have time to do, nearly all say they would do it anyway. Why? Hallie, a freckle-faced fourteen-year-old, neatly summed it up with a "duh, that's so obvious" shrug: "No one wants their friends to think she's a bitch. I mean, *no one*."

The internal pressure to say yes only gets stronger as we grow up. Like Dina, who works long hours as an attorney but somehow felt guilted into agreeing to be her son's class parent. So many of us give our time, attention, maybe even money, to people or causes that are not a priority to us because we don't want to hurt anyone's feelings (mostly, though, because we don't want them to think badly of us).

Boys, and the men they become, rarely feel this way. Janet, a forty-four-year-old manager at a clothing store, cringes anytime she reads an email that her husband, a general contractor, sends for work because she thinks his directness sounds harsh. He bluntly asks for what he needs or states his opinion, never softens critical feedback, and signs his emails without any salutations. No "best wishes" or even "thanks." When she once suggested he soften the tone of an email to a vendor he worked with so as to not piss him off, he told her, "It's not my job to be liked. It's my job to get my point across."

She, on the other hand, peppers her emails to her boss and coworkers with friendly lead-ins, praise, and, occasionally, a smiley face emoji. She reads over every email at least three times, editing and reediting it before she hits send. "My husband thinks I'm being neurotic when I do that," Janet told me. "I think I'm being thorough. But if I'm being really honest, I'd say I'm being cautious so I don't annoy or offend anyone."

I work with an executive coach who tells me all the time that being liked is overrated. She does not say this to the über-successful male CEOs she coaches; she doesn't have to. After all, their role models are men like Steve Jobs and Jeff Bezos who are notorious for not being people pleasers, so they don't give a damn whether they're liked or not.

Despite my coach's urgings, I *do* worry about being liked. Running for office, especially in New York City, I built a pretty tough skin when it comes to public criticism. But on a day-to-day level, I care whether my team likes me. I care a lot. I want them to think I'm the most amazing boss they've ever had—which makes giving them critical feedback really hard. I do it, because I know I have to be the CEO, but *ugh*. In my personal life, I get completely twisted up inside if I have a disagreement with a friend or if I sense my parents or husband are upset with me. I've definitely spent nights worrying about how a colleague, an acquaintance—even a complete stranger!—may have interpreted something I've said, and I've soft-pedaled way too many times when I really should have ripped someone a new one.

Just yesterday a guy cut in front of me in line while I was buying a sandwich and even though I was pissed, I didn't say a word because I didn't want to be rude—and this was someone I didn't even know and would likely never see again. And I too have been guilty of saying nice things even when I secretly think the exact opposite, so as to not offend (hello, salty lemonade). Haven't we all?

The result of all this toxic people pleasing is that your whole life can quickly become about what others think, and very little about what *you* genuinely want, need, and believe—let alone what you deserve. We've become conditioned to compromise and shrink ourselves in order to be liked. The problem is, when you work so hard to get everyone to like you, you very often end up not liking yourself so much. But once you learn to be brave enough to stop worrying about pleasing everyone else and put yourself first (which you will!), that's when you become the empowered author of your own life.

The "Softer" Sex

One sunny Saturday morning in late May, I sat on a bench in a playground in downtown Manhattan watching my husband, Nihal, and our then sixteen-month-old son, Shaan, play. Or, rather, I was watching my son bop from the monkey bars to the jungle gym and back again while Nihal stood a decent distance away and watched. Shaan's shirt was smeared with strawberry ice cream and his nose was filled with boogers, but he didn't care—and neither did I. Still new to the whole vertical coordination thing, Shaan toppled over a couple of times as he waddled from one end of the playground to another; each time, rather than run to his rescue, Nihal calmly waited for him to get up and keep going. At one point, I looked over and saw him coaxing Shaan, who was a little scared, down the big slide. "You can do this . . . you're a big boy . . . you're not afraid!"

Nearby, a few older boys were play-fighting using sticks as swords and chasing one another. Lots of happy hollering and a sea of dirty, scabby knees and elbows: a classic case of grade-school boys at play.

Meanwhile, over at the sandbox, five girls who looked to be around three years old were playing quietly. No ice-cream-smeared shirts or booger-encrusted noses there. Wearing cute coordinated outfits, they took turns scooping piles of sand to make a pretend cake, while their moms watched intently from a few feet away. In a ten-minute span, three of the five moms jumped up from their perches and climbed into the sandbox—one to straighten her daughter's headband and another to reprimand her daughter for being "rude" by taking the shovel from another girl. The third mom rushed to her daughter's aid after her sand "cake" fell over and hurriedly helped her daughter rebuild it while making soothing noises and wiping the tears from the girl's face. When the cake was fixed, the little girl smiled and her mom beamed with pride, "There's my happy girl!"

You can't make this stuff up.

Nearly everything I'd read, researched, witnessed, and interviewed experts about over the past year was playing out right in front of me. Go figure: a classic illustration of how boys are socialized to be brave and girls to be perfect, right here on a little asphalt playground less than ten minutes from my apartment.

At the same time we're applauding our girls for being nice, polite, and perfect, we are also telling them in not-so-subtle ways that bravery is the domain of boys. What I saw that day on the playground reminded me of another scene I'd witnessed just a few months earlier in Shaan's swim class. Parents were encouraging their timid sons to "be tough," and shouting with glee when their boys jumped into the deep end. If one of the little girls in the class was afraid to jump in, however, her fears were met with soft, reassuring coos: "It's okay, honey . . . just take my hand . . . you don't have to get your face wet." This one really made no sense to me; I mean, how do you go swimming without getting wet?

This isn't just casual observation on my part. Studies

show that parents provide much more hands-on assistance and words of caution to their daughters, while their sons are given encouragement and directives from afar and then left to tackle physical challenges on their own. We start with protecting girls physically, and the coddling continues on from there.

So many of these patterns are perpetuated because as parents, we're punished socially for violating them. A woman named Kelly told me a story about a group excursion she took to Oregon with her son and daughter, along with several other families. After taking a mountain bike ride, they hiked up a cliff where the rocks create a natural slide into the water. Their guide, Billy, helped all the kids out onto the rocks and offered them a push down the slide. The boys all went right away, but Kelly's usually courageous daughter was nervous. Instead of encouraging her the way he had done with the boys—that is, by just giving them a little shove—Billy helped her off the cliff and gently assured her that she didn't have to go if she didn't want.

Meanwhile, Kelly, knowing that her daughter is usually fearless, was hollering from the bottom, "Go, Ellie!" When it became clear that Billy wasn't going to give her a nudge as he did for the boys, she screamed up the cliff, "JUST PUSH HER!" Everyone around was *horrified*. "Every adult on the tour gave me the side-eye," she remembers. "They didn't even try to hide their judgment about how I was encouraging someone to push my daughter to be brave. We're not supposed to do that to our daughters."

The belief that boys are tough and resilient while girls are vulnerable and need to be protected is both deeply and widely held. In 2017, the World Health Organization released a groundbreaking study done in partnership with Johns Hopkins Bloomberg School of Public Health. Across fifteen countries, from the United States to China to Nigeria, these very gender stereotypes proved to be universal and enduring; and the study found that children buy into this myth at a very early age.

This "girls are softer" mentality extends beyond the playground, often straight into the classroom. One problem is what girls focus on when they're given difficult feedback. When girls are told they got a wrong answer or made a mistake, all they hear is condemnation, which sears like a flaming arrow straight through the heart. They go straight from "I did this wrong" to "I suck" to "I give up," rarely stopping at "Oh, I see how I could do this better next time."

The bigger problem, however, is how adults respond. To spare the girls' fragile feelings, we naturally temper anything that sounds too critical. More protection, more soft-pedaling, more steering girls to what's "safe," more feeding the self-fulfilling prophecy of girls as vulnerable. But if they are constantly shielded from any sharp edges, how can they be expected to build any resilience to avoid falling apart later in life if (more like when) they run up against real criticism or setbacks?

Boys, on the other hand, have repeatedly been shown to bounce right back from criticism or negative feedback, so we don't hold back. Brad Brockmueller, one of our Girls Who Code instructors who teaches at the Career and Technical Academy in Sioux Falls, readily admits that teachers feel they need to tailor their feedback differently for boys and girls. "If boys try something and get it wrong, they'll just keep trying and coming back," he said. "With girls, I have to focus on what they got right first before telling them what doesn't work, then encourage them." He recalls the time he had the class making network cables and one of the girls got frustrated because she couldn't get it right. "She wanted to give up, but to keep her going, I had to reinforce how much of it she'd gotten right and how close she was to nailing it. Some of the boys came up to me with a cable that wasn't well done and I literally took a scissors and chopped off the end and said, 'Nope, not right; try again.' And they did."

Brad also currently coaches the girls' basketball team, which he's found to be much different from his experience coaching the boys. "With girls you have to stay constantly positive," he says. "If you go negative or critical, they just shut down and there's nothing you can do to pull them out of that funk. If boys lose, it's just a game . . . they figure they'll play hundreds of games in their high school career, they'll get over one loss. For girls, a loss is personally defeating. They think, 'Why am I even playing basketball at all?'"

Debbie Hanney is the principal of Lincoln Middle School, an all-girls school in Rhode Island. She sees many parents caught between wanting to teach their daughters resilience and wanting to shield them from the sting of failure. She describes how, when a girl gets a 64 on a test, parents immediately swoop in and focus on how their daughter can get that grade up or take the test over. "We try to explain it as one thing on the continuum, but parents are understandably nervous in this day and age. It's hard trying to encourage them to let their daughters fail," she says.

It's deep stuff, this urge to protect and shield girls from disappointment and pain. Even more profound are the long-term effects, which many of us feel today as grown women. If we think about how horrified we are by the idea of failing, whether it's a serious rejection or a little mistake that we ruminate over for days, we can see how avoiding disappointment in our early life sliced into our resilience. We just didn't get the practice we needed to give us the bounceback that life demands. The good news here is that it's never too late. We can build resilience through bravery, and in later chapters, I'll show you how.

Perfection or Bust

When girls first walk into our Girls Who Code program, we immediately see their fear of not getting it right on full display. Every teacher in our program tells the same story.

At some point during the early lessons, a girl will call her over and say she is stuck. The teacher will look at her screen and the girl's text editor will be blank. If the teacher didn't know any better, she'd think her student had spent the past twenty minutes just staring at the screen.

But if she presses "undo" a few times, she'll see that her student wrote code and deleted it. The student tried. She came close. But she didn't get it exactly right. Instead of showing the progress she made, she'd rather show nothing at all.

Perfection or bust.

Dr. Meredith Grossman is a psychologist on the Upper East Side of Manhattan. With its concentration of highly competitive private schools, it is arguably the high-pressure-school capital of the world. She works with many girls to help them manage anxiety, and I asked her to tell me a little about what she sees on a daily basis.

"What's fascinating is the extreme amount of work they put into everything, and how much they underestimate their performance," she said. "I work with a lot of highly intelligent girls, and the quality of their writing is superior to what most adults can produce. But I constantly hear, 'I couldn't possibly turn that in.' They write and rewrite five times. They'd rather ask for an extension than turn something in they think isn't perfect."

As soon as one paragraph or paper is polished to perfection, it's on to the next. There's no break in the cycle because it's rare that their extreme efforts don't pay off. "Perfection begets more perfection," Meredith explained. "Every time a student overstudies or rewrites something five times and gets a good grade, it gets reinforced that she needs to do that again to succeed."

For every girl who writes and rewrites her papers until she's bleary-eyed, there's a woman who reads (and rereads, and rereads . . .) an email, report, or even a simple birthday card before sending it to make sure it hits precisely the right note, or spends weeks planning the ideal dinner party or a family trip to make everyone happy, or changes her outfit six times before leaving the house. We revise, rework, and refine to get things just right, often to a point of obsession or frustration that takes us out of the game.

Whether I'm speaking at a private school in New York City or at a community center in Scranton, Pennsylvania, I ask the girls in the audience the same question: "How many of you strive to be perfect?" Almost without exception, 99 percent of the hands in the room shoot up. Not with embarrassment— with smiles. They *know* they're trying to be perfect and are proud of it! They're rewarded for that behavior so they see it as a virtue. We heap praise on our girls for getting good grades, being well behaved and well liked, and for being good listeners, polite, cooperative, and all the other qualities that earn them gold stars on their report cards. We tell them that they're smart and talented, pretty and popular. They respond to these messages positively and wear them like a badge of honor. Is it any wonder that they see perfection as the only acceptable option?

In perfect-girl world, being judged harshly by their peers is the ultimate mortification; many girls and young women told me they won't post pictures on social media that are anything short of perfectly posed and meticulously edited. They'll take and retake a picture dozens of times to make sure it's flattering. One seventeen-year-old who suffers from a mild case of scleroderma, an autoimmune disease that caused a small patch of hardened skin on her forehead, admitted that she will anxiously spend up to an hour trying to take the perfectly arranged selfie in which her "patch" is 100 percent concealed by her long bangs. To make matters even more agonizing, the new thing is to go in the complete opposite direction and post "no filter" photos, which becomes a whole other level of pressure to capture that selfie that's "perfectly imperfect" *without* filters.

Girls will freely admit that they're afraid to blemish their records, so they don't take classes they aren't certain they can get a high grade in—no matter how interested they are in the subject. This continues through college, as they automatically close doors to career paths they could potentially love. It's not a coincidence that male economics majors outnumber women three to one; research done by Harvard economics professor Claudia Goldin revealed that women who earn B's in introductory economics are far more likely to switch majors than those who earn A's (while their male counterparts stick with it, B's be damned).

Appearing stupid is a huge concern. In perfect-girl world, being judged harshly by one's peers is the ultimate mortification; and it's been shown to be one of the main barriers girls face when they think about doing anything brave. For Destiny, math had always been a challenge. But the boys in her middle school made her feel far worse about it. "I'd be up at the board for a long time trying to work out a problem, and they'd say something like, 'You're so dumb,' or they'd laugh, and I'd get all flustered. It made me not even want to try to do math anymore. Why put all this effort in, just to get it wrong, and get yelled at by the boys?"

I know how she feels. When I was in law school at Yale, I remember sitting in my constitutional law class wanting desperately to contribute but feeling too intimidated. I mean, I was a girl from Schaumburg, Illinois, who was one of the first in my community to go on to an Ivy League grad school. All my classmates seemed so smart and impeccably articulate, and I didn't want to seem stupid in comparison. So I'd write out in my notebook exactly what I wanted to say, then I'd rewrite it three, four, a dozen times. By the time I worked up the courage to raise my hand, class was usually over.

Of course, the fears of not measuring up extend beyond the classroom. Amanda wanted to try lacrosse in high school but didn't because she's "not athletic." She summed up in two sentences a familiar sentiment I heard expressed in so many different varieties: "I just felt like if I couldn't do it well, I didn't want to do it at all."

It's important to understand that for girls, failure is defined as anything that is less than the proverbial A+. It's black and white: you either totally rock or totally suck. To them, failure isn't just painful—it's colossal, devastating, and to be avoided at all costs. So if they can't rock it, they skip it.

The Fixed Mindset

When Amanda declared that she didn't dare try lacrosse, she fell victim to a type of thinking that Stanford psychologist

Carol Dweck famously outlined in her brilliant book *Mindset*. In a nutshell, Dweck identified two different belief systems about ability and intelligence.

The first is a *fixed mindset*. A person with a fixed mindset believes that their abilities are innate and unchangeable. You're either smart or you aren't, talented or untalented, athletic or not at all, and there's not much you can do about it. The other is a *growth mindset*, which is based on the belief that abilities can be developed and cultivated through effort. Regardless of whatever natural level of ability or talent you are born with, you can learn skills and improve.

These are the hallmarks of a fixed mindset:

- An urgency to prove oneself again and again.
- Deep concern about making mistakes and failing.
- A reluctance to expose deficiencies.
- Seeing imperfections as shameful.
- The expectation that one will do well on something right away and if one doesn't, the loss of interest or self-admonishment for having put in the effort.
- The tendency to see failures as a measure of one's worth and allowing those failures to define the person.
- Being solely focused on the outcomes. It doesn't matter what one achieved or learned along the way. Not hitting the final mark means failure. And failure means that one isn't smart, talented, or good enough.

Sound familiar?

When you tell someone with a fixed mindset that they are smart or talented, they etch these messages into the "this is how I am" truth in their minds. That sounds like good, positive self-esteem building, but the problem is that after being showered with such praise of their perceived innate abilities, they fall to pieces when they encounter setbacks. Why? Because they take any failure, however insignificant, as a sign that maybe they aren't as innately smart or talented as they thought.

A fixed mindset also holds us back from trying anything outside our comfort zone. How many times have you begged off doing something spontaneous and potentially fun with, "I'm just not adventurous," or turned down an invitation or opportunity because "that's just not who I am"? That's the fixed mindset at work.

Not surprisingly, girls are more prone to a fixed mindset than boys. This is partially because, as Dr. Dweck's research showed, parents and teachers tend to give boys more "process praise," meaning they reward them for putting in effort, trying different strategies, sticking with it, and improving, rather than for the outcome. In the absence of this kind of process praise, girls come to believe that if they can't get something right away, they're dumb. You can see how this impacts us later in life, as we take even the smallest daily mistakes as indicators of fundamental limitations. We forget to pick up the school supplies our kid asked for = we're bad moms. We get a ticket for a broken taillight that we'd been meaning to take care of = we're idiots. We see a failure as a definitive condemnation of our worth, rather than seeing ourselves and our abilities as works in progress.

The single best example I can point to of girls being trapped in a fixed mindset is in relation to STEM subjects (science, technology, engineering, math). As you might imagine, being the founder of an organization that teaches coding to girls, I hear the refrain "I'm just not good at math" a lot. Like Destiny, who cringed when the boys made fun of her for taking so long up at the board to solve a math problem, or like the girls who delete their work in coding classes, it isn't a lack of interest or capacity in these subjects that scares them off, but a perception that they're fundamentally bad at it. After being told outright—or subtly, through the micromessages we'll talk about in the next chapter—that boys are naturally better at math and computing (they aren't) and that girls are innately more suited for humanities (again, not true), they believe to their core that their abilities in these subjects—or lack thereof—are carved in stone.

Of course, they aren't. Carol Dweck points out that no one is born with a fixed mindset; in fact, we all come prewired with a desire to learn and grow. It's only once children begin to evaluate themselves (I'm smart/not smart) that they become afraid of challenges. Thankfully, as adults, we *can* undo that long-ago wiring by taking on the practice of bravery in the here and now.

Silenced Voices

On a gray afternoon in late January, I sat around a conference table talking with a group of high school girls from Harlem. Kim, the most opinionated of the group, sat up straight with unusual presence for a girl her age. All outward signs pointed to a confident, secure young woman so I was surprised when she shared her inner reality with us.

"I feel like whenever girls speak up for themselves, we get slapped down for it because it seems like we're being bossy," she said. "Especially if I stand up for myself as a black woman specifically, boys really don't get it. If a boy does it, it's like he's a boss man . . . but if it's me, I'm just an angry black woman. Boys will say dumb stuff like they only like light-skinned girls . . . if I speak up to them, they tell me I just like to complain and dismiss me."

"But you're pretty outspoken," I said. "Does their reaction have an effect on you?"

"Please . . . you think I want to be smacked down for what I think all the time?" Kim put on a good show of sounding tough as she spoke, but I could hear a tiny tremor in her voice. Her bravado didn't quite match the vulnerability peeking through. After a beat and a few hard blinks of her eyes, she explained that she just found it easier to stay quiet than deal with the boys trying to put her down. "Everyone thinks I don't care but I do," she continued. "I feel like anything I say will just turn into a whole big thing, and then everyone will get into it and turn on me, too, so I don't bother."

The other seven girls around the table all nodded knowingly. Don't be too much, don't say too much, and definitely don't say anything that makes you sound angry or bossy. Got it.

From the time girls are young, they're trained to keep a lid on anger in the face of an affront, unlike boys who are trained to stand up for themselves, or retaliate. This explains why girls (and women) will do almost anything to avoid rocking the boat, and why they choose to downsize their personal power and swallow negative feelings, rather than be seen as boastful or face the horror of confrontation. Praised on the one hand by parents and teachers for being polite, agreeable, and "well behaved" and, on the other, punished by their peers for speaking out, the docility girls are rewarded for as children translates directly into a lifelong habit of suppressing their instinct to speak up and take a risky stand. Mansplaining and dominance plays aside, it's not surprising that findings show women speak less than 75 percent of the time than men do in conference meetings.

Modesty—another prized virtue for girls—also plays a hand in keeping us quiet and meek. I recently heard a story about a sixth-grade graduation ceremony in suburban Ohio, where a handful of kids were presented with awards for academics or leadership. A mom of one of those students described the scene for me: When a boy won an award, he would saunter up to the stage with a swagger. More than one "dabbed"–a hip-hop dance move that lots of pro athletes use in moments of triumph. When a girl won, she would throw her hands up to her face feigning a look of shocked surprise as if to say, *Who, me? You want to give an award to* me?

So why don't girls dab, too? Because if being a confrontational bitch is the first cardinal sin for girls, being seen as conceited runs a close second. So they downplay, demur, and hold back. Add ten, twenty, thirty years to this story and we see that modesty devolved into an uncomfortable meekness. It makes us squeamish to self-promote our professional accomplishments (possibly because we know other women will judge us for it, just like we'd judge them), yet our male colleagues proudly trumpet theirs. We underestimate our abilities and hold off going for a job unless we are *absolutely* sure we're 100 percent qualified, while men charge ahead if they come in around 60 percent qualified. We undervalue our contribution to a collaborative project and give more credit to our male teammates, as a fascinating study from Michelle Haynes of the University of Massachusetts and Madeline Heilman of New York University revealed.

At age thirty-eight, Vanessa is a successful dermatologist. She's one of those people who radiates competence, so you wouldn't think that she'd fall prey to the same trepidation about touting her accomplishments. Yet on a routine visit to get her teeth cleaned, her (older, male) dentist, upon hearing what she does for a living, immediately launched into a story about his son who was a resident in medical school. "I just sat there as he went on and on about how I should call his son because he could probably give me some good advice about the business," she said. "I was thinking, *huh?* Never mind that I own my own practice with three associates, or that I've been listed as a top doctor in national magazines. I still sat there not feeling brave enough to tell him it was probably his son who should be calling *me* for advice."

Caught in the "double bind" that says we need to be assertive and confident if we want to get ahead, but knowing we'll get heaped with disapproval if we do, we tread lightly. When someone compliments us, we humbly deflect. This is one I definitely struggle with. Every time someone introduces me before a speech, they inevitably read off the awards I've won. Then I'll get up there and make a joke about how my dad probably put them up to it. I'm pretty sure no guy would ever do that.

Quiet. Contained. Modest. Diligent. Likable. Easy to get along with. You can see how all these accolades might have earned us high praise in girlhood but aren't necessarily doing us any favors as grown women.

Now, if you're a parent reading this and thinking, *I've totally screwed up my daughter*—or are getting ready to blame your own parents for doing a number on you—let me stop you right there. The pressures on girls to be perfect does NOT all come down on the parents. It's important that we understand how ingrained these cultural norms are, and how hard it is for them *not* to become internalized. As you'll read about in the next chapter, more and more it's about the messages girls are getting from the culture we live in, and their parents are caught with them in the same tangled net. But don't despair—all hope is not lost, for you or for your daughter! As psychologist Dr. Meredith Grossman says, "It's not about parents screwing up. It's about becoming aware of these internalized beliefs and making different choices."

We *can* reverse and relearn these habits—and help our daughters do the same—with just a little awareness and practice. And in Part Three I'll share my best tips, ideas, and strategies for doing exactly that.

2

The Cult of Perfection

We are living in the era of girl power. From fiery Beyoncé anthems to powerhouse athletes like Serena Williams to badass literary and on-screen heroines like Katniss Everdeen and Wonder Woman, our culture is on a crusade to rally girls and tell them they can be and do it all. Of course we want our girls to know they can accomplish anything and everything they set their minds to! Right?

All this "positive" messaging, however, turns out to have a dark side. We hold up these larger-than-life women as role models with the goal of empowerment, but for many girls it lands as crushing pressure to excel in everything. We may be saying, "You can do and be anything," but they hear, "You *have to* do and be everything" What we might see as inspiration, they take as expectation.

My friend Rachel Simmons, one of the country's leading experts on girls and the bestselling author of *The Curse of the Good Girl*, points to this mentality as a factor contributing to the significant mental health crisis we see in today's young women. Rates of depression and anxiety are skyrocketing, and she says part of the problem is the role conflict girls today live with on a daily basis. "We've only added on to what it means to be a successful girl," she explains. "We didn't update

it. If you're expected to be in the library for six hours studying, how are you also expected to have a really great body
and great weekend plans?" Now they need to be nice, but also
fierce; polite but also bold; cooperative but trailblazing; strong
but also pretty. All this plus, in a culture that lauds effortless
perfection, making it look like they're not trying—not even
a bit.

Sophie is a perfect example. At fifteen, she is tall and lanky,
with unblemished skin and a gorgeous smile that reveals two
perfect rows of straight, white teeth. She's a star soccer player,
she's been on the varsity team since she was in seventh grade,
played Belle in her eighth-grade production of *Beauty and the
Beast*, and got elected to the student council in ninth grade—a
highly competitive and coveted post in her school. No surprise,
she also gets straight A's. If you met her, you'd immediately
be struck by how poised and articulate she is. Sophie's mom,
Dina, is proud—but also very worried. She talked about how,
despite her parents' urgings to take it easy, Sophie pushes herself relentlessly, waking up at the crack of dawn every morning
to work out at the gym before she goes to school and often
staying up until well past midnight to get her homework done
(while wearing teeth whitening strips and acne-fighting face
masks). To everyone else, it seems she's got it together; it's only
her family that sees her cry nearly every night in frustration or
sheer exhaustion. There isn't a single minute of Sophie's week
or energy that isn't consumed with practicing, studying, working on student council issues, and perfecting her appearance—
all without ever showing anyone other than her parents what
really goes into her all-star packaging.

Be bold and brave . . . but make sure not to step on any
toes or offend anyone. Go for what you want . . . as long as
it's what we expect of you. Speak your mind . . . but make

sure to smile when you do. Don't settle for less than you're worth . . . but ask for it nicely. Work hard . . . but make it look easy. This chapter is a glimpse inside how popular culture shapes the Perfect Girl, and what happens when she comes up against the confusing messages lobbed her way in the era of girl power.

Pretty like Mommy

Remember, we can't exclusively blame parents for creating generations of girls who are afraid of failing, or speaking up, or stepping out of line. The socially accepted gender beliefs that we—and our parents, and their parents—grew up with are so deeply etched into our psyches that it would be shocking if they *didn't* show up in our parenting. No, we need to look deeper into the culture we live in to find where the gender expectations are still flourishing and reseeding themselves in the next generation.

The cultural indoctrination starts early, with toys. Kids learn gender roles as early as thirty months old, and the toys and other merchandise they are nudged toward play a big role in that education. Studies show that play choices for boys and girls can have lasting effects on how they view themselves and their abilities, including what they believe they will be good at professionally when they grow up. It's almost hard to believe that child play can have that powerful effect, but it does. This goes way beyond trucks versus dolls or pink versus blue. The skills these toys teach set the gender narrative for what kids are "supposed" to like and excel at. The majority of toys and games created for boys like LEGOs and *Minecraft* are geared toward developing large motor skills like running and kicking and spatial skills, which are the 3-D visualization skills that are said to predict a child's achievement in STEM subjects. Toys for girls, on the other hand, generally build fine motor skills such as writing and making crafts, language development, and social interaction. Just in case you're thinking we've evolved past this, research from scholar Elizabeth Sweet at UC Davis shows that the gender marketing of toys is even *more* pronounced today than it was fifty years ago, when gender discrimination and sexism were as baked into our culture as apple pie.

We can't talk about the influence of toys without mentioning princesses. The effect the princess movies and paraphernalia has on girls has been hotly debated in recent years. Of all the conversations and articles out there, it was a study done at Brigham Young University that resonated the most for me. Professor Sarah M. Coyne observed 198 preschoolers and found that a full 96 percent of the girls engaged with "princess culture" in one way or another. That's not a huge surprise, but more interesting is how, when she observed these same kids one year later, she found that the more these girls watched princess movies and played with princess toys, the more they exhibited stereotypical female behavior like playing nicely and quietly, avoiding getting dirty, or being submissive, passive, physically weak, and valuing qualities such as being nurturing, thin, pretty, and helpful. This sticks with us in profound ways, whether we know it or not. A related study showed that grown women who self-identify as "princesses" are less interested in working, give up more easily on challenges, and place higher value on superficial qualities like appearance.

Here's a particularly horrifying example of the messages girls receive from the world of toys. In 2014, Mattel released a Barbie book called *I Can Be a Computer Engineer*. Sounds empowering, right? But just wait. A few pages in, Barbie is having a conversation with her little sister, Skipper, about her robot puppy. Skipper says, "Your robot puppy is so sweet, can I play your game?" Barbie laughs and says, "I'm only creating the design ideas, I need Steven and Brian's help to turn it into a real game."

No, I'm not joking.

In a few words Barbie told girls: "You're not good enough or smart enough. Computers are a boy's thing so if you're going to build something technical, you're going to need their help." Leave it to Barbie to articulate some of the worst stereotypes that girls and women face when it comes to technology.

Eventually, playtime ends, but once we are done with toys, popular culture swooshes in to reinforce those gender constructs. For the majority of their waking hours, kids get bombarded with not-so-subtle images and messages about what's expected of them and how they are supposed to behave. These messages are everywhere they look, from fashion to movies to headline news. They see T-shirts in the window of Gymboree emblazoned either PRETTY LIKE MOMMY or SMART LIKE DADDY, and older teenage girls (whom they idolize) wearing the popular T-shirt from Forever 21 that says ALLERGIC TO ALGEBRA. They watch a viral video of a principal in South Carolina telling girls that unless they are a size 0 or 2, wearing leggings will make them look fat, and they hear about how presidential candidate Hillary Clinton was called a "nasty woman" for speaking boldly during a debate.

Needless to say, media and pop culture support a completely different reality for men. The images that boys see, from Marvel superhero movies to HBO's Silicon Valley, reinforce the same messages they get early in life: that they need to be daring and brave—physically, intellectually, and otherwise. That part isn't news, but this gets interesting when we see how we can trace a straight line from the messages men have absorbed about masculinity to their behavior. In one experiment, a researcher at University of California-Berkeley's Haas School of Business assessed his male subjects' risk tolerance with a gambling assignment, then had them read about "masculinity." Then he assessed them again. Just by *reading* about masculinity, the men, on average, become substantially more risk-tolerant than they had been before they read the material.

Comedian Amy Schumer highlighted the glaring differences in the messages boys and girls receive when she posted a photo on Instagram of a newsstand display showing *Girls' Life* and *Boys' Life* magazines right next to each other. The cover of *Boys' Life* said in bold letters "Explore Your Future" and was covered in photos of airplanes, firefighter helmets, microscopes, computers, and a human brain. The cover of *Girls' Life* featured a blond teenaged cutie surrounded by the taglines "Wake Up Pretty!," "Fall Fashion You'll Love: 100+ ways to slay on the first day," and "Best. Year. Ever. How to Have Fun, Make Friends and Get All A's." These might sound like quaint vintage headlines from the 1950s, but nope, they were proudly displayed without a hint of irony in 2017. Schumer's one-word comment neatly summed up the disgust I feel at this messaging: "No."

In my research for this book, I came across shortstoryguide .com, a website to help middle- and high school teachers and students find stories organized by theme. I typed in the word *bravery*, and of the seventeen stories listed, only four featured female protagonists. One was a princess who pretends to be ashamed for shooting a lion who lunged at her. Another, an aspiring astronomer, "has to help her family during the *charreada*, a Mexican-style rodeo. She is caught between her own desires and tradition." Meanwhile, the male protagonists in the remaining stories bravely confront violent gangs and a Nazi spy, go bear hunting and capture a Russian fort—free of shame, or family obligations.

A study done by the *Observer* in conjunction with Nielsen that assessed the one hundred most popular children's books of 2017 revealed a few casually sexist trends that stubbornly prevail in modern literature. Male characters are twice as likely to take leading roles while females play the sidekick; when the characters took the form of animals, the powerful, dangerous bears, dragons, and tigers were mostly male while the smaller and more vulnerable birds, cats, and insects were female. One-fifth of these books had no female characters at all.

Boys and girls will model themselves after what they see, and even what they don't see; as children's rights activist Marian Wright Edelman famously said, "You can't be what you can't see." There's a running theme in movies and on television about the nerdy guy who gets rejected and goes on to become Mark Zuckerberg, but there's no similar narrative for girls. We muse and debate why there aren't more girls interested in tech, but for one key factor, just look at the media's depiction of the "brogrammer"—the brilliant but socially awkward white guy in a hoodie who is obsessed with computers—that girls look at and say, "Um, no thanks. I don't want to be him."

Instead, they watch as women backstab and screech at each other while hurling over tables on *The Housewives of New Jersey* (and *New York* . . . and *Beverly Hills* . . . and *Atlanta* . .), and catfight their way to the final rose ceremony on *The Bachelor*.

Needless to say, these are not the best role models. Women who take power roles on-screen are usually depicted as cold, ruthless bitches, like Daenerys Targaryen on *Game of Thrones* and Cheryl Blossom on *Riverdale*, or as volatile crazies, like Frances McDormand as a grieving mother in *Three Billboards Outside Ebbing, Missouri* or Viola Davis as the formidable but unstable lawyer on *How to Get Away with Murder*.

When brave women are portrayed, they are often almost cartoonish in their depiction. Granted we had the amazing *Wonder Woman* movie, with a fierce and kind heroine who spoke twelve languages and literally did not know what the men were talking about when they told her she couldn't do something, but she was a superhero demigod who isn't exactly relatable on a human scale. Ditto for the lead character Bella in the *Twilight* series; she is a meek and needy mortal for the first three-quarters of the story, gaining supernatural strength and ferocity only after she morphs into a vampire. In the re-boot of the cult-classic movie *Tomb Raider*, Alicia Vikander's Lara Croft is a hard-bodied badass, but what real-life woman do you know who survives crash landings, parachutes off the top of a waterfall, and fights off machine gun attacks with a bow and arrow—all while managing to look camo-chic and sexy?

It's important to see people like you on-screen; the un-bridled, infectious joy we saw spread across the Internet after Jodie Whittaker was cast as the first female Dr. Who makes that clear. I decided I wanted to be a lawyer when I was thir-teen years old and saw actress Kelly McGillis kick serious ass in the movie *The Accused*. That was the first time I'd seen a female character in a movie go up against the big boys with-out pulling any punches. As my father and I left the movie theater, I turned to him and said, "Dad, I want to be her."

Think about all the young girls now who know who Katherine Johnson is because of *Hidden Figures*, and who now see being a NASA scientist as a possibility; these are the kinds of realistic role models we need for our girls.

#perfectgirl

Today, social media feeds the expectation of polished perfection, perhaps more than any other influence out there. Girls spend up to nine hours each day scrolling through endless feeds of their friends' flawless photos and posts—all doctored and edited to show the world how popular, carefree, smart, pretty, and cool they are.

Listening to some of the millennial women I met with, I couldn't help feeling terrified for them. It was astonishing to hear how relentless but utterly normalized the pressure is for them to project an image of perfection in their online life—way beyond what I even imagined. The "personal branding" phenomenon has become an obsession for them; taking and editing the perfect photo consumes their time and efforts like nothing else. I listened to a group of friends in their midtwenties debating who was most obsessed with getting the ideal shot; they were torn between Sasha, who practices her photo faces in front of the mirror every morning to see what works best with her "look" that day, and Layla, who routinely makes her boyfriend wake up with her at sunrise for an early morning photo shoot in order to capture herself in the flattering light of dawn. Other girls told me about how the "ugly" pictures that someone had posted of them haunt them, or about how they felt panicked that they need to positively document every little thing they do to stay relevant in the eyes of their peers.

Perhaps as a way to preserve a sense of their true self, they literally separate themselves into two identities: their polished, carefully cultivated online persona, and the real them. Many set up separate Instagram or Snapchat accounts, and it's only on their private accounts accessible to only their closest friends that they'll post pictures of themselves in sweatpants, share a goofy video of themselves learning to hoop dance (it's a thing), or post a message expressing grief when a relationship ends.

They know this identity splitting isn't healthy but feel powerless to do anything about it. Positive and pretty: that's what's expected of them, and if they don't comply, it's a one-way ticket to judgment city. Anna, a twenty-five-year-old grad student, used the phrase "negativity shaming" for the pushback they often get if they post anything too raw or real. Anna recounted a time when she was really down after a breakup with a boyfriend; she posted something about how down she was feeling, and instead of rallying around to support her, people commented that she was being "superintense." She removed the post within an hour.

It's safer and easier for girls to stick to the stuff that gets them the most likes, because that's their currency. The more you play by the rules, the more followers and likes you have, and in perfect-girl world, the more followers and likes you have, the more valuable you are. Curating is everything.

So is comparing. According to Catherine Steiner-Adair, psychologist and author of *The Big Disconnect: Parenting, Childhood, and Family Connection in the Digital Age*, it takes only nine minutes of scrolling through everyone else's profiles and pictures for girls' anxiety to spike. Their FOMO—fear of missing out—is very, very real. Every post of a fun gathering they weren't a part of makes them feel ostracized and unwanted, every perfectly polished photo causes paroxysms of inadequacy. They are constantly competing in the never-ending game of *who has more followers, whose photo got more likes,* and so on. Hey, I get it; I'm forty-two years old and I still find myself refreshing Instagram posts obsessively to see how many likes I have.

Catherine recalled one girl she interviewed who frequently goes on nice vacations with her family. After one such trip, she came back and told Catherine, "I had had this awesome vacation until I saw where this other girl went. I started thinking, Are we poor?" Catherine initially thought maybe she was kidding, but she wasn't. "First world problems, of course, but the idea that the comparison would dampen the meaning and enthusiasm of her great family vacation is terribly sad," Catherine commented.

Then there's the truly nasty side of all this, the fallout that can range from hurt and embarrassment to serious psychological damage. Unfortunately, the shaming and bullying are not new; even shaming and bullying on social media are not new. But what *is* new is how young it starts. These days, girls as young as seven years old are on Instagram, Facebook, and Snapchat, far too young to have developed strategies to cope with the judgment they find there. A mom of a ten-year-old told me a story about her daughter, whose first Instagram post two years ago was a photo of a bowl of chocolate ice cream. A girl from school commented, "Ewww . . . is that poop?" Shamed and embarrassed, her daughter hasn't posted a single thing since.

Another mom told me—her voice shaking through her tears—that her thirteen-year-old is struggling with an eating disorder, which began shortly after she posted a picture of herself in a bathing suit and towel; a group of boys screen-shot and circulated her picture with the tagline, "Pig in a blanket." I recently read about a horrifying Snapchat craze in which middle-school kids competed to see who could post the cruelest insult about another kid's personality or appearance.

As if girls didn't have enough to contend with, many can't resist logging on to sites like www.prettyscale.com to upload pictures of themselves and receive the answer promised by the site's provocative tagline, "Am I beautiful or ugly?" (the helpful small print below says, "Please do not start if you have low self-esteem or confidence issues," which would seem to rule out all preteen and teenage girls), or sites where you can post anonymously like ask.fm, Kik, and Voxer. Anonymous sites, not surprisingly, are fertile ground for the cruel cyberbullying that has been linked to tragic suicides, such as that of twelve-year-old Rebecca Ann Sedwick, who killed herself at the repeated urging of a group of middle-schooler bullies. It's heartbreaking. If ever there was a reason for us to learn to be brave, it is so we can teach the next generation how to make empowering choices in the face of messages and challenges like these.

Changing the Code

Looking at all this, we start to see how deeply we as adult women have been wired to play it safe and to color well inside the lines of perfection—and what it costs us. It's like a code that has been programmed into us, over many years of perfect-girl training. But take it from someone who actually now does know a thing or two about coding: all code can be revised and rewritten—including the one that dictates whether you choose the path of perfection, or bravery.

3

Perfection 3.0: When the Perfect Girl Grows Up

*I*f life were one long grade school, girls would rule the world."

This famous quote by Carol Dweck hits hard for all of us who were primed to be perfect girls. Of course, she's right: in school, the quest for perfection may have served us well, but in the real world, there are no straight A's. Inevitably, we grow up and discover very quickly that the rules have changed; suddenly, everything we've been taught backfires on us. The very same behaviors that used to pay off—like being nice, polite, and agreeable—suddenly end up costing us big-time, both literally and figuratively.

Playing nice doesn't get us the promotions or positions of power—and it certainly doesn't get us raises. Being overly accommodating lands us in situations and relationships we don't necessarily want to be in. Minding our manners and staying quiet leaves us feeling queasy knowing that we didn't tell our uncle Joe to shut it when he told one of his usual racist jokes, or call foul when a colleague took credit for an idea that was ours. Being sweet and ultrameticulous may earn us gold stars in the classroom, but by the time we hit the real world, those stars aren't exactly raining from the sky.

I once met a woman at a conference in California who

asked me, "How can I not strive to be perfect, when the world rewards perfection?" My answer to her was that maybe high school or college rewards perfection, but in the real world, it's different. The real world rewards bravery.

The pursuit of perfection may set us on a path that feels safe, but it's bravery that lets us veer off that "supposed to" path and onto the one we're authentically meant to follow. Perfection might win us points for popularity at the office, but it's bravery that lets us speak up and take a stand when we're hit with workplace sexism or harassment. Having a 4.0 GPA, an impeccable interview outfit, and a charming smile may get us in the door, but we need bravery to get our work recognized and advance beyond entry-level. Having perfect hair or the perfect body might land us a date, but it takes bravery to fall in love, and to do it all over again after our hearts have been broken. Trying to be the perfect mom might win us tacit approval on the playground, but it takes bravery to give our child the freedom to explore and make mistakes even though we desperately want to wrap them in bubble wrap to protect them forever. Perfection might feel good for a few fleeting moments, but bravery powers us through the difficult times and deep losses that can feel insurmountable. By being brave, not perfect, we get to create and live lives that don't just *look* good but are authentically, joyfully, messily, and completely ours.

How Did I Get Here?

"I didn't know until I was in my late twenties that I had choices in life," Ruth told me. She and I met while sitting side by side at a nail salon and struck up one of those unusually intimate conversations the way one sometimes randomly does with a complete stranger. Ruth got the message when she was young that an appropriate path for her was to become a teacher, get married, have kids, and then stay home to raise them. It didn't even dawn on her that she had other options—that is, until she was twenty-eight and a friend of hers joined the Peace Corps and moved to South America. "All of a sudden I thought, wait a minute . . . you mean I can do that?!" At age sixty-two, Ruth says she sometimes wonders what turns her life might have taken if she'd looked within and asked herself what she really wanted.

All the lessons we learn as little girls have real consequences on our life choices. So many of us have been trained to please others—first and foremost our parents—and so we follow the "expected" path without questioning if it's genuine for us. For some, like Ruth, it was getting married and having babies; for others, it's working tirelessly to get ahead. I see this a lot in young women raised by immigrant parents like Yara, whose dad grew up in a tiny city in Holland, with a bed that came down out of the wall. "When he moved their family here, there was no question—none—that I had to succeed at everything," she said. "It's what he came here for."

Julianne is first-generation Asian American. At the age of thirty-one, her family's disapproval of her life choices still stings. Her parents wanted her to become a doctor, but she got to a certain point in her training when she realized that wasn't how she wanted to spend her life, so she quit medicine and chose something that she really likes. In the back of her mind, she still wonders if she's a failure. "Anytime we have a family reunion," she told me, "there's a passive-aggressive undercurrent of 'Why did you choose that . . . could you not make the other path?'"

As a daughter of immigrant Indian parents, I totally relate. I thought if I did everything perfectly, got straight A's, was number one on my debate team, and valedictorian in college that all the sacrifices my parents made as refugees would be worth it. So, even though I secretly dreamed of being in public service, I went to work at a prestigious law firm, knowing it would earn my father's approval and praise. I hated my job, but I never let that show. I moved on and up to a high-paying job at a marquee-name financial firm, even though, for me, making money was only a means to an end (as in, to pay off my student loans and then go on to make a difference). Yet I made choice after choice like this, climbing up rung after rung on corporate ladders and making myself more miserable by the day. I spent all my free hours volunteering on political campaigns and giving back, but my day job in finance was completely disconnected from that. By the time I hit my early thirties, I was waking up most mornings curled in the fetal position, nursing the sick realization that my professional accomplishments were hollow. On paper you would have thought I had it made, but in reality I was way, way off my dream path.

That was a dark time in my life. My body and soul exhausted, I would often come home from work, change into comfy sweats, pour a glass of wine, turn on CNN, and just cry. I felt so stuck, not knowing what to do next and too scared to quit and free myself of the trap into which I'd fallen.

Until the day in 2008 when everything changed.

I remember so vividly it being one of those stifling hot August days in New York City, when the streets are gooey and standing on the subway platform makes you feel like you're being roasted. I was sitting in my hermetically sealed, frigidly air-conditioned office on the forty-eighth floor in the heart of

Midtown Manhattan in a fitted blue suit and four-inch heels that were killing me, trying to hold back the tears. Even my afternoon cappuccino tasted like fear and regret.

Less than two months earlier, I'd gone down to Washington, D.C., to offer support for my mentor Hillary Clinton as she gave her concession speech, ceding the 2008 Democratic nomination to then senator Barack Obama. I'd worked so hard volunteering on her campaign and, like so many others, felt disheartened and deflated. As I watched her speak, with tears streaming down my face, one message particularly stuck with me: that just because she failed doesn't mean that the rest of us should give up on our goals and dreams. I'd felt like she was speaking directly to me.

On that sweltering August day, I was replaying Hillary's speech in my head—as I had many times in the weeks since—when my phone pinged. It was Deepa, one of my best friends from law school. She knew me when I was still a bright-eyed graduate who believed I could do and be anything (she once walked in on me standing on her balcony practicing my presidential acceptance speech). I was never so happy to see a name light up on my phone! I quickly walked across the somber, hushed office into a windowless conference room in the back, closed the privacy blinds, kicked off those miserable heels, and picked up the call. The instant I heard Deepa's voice, the flood of tears came rushing out. I must have sounded a little nuts, sobbing and hiccupping as I told her I couldn't take this corporate job anymore . . . that I felt so empty . . . that my life had no purpose. She listened patiently until I was finished, paused, and then she said, simply and quietly, "Just quit." Maybe it was the inspiration from Hillary's strength and resilience, or hearing my best friend give me permission to do something I was terrified to do, but for the first time in as long as I could remember, I felt a glimmer of hope.

Shortly after that, I worked up the courage to tell my father that I wanted to quit my job and run for office. I was worried that he would say I shouldn't do it, which would have tapped right into my fear of his disapproval and made me give up on the idea entirely. When I dialed the phone to call him, I was so nervous that my hands were shaking; I *really* wanted this and didn't want anything to dim my excitement. You know what he said? "It's about time!" I never felt more proud to be my father's daughter than I did that day—and never wanted to kick myself harder for not going to him with my truth earlier. In the long run, I ended up making his American dream come true by going after my own.

I've met so many girls and women who made the same early mistakes I did. Like Melissa, an art history major who let her dream of being an artist waft away when she got married at twenty-two to her nice (but boring) Jewish boyfriend at the none-too-subtle urging of her religiously conservative parents. Almost on autopilot, she moved into a nice-size house and built a social life that was a mini-replica of theirs, including joining their synagogue. For a couple of years, she cheerfully played the part of gracious hostess and suburban wife, until the *Is this it?* feeling started to creep in. At twenty-five, she woke up one morning, looked around at her pristinely manufactured home and life, and thought, *Oh, hell no. This isn't where my story ends.* By her twenty-sixth birthday, Melissa was single, working for almost no money as a receptionist in an art gallery, and living in a tiny walk-up in Brooklyn. Was her life perfect? No. But she'd never been happier, because she'd let go of the expectation that it had to be.

The Myths of Perfection

Something interesting happened when I first started talking with women about perfection. I'd start off by asking them what I thought was a softball question to open the conversation: "Do you believe you need to be perfect?" I assumed the answer would obviously be yes, but nearly all of them said the exact opposite. I began to wonder if maybe I had it all wrong.

Then I realized they were answering the question from the very same style of thinking I was trying to unravel. They were giving me what they assumed was the *right* answer—the perfect answer—the answer that said *of course* they know that the pursuit of perfection is a demoralizing waste of time and energy. And yet all the stories I was hearing were telling a very different tale.

So from then on, when I spoke to groups of women, I changed the question. Instead of a binary yes or no question, I asked them instead to rate themselves on a scale of 1 to 10, 10 being that they were strongly driven to do everything in their lives to perfection. Just as I suspected, once I eliminated the suggestion of a "right" answer, a different picture began to emerge; the average answer was between 8 and 10. Once the floodgates began to open, I asked them if friends and family ever suggested that they were holding themselves to unreasonable standards; the answer was usually yes. I asked them if they believed that no matter what they did, they should've done better. That one scored an almost unanimous yes.

After talking to hundreds of women ranging from teenagers to senior citizens, from all backgrounds and walks of life, I've learned that perfectionism isn't simple or one-dimensional. It's a complex knot of lifelong beliefs, expectations, and fears. Our attitudes toward it are confusing and inconsistent; we nurture and feed it but wish like hell we could shake it. It can be an unforgiving taskmaster, naysayer, and critic all rolled into one. It greets us every morning as we stare in the mirror and keeps us awake, rehashing and ruminating over our mistakes, long into the night.

Sometimes perfectionism tells us that other people won't accept or value or love us unless we're perfect (what psychologists call "socially prescribed perfectionism"); other times it feels like we're the ones pushing ourselves to reach our own impossible standards ("self-oriented perfectionism"). Either way, it's a nagging presence that whispers in our ear, constantly reminding us of all the ways we failed others and ourselves.

Perfect-girl training aside, we're now smart, savvy women who intelligently know the pursuit of perfection is absurd. Yet it still rules our lives. Why? Because whether we're consciously aware of it or not, we still buy into some outdated myths about what being perfect will do for us. It's time to drag out these stubborn lies and kick them to the curb once and for all.

Myth #1: Polished Equals Perfect

From a very young age, we're taught that if we're polished on the outside, we'll get the perfect job, the perfect man, the perfect life. But polished doesn't equal perfect, and it definitely doesn't guarantee the happy ending. Believe me, I should know.

The delusion we harbor is that if we're perfect in how we look, sound, or behave, our secret—that we are actually *not* perfect—is safe. If we come off as flawless, we are beyond reproach: shielded from judgment or criticism. So we obsessively polish our veneer to keep any ugly insecurities, feelings, or flaws hidden from view.

Early on in my run for Congress, I was a wreck. A very worried wreck. I was nervous about whether I really had what it took to hold office. I felt like I needed to be an issues expert on everything from Iraq to potholes—what if someone asked me a question and I didn't have the answer? I already had my young age and lack of experience stacked against me; would I be seen as incompetent, not smart enough to do the job? I may have seemed tough and composed on the surface, but inside I was riddled with anxiety and self-doubt.

So I focused on the only thing I could control: my stump speech. Oh my god, I was so obsessed with that stump speech. I wrote and rewrote it dozens of times and memorized every word. I watched countless videos from great orators and rehearsed it over and over in my head while lying in bed, while brushing my teeth, while walking to the subway. I convinced myself that if I gave a flawless speech, I would appear flawless and spare myself the wrath of critics. I thought my flawless speech would be like a shield, that it would put me in control of how I was perceived. Needless to say, I was wrong. The haters still found plenty to hate on, from my words to my footwear. It wasn't until years later that I learned that the only thing that can truly protect me is my inner bravery.

For many of us, our appearance is our armor. If our outfit, hair, makeup, jewelry, shoes, and everything else are perfect, we feel in control. Yet this is an illusion that assumes we have power over how other people view and respond to us. One petite blond entrepreneur told me she gets her hair and makeup professionally done before she pitches to potential investors. "It's as if they can't fuck with me if I have a blowout," she said with a laugh. But the reality is that we're never really in control. Not of what people think of us in their private thoughts, and definitely not of what happens once we step away from the primping mirror or our carefully crafted notes. Of course anyone can fuck with you, with or without a blowout.

It wouldn't be possible to talk about women and perfectionism without mentioning the most obvious and insidious way we torture ourselves: our bodies. On average, a woman spends 127 hours per year fretting about her weight and how many calories she consumes. Over a lifetime, that adds up to *one full year* that we give to obsessing over the size and shape of our bodies. It's been estimated that between 80 and 89 percent of women are unhappy with their weight. Ten million women in this country have eating disorders. Even more disturbingly, the National Eating Disorders Association reports that 81 percent of *ten-year-old* girls are afraid of being overweight.

A few days following a packed focus group I did in New York City, I got an email from a participant named Marta who had sat quietly on the floor throughout the evening. But in her email she wrote candidly about how the whole experience had been very "meta" for her—here she was at an intimate gathering to talk about how perfectionism and fear hold us back, and she was too intimidated by the accomplished women sitting on the sofa across from her (she called them "the couch women") to speak up. I told Marta I was grateful to her for reaching out to me, as the story she then shared is one I think many of us can relate to in one way or another.

At a young age, she'd internalized the pressure to maintain a perfectly polished exterior from her mother, who had never, in the thirty-two years Marta had been on this earth, been outside of their house without a full face of makeup on. She was thin and very pretty and had always been in good shape, and Marta described to me how, in high school, boys would tell her that her mom was "hot," which made her feel nauseated and like she'd never measure up. "I was too big, my hair was too curly, my nose was too broken," she wrote.

These deep insecurities drove her to fix her nose when she was sixteen, which was also around when she stopped playing basketball, a game she had loved since childhood. "At seventeen, I tried straightening my hair (once) and literally cried about it," Marta recalled. "At eighteen, I left for college and immediately gained ten pounds by eating and drinking like a frat boy; and then gained another ten pounds soon after by 'going on a diet' that consisted of eating my dessert *before* my dinner. As I got heavier and heavier my freshman year, I learned that a really easy way to forget that you've lost all control is to get blackout drunk and lose all control. So I did that for a few years, ashamed of my body, feeling hopeless."

Marta told me that for as long as she could remember, the idea of trying hard to look "perfect" (working out, eating healthily, wearing makeup) made her feel pathetic—so she just let it all go. "I felt like if I couldn't be perfect, there was no use trying," she said. She added that over the years she'd made a lot of progress in terms of how she felt about her body and her weight, but admitted that those childhood messages had been hard to shake. "Even now, at thirty-two, I have to consciously remind myself that I am more than my body," she said. "That if I can't fit into a pair of jeans, I still have a meaningful career and friends and family whom I love and who love me. I have to *remind* myself of these things. And that feels insane."

Unfortunately, the pressures to appear flawless are definitely not in our imagination. And neither is the fact that it's not the same for men. Hillary Clinton once remarked that during her 2008 presidential race, Barack Obama could just "roll out of bed and into a suit," while she spent hours prepping hair, makeup, and wardrobe before every appearance. When you're a woman on that size stage (I'd argue on any stage, for that matter), there's no room for error in how you look.

The examples are endless. Rihanna is photographed in baggy jeans one day and a sportswriter dedicates an entire blog post to how she "looks like she is wearing a sumo suit" and wondering whether she was "going to make being fat the hot new trend"? (Thankfully, the blowback was swift and he was summarily fired.) Jennifer Aniston once dared to eat a cheeseburger shortly before being photographed in a bikini and the entire Twittersphere was abuzz speculating whether she was "just gaining weight," or pregnant.

Just to add a little more fuel to the insecurity fire, these days we're not only supposed to look flawless, we're also supposed to pull off being thin and toned with straight white teeth, radiant skin, and glossy hair without looking like we're even trying. Seems growing up doesn't make us immune to the pressure of "effortless perfection" that plagues our girls. As a recent article by Amanda Hess in the *New York Times* points out, society now puts the onus on women to look within to overcome crises of beauty confidence, as if it's entirely self-generated and the unreasonable standards thrown at us from every direction don't exist. "The reality is that expectations for female appearance have never been higher," writes Hess. "It's just become taboo to admit that."

While most of us don't have to worry about our appearance being picked apart in the pages of *US Weekly*, we all feel body and beauty pressure in our own way. What's important here is to recognize how closely and incorrectly we've linked having a killer wardrobe, unblemished skin, and a toned booty with being perfect—and how false and fleeting the sense of control that gives us is.

A lovely woman named Evelyn told me a story about having to see her ex-husband and his new (much younger) wife at her daughter's wedding. She was so tied up in knots about it that she spent three months leading up to the event "perfecting" herself. She went on a strict diet to lose ten pounds, dyed her hair, and tried on countless dresses and shoes until she found the "perfect" combination. When the day of the wedding came, she looked spectacular—and still felt sad, jealous, and all the other emotions she was hoping to keep at bay. "Don't get me wrong," Evelyn said. "I felt like a million bucks, and that helped. But it wasn't a miracle cure—not by a long shot."

Obviously, I'm not suggesting we should all let ourselves go and start showing up for events or meetings looking like we don't give a crap. Appearance does matter, at least to a degree in terms of making a good impression. But having said that, there's a big difference between being appropriate and torturing ourselves in an attempt to look "perfect." If looking fabulous gives you a boost of confidence, by all means do it! Beauty is meant to be a joyful form of self-expression, and I'm the first person to admit that a bold red lipstick makes me feel on point. It's when we start obsessing and clutching on to flawlessness as a security blanket that we know we've tipped over into unhealthy territory.

Myth #2: Once Everything Is Perfect, I'll Be Happy

I once read that the amount of money a person needs to be happy is always 10 percent more than they have. That seems like a great analogy for how we chase the elusive carrot of perfection.

The thinking goes something like this: *If I look the right way, have the right job, land the right partner, everything will fall into place and I'll be happy.* I've fallen prey to this flawed logic myself. When I was younger, I thought if I worked out five times a week to have the "ideal" size 2 body like my sister's and went to Ivy League schools, I would meet the perfect guy who loved my brains and would support me unconditionally. We would have three perfect children and I'd become the president of the United States. I thought I could plan my life to be exactly as I dreamed, but only if I followed the script as perfectly as possible. I'm far from alone in this skewed perception.

To achieve our perfect ideal, we log our ten thousand steps a day, work out seven times a week, cut carbs out of our diets. We read endless articles, blogs, and books on how to advance in our careers, find work-life balance, attract the ideal partner. We go after the hot job or role in our community that everyone tells us we'd be perfect for. We have two point five kids, buy the perfect house, acquire all the right stuff.

And yet, are we happy?

The numbers say no. According to the National Institute of Mental Health, one out of every four women will experience severe depression in her lifetime. A seminal study done in 2009 at the University of Pennsylvania called "The Paradox of Declining Female Happiness" (how's that for telling?) showed that although women's lives have improved over the past thirty-five years in terms of increased opportunities, higher wages, and freedom from domestic drudgery via technological advancements, their happiness has declined. We *should* be happier, but we're not.

When we're chasing perfection, we can end up in jobs, relationships, and life situations we don't necessarily want to be in. We think that checking all the requisite boxes will lead to joy and fulfillment, but eventually we get to the bottom of the list and think, *Oh, shit . . . why am I not happy?*

Tonya is a talented illustrator who gets paid big bucks for her work. For more than twenty years, she's been regarded as one of the best in her business, with several prestigious awards to show for it. Her career provides her with lots of praise and admiration from others, not to mention good money. The only thing it doesn't bring her is joy.

Tonya doesn't hate her job; she's quick to point that out. But she doesn't love it, either. The spark went out of it for her a few years ago, and she's just going through the motions. She's got a decent amount of money saved, so that's not a major issue, but when I asked her why she didn't stop doing it and try something else that turned her on, she just sighed.

I know that sigh. I remember heaving it myself back when I was a young rising star at a fancy law firm, earning lots of praise and a big paycheck but hating every second of it. I've heard that sigh from many other women who feel stuck in roles in which they're "successful." I know it sounds funny to talk about being trapped by something we excel in. First world problems, right? But all problems demand we develop our bravery if they are ever to get solved.

One of the hallmarks of happiness is having close, mean-ingful connections with others. But keeping up a façade of having it all together keeps us isolated, because it keeps us from forging real, honest, deep relationships where we can fully be ourselves and feel accepted exactly as we are.

It's not that there's anything objectively wrong with our jobs, relationships, or lives—unless they are ones we didn't authentically choose; unless they are a reflection of every-thing we *believed* we were supposed to pursue rather than our real passions. After a lifetime of chasing other people's dreams (whether we're actually aware that's what we're doing or not), worrying about what others think, or following a prescribed formula for what we think our lives "should" look like, our own desires and goals get blurred. It's like driving a car with the navigation system yelling out dozens of different instructions all at the same time. Go right, go left, make a U-turn . . . eventually your own sense of direction gets drowned out.

We choose partners who fit the bill, even if we aren't genuinely in love or happy. (While this is speculation on my part, I don't think it's coincidental that the percentage of married women who report having affairs has risen 40 percent over the past twenty years.) We move into idyllic homes or lives—whatever form that takes for us—then feel disappointed that everything feels forced and plastic. Even with the people closest to us, we feel like we need to hide the truly ugly, messy, real stuff behind a glossy façade; then we wonder why our relationships feel hollow. We pursue opportunities or degrees that loved ones encourage us to do, believing that's the ticket to our happiness. Or, like a lot of women I met, we stay years too long in a career we don't love simply because we're good at it. Even when we wake up and realize that we are in the wrong career, or relationship, or life, the idea of making a change is terrifying, partly because we take it as a sign of failure and partly because it means we may have to go *way* outside our comfort zone to start over.

When I give talks at colleges, I often tell the story about how I spent so many years climbing the corporate ladder without ever questioning whether it was truly what I wanted. Once, after a speech I gave at Harvard, a young woman of color came running up to me as I was getting into a cab to say, "Everything you just said in your speech was ME." She told me about how she'd done everything she could to get to where she is pursuing a Ph.D. in early learning education, never asking herself if that was going to make her happy. She realized now that wasn't at all what she wanted to do, but she was doing it because it was simply the next credential she was tracked to earn.

Cindy is a stunning woman who literally looks like she stepped off the pages of a fitness magazine. She told me about how she'd finally reached the state of absolute physical perfection that she'd always wanted, but it ended up feeling empty. She wasn't any happier, her marriage wasn't any better, her teenage son's mental health issues were not any more under control. It seems that even if you do get to flawless, not much changes. No fireworks, no trophies, no guarantee of happiness—nothing but a vague sense of dissatisfaction and a feeling of *Is this it?*

We are trained to assume that if we connect all the perfect dots, it's going to bring us fulfillment. We don't even know how much of this in so ingrained in us. The thought is revolutionary when it hits us: Maybe "the perfect life" isn't really all that perfect after all.

Myth #3: If I'm Not Perfect, Everything Will Fall Apart

When flawlessness is the ideal, flaws by definition cannot be tolerated. It's not so much the mistakes we make that get to us; it's what we make them mean. In the mind of a perfectionist, a mistake is a sign of a personal flaw. The internal spin happens fast: It's not just that I rambled a little in a meeting;

it's that my colleagues will now forever think I'm stupid. It's not that I forgot to send in the permission slip for the class trip; it's that my kid's teacher—and probably my kid—now thinks I'm a shitty parent. It's not just that my date will be disappointed that I had to cancel on him at the last minute; now he'll never ask me out again and I'll die alone.

Lilly, an assistant to a publicist, spent an entire weekend in the throes of panic because she hadn't answered an email as soon as she should have, and she was sure her boss would be upset when she found out. "On Saturday I went to lunch with a girlfriend and spiraled all the way into, 'Maybe I should just forget working and go back for my master's . . .' I was so scared I was going to get fired, I came in at seven a.m. Monday morning and organized everything in sight so I could be beyond reproach."

I came across a recent study done by a professor at Auburn University which found that fewer women than men believe they meet their own standards in terms of family and work commitments. One expert commenting on the study added that women experience a lot of guilt as they try to juggle their work and home life. No disrespect meant here, but my immediate response when I read these shocking newsbreaks was, "Well . . . *duh.*"

I don't think the pressure to do everything perfectly shows up anywhere more profoundly than for working moms. Let's be serious: even when we have amazing 50/50 spouses or life partners, we are usually the ones who know what's in the diaper bag, or remember to grab the pacifier, or have the babysitter's numbers on speed dial. We've done a great job of internalizing the message that anything less than a perfect mom equals a bad mom.

I travel a lot for my work and feel unrelenting pressure and guilt about spending too much time apart from my kid. So I am constantly editing and reediting my schedule to minimize the time I'm away. When I'm in town, I'll get up at 5 a.m. to go to the gym so I'm done before my son gets up and I can sit with him while he eats breakfast and get him dressed for school. My husband is a great dad, but he doesn't have that same kind of guilt. If he has an early meeting and I'm not in town, he has no problem letting the babysitter do the breakfast and dressing routine. Even our bulldog, Stan, activates my mom guilt: when she's up and howling to go out at 7 a.m., I'll take her, even though I know that when I'm away, she'll happily snooze until 10 a.m. when Nihal is showered, shaved, and dressed.

Women are the ones who give away all of our "me" time to our partners and our children. But let's be brutally honest here: we often bring this on ourselves. Could our partners pack the diaper bag and make the kids' breakfast and make arrangements with the babysitter? Absolutely. Will they do it exactly the way we want them to? Probably not. But if we assume they won't do it 100 percent right, we figure we'll just do it our damn selves.

A national survey designed by the Families and Work Institute revealed that much of the time pressure women deal with is self-imposed because they have trouble delegating or letting go of control. Some have argued that women take on more of these parenting tasks because they are more nurturing by nature. But how much of what we're talking about here is really fundamental nurturing? When I think about nurturing, I think of tending to my son's physical and emotional well-being: caring for him when he spikes a fever, comforting him when his favorite stuffed froggy goes missing. It's our modern-day obsession with being the perfect mom—or what feminist sociologist Sharon Hayes dubbed "the ideology of intensive mothering"—not a nurturing instinct, that tells me I have to have every one of the necessary (and very best) school supplies on hand, feed him organic snacks, and teach him the alphabet before he turns twenty-one months old because we (okay, I) read somewhere that that's a sign of genius.

Dads, for the most part, don't feel that same pressure. They don't feel the same soul-crushing guilt if they don't nail the parenting minutia, because they never aimed for that perfection marker in the first place. I laugh every time I see the Pedigree Dentastix commercial featuring a young dad supervising his very messy toddler eating in the high chair. The child ends up with food all over his face, so the dad runs out of the room to get a wet towel to clean him up. By the time he gets back, the family dog has licked the baby's face clean. Dad pauses, assesses the situation, then shrugs and cheerfully responds, "That'll work."

Can you imagine how freeing it would feel to be like that?

The image of washing your kid's face with doggie slobber aside, I want to emphasize that giving up the expectation of perfection is *not* the same as being a bad parent or lowering your standards. It isn't the standards at all that we need to change, but our thinking about what it means if we do or don't reach them. It's great to want to feed your kid healthy meals. At the same time, he will not keel over from malnourishment if you feed him frozen chicken nuggets for dinner now and then. Punctuality and routine are good parenting practices. That being said, if you are unintentionally late to pick your kid up from day care because your rideshare was trapped behind a garbage truck, chances are you won't have done permanent psychological damage.

Being able to handle it all doesn't require perfection. It

demands bravery. It takes bravery to let go of control and delegate, to aim for 100 percent but be okay if you come in at 90, to make mistakes and own up to them without sliding into shame. It takes bravery to take care of yourself and say no when that voice in your head is telling you to sacrifice *everything* for your job and family (and your friend who calls for relationship advice six times a week . . . and your kid's PTA . . . and your neighbor who asked you to walk his dog while he's away . . .). It takes bravery to give yourself a break and refuse to let guilt dictate your daily life, and to model self-compassion for your kids by letting them see it's okay to screw up.

It takes bravery to retire our perfect girl and trade her in for the new model of brave woman. But it's worth it.

Myth #4: Perfection Is the Same as Excellence

It's easy to tell ourselves that we're aiming to be perfect because we have high standards and want to excel. What could be wrong with that? But our perfect girl training has muddied the waters here. The truth is we can be excellent *without* being perfect; they aren't one and the same.

The difference between excellence and perfection is like the difference between love and obsession. One is liberating, the other unhealthy. Perfection is an all-or-nothing game; you either succeed or fail, period. There are no small victories, no "A" for effort. If you're a perfection seeker and you fail at anything, it can really take you out.

When you are pursuing excellence, on the other hand, you don't let failure break you, because it's not a win or lose kind of game. Excellence is a way of being, not a target you hit or miss. It allows you to take pride in the effort you put in regardless of the outcome. I'll be the first one to tell you that it's great to have high personal standards. You *should* prepare well and strive to do your best in that interview, meeting, event, speech, game, or project—personal or professional. There's nothing wrong with having a healthy desire to excel, even to win. What's *not* okay is setting impossible goals and expectations or beating yourself up if you don't get the ideal results.

You know you're crossing the line from the pursuit of excellence into perfectionism when you feel like nothing is ever enough. A big clue is if you don't know when to celebrate. I still have to watch myself on this one. People will say, "Wow, Reshma, you've accomplished a lot," and immediately a needling little voice in my head says, *Not really.* That's the ghost of perfectionism talking, and it sucks all the joy right out of the experience. But if you chase excellence instead of perfection, you get to actually feel proud of your achievements. These days, I'm working on taking moments to celebrate when I accomplish something. I'll turn up my girl Beyoncé really loud and dance around my living room, get one of those decadently good chocolate chip cookies from my favorite bakery, or even tweet a little congratulatory note to myself.

Perfection can really ruin a good thing. Instead of allowing us to see everything we did right, it demands that we hyperfocus on the one thing that wasn't 100 percent. For example, my TED talk has had over almost four million views; countless women have emailed to tell me how much it moved them, and *Fortune* magazine even called it one of the most inspiring speeches of 2016. But you know what I saw when I watched it? Overly curled hair and makeup that looks ridiculously vamped up. There I was making an impact on the lives of millions of girls and women, and all I could think was, *Why didn't anyone tell me I looked like I was going clubbing instead of getting onstage to give a speech in front of millions of people?*

When my friend Tiffany Dufu published her amazing book, *Drop the Ball*, it received glowing reviews and was hailed by Gloria Steinem as "important, path-breaking, intimate and brave." Instead of reveling in this incredible praise, she became fixated on a couple of negative Amazon reviews (even though they were far outnumbered by positive ones). "You'd have thought my world was falling apart every time anyone wrote something critical," she said. Another case of perfectionism robbing us of pride in excellence.

It's become a bit of a cliché to call yourself a perfectionist in a job interview, thinking it implies a strong work ethic and high attention to detail. The irony is that perfectionism actually *impedes* excellence. It causes us to overthink, overrevise, overanalyze: too much perfecting, not enough doing.

You might be thinking, *Sure, some imperfection is fine in some jobs, but we all want our trusted professionals, like doctors or lawyers, to be perfectionists, right?* But the research makes a compelling case for why that thinking is upside down. For example, a 2010 study of twelve hundred college professors found that those who strive for perfection are less likely to get published or receive citations. Research confirms that the most successful people in any given field are *less* likely to be perfectionistic, because the anxiety about making mistakes gets in your way, explained psychologist Thomas Greenspan in a *New York* magazine article. "Waiting for the surgeon to be absolutely sure the correct decision is being made could allow me to bleed to death."

Myth #5: Failure Is Not an Option

If failure isn't an option, then neither is taking risks. That, right there, is how perfection strangles bravery.

The fear of failure is so huge. We're afraid that if we try something outside our comfort zone and fall short, we'll look foolish and forever be identified with our failure. We're afraid it will be proof that we'll never meet our expectations of ourselves—or the expectations of others. We will end up disgraced, ashamed, emotionally and professionally decimated. What if it breaks us and we can't pick ourselves back up?

When I lost my congressional race, I thought I was done, washed up for good, my dream to be a public servant on a national scale dead in its tracks. I woke up the morning after in the hotel room my staff had (rather optimistically) decorated with congratulatory balloons and congratulatory notes stuck everywhere on Post-its, feeling sick to my stomach. I'd let down all the people who had invested in and supported me, my voters, my friends, my family. As a candidate, I was sure my career was in ruins; as a human, I felt utterly and sickeningly like garbage.

It took me a few months of nursing my wounds before I was ready to pick up my head. Once I did, I discovered a new dream that has allowed me to serve and make a difference in exactly the way I can now see that I was meant to. I'd always thought my calling was to be on Capitol Hill, but I found that if I wanted to innovate and make a real difference, my path would be through creating a movement of girl coders who will grow up to solve our nation's and our world's most pressing problems. And here's the thing: I never would have learned that if I hadn't tried something and failed. If I had never run for office, I never would have visited classrooms on the campaign trail and seen the gender divide in schools and the potential talent our economy was missing out on. I never would have had the idea for Girls Who Code and I never would have had the privilege to help tens of thousands of girls around the country believe that they can do anything. Nor would I have cultivated the rock-solid belief that *I* can do anything.

In start-up world, failure is celebrated as a necessary part of innovation, and the entrepreneurial "fail early and often" mentality is beginning to spread. These days, we're seeing a lot of momentum to destigmatize failure both in education and in the world of business, and I love it. Smith College, for example, recently launched a program called "Failing Well" to teach high-achieving students how to deal with and even embrace setbacks, and Stanford, Harvard, Penn, and others have followed suit with similar initiatives. At the NYC-based media start-up theSkimm, founders Danielle Weisberg and Carly Zakin instituted a "Fail So Hard" hat ritual in which they pass around a hard hat at staff meetings for anyone who tried something new and failed that week to proudly wear while sharing their story.

I'm here to tell you that failing IS an option. I didn't just fail when I lost my race for the US Congress, I also did it again in 2013, in an unsuccessful bid for the office of public advocate of New York City. I failed last month when I spaced and forgot my niece's birthday, and again this morning when I put on my son's diaper and he peed on me. By failing, I learned how to embrace imperfection. I'm not afraid of either anymore. In the words of Hillary Clinton, I'd rather be "caught trying" than not at all.

Myth #6: I Need to Be Perfect to Get Ahead

Sadly, it is still true that women need to work twice as hard to earn the same respect as men in their work. Being the ultimate overachievers, most of us take that to mean that to succeed we need to not just be excellent—we need to be perfect.

The problem here is that perfection *doesn't* get us ahead. In fact, it sabotages us in more ways than we even realize.

A study released in 2015 from LeanIn.org and McKinsey & Co shows that women don't step up to positions of senior leadership not because of family obligations, but because they don't want the stress and pressure that comes along with that level of responsibility. As the *Wall Street Journal* reported in a summary of this study, "The path to senior positions is disproportionately stressful for women." I believe this is true, but I think this disproportionate stress arises in part because women think they need to do the job perfectly.

How many career opportunities have we passed up because we were afraid of being rejected or failing? How many times have we begged off an assignment or promotion saying, "I'm just not good at that"? No question that the glass ceiling and double bind are factors in women's advancement, but I believe our perfect-girl hardwiring is also a significant part of the reason women are underrepresented in leadership positions in the corporate world, in government, and elsewhere. Women don't run for office because they believe they won't fare as well as men, even though the research proves that's not at all the case. It's the fear of exposing our less-than-perfect selves or the belief that we don't have the ideal leadership skills that interferes, not capability.

I have worked with many men in law, in finance, and now in the tech industry, and one trait they all seem to have in common is a willingness to step up to take on a challenge—regardless of whether or not they're ultraprepared for it. If I ask my team at Girls Who Code who wants to spearhead a new business opportunity, without fail the dudes around the table will immediately step up—even the ones who've never done anything in that area before. Like the time my VP of finance, for example, eagerly volunteered to take over Human Resources even though he had zero prior HR experience and the organization was looking to grow by 300 percent over the next year. If I ask one of my female employees to head up a big project in new and unfamiliar territory, however, more often than not she'll question whether she's qualified to take the lead or ask if she can sleep on it (which most of the time comes back with a no).

I've seen countless men launch entire businesses without worrying about having the relevant training or expertise. Jack Dorsey, a cofounder of Twitter, started Square because he was curious about finding a way to make payments easier, not because he was knowledgeable about mobile payment. He had no experience building a financial services company, but that didn't stand in his way. Three tech dudes in their twenties founded the cool and successful beauty product app Hush when they realized—almost by accident—that makeup was the top seller on their bargain-driven site. Instead of saying, "We're guys . . . we don't know anything about makeup," they went out and put together a staff that was 60 percent women to steer them in the right direction.

This is in stark contrast to Tina, the smart, talented woman who cuts my hair. Tina wants to open her own salon, but because she doesn't know how to build a website or start a company, she's resigned herself to staying where she is. So much of this is tied into the "effortless perfection" ideal we've been taught as girls. As Rachel Simmons points out, when you believe you're supposed to make it all look easy, and pretend like you've got a handle on everything, you lose out on building a very important skill: admitting you need help. Instead of asking for help with her idea, Tina talked herself out of it. At some time or another, most of us have done the same.

The perfection ideal also hits us squarely in the paycheck. There has been a lot of talk about why there is a persistent wage gap between men and women. Is the gender and structural discrimination women face an insurmountable barrier? Are women simply picking industries that pay less? Or is it the pressure we put on ourselves to do the job perfectly that makes us opt out of high-paying opportunities? There's also the negotiation factor to consider when we think about money we may be leaving on the table. It's difficult to press for more when you're worried about seeming pushy.

This fear lurks in the majority of women, no matter how accomplished or powerful. When Academy Award–winning actress Jennifer Lawrence discovered that she earned significantly less than her male costars on the blockbuster hit *American Hustle*, she blamed herself for not having pressed for her fair share because she'd been worried about how she would be perceived. "I would be lying if I didn't say there was an element of wanting to be liked that influenced my decision to close the deal without a real fight," she wrote in the feminist newsletter *Lenny*. "I didn't want to seem 'difficult' or 'spoiled.' At the time, that seemed like a fine idea, until I saw the payroll on the Internet and realized every man I was working with definitely didn't worry about being 'difficult' or 'spoiled.'" That's exactly why we need to cultivate the courage to demand and earn the money we deserve.

The only thing Perfect Girl 3.0 can tolerate less than making mistakes is getting negative feedback. Nora works at the front desk of a hotel, where she's given quarterly performance reviews. Even if 90 percent of her review is positive, she zooms right in on the 10 percent her boss says needs improvement. Even though it's meant to show how and when she can better serve the hotel guests, all she hears is how she's screwed up and disappointed her boss. "I take it well up front, but I die inside," she said. "It eats me alive for days."

Stand up straight . . . fix your hair . . . don't mumble. But wait. If we're used to getting this kind of needling input throughout our young lives, why do we then fall apart later in life when we get less-than-glowing feedback? Why didn't that chorus of criticisms translate into grit? Likely because we're getting that input when we're too young to hear it as anything but disapproval. We don't see it as constructive advice from a loving parent trying to teach us how to present ourselves, but as disapproval. So naturally, later on, we experience the smallest criticisms as an indictment of our character.

This inability to tolerate negative feedback holds us back professionally, because it prevents us from taking in *constructive* feedback that could actually help us improve. I've had more than one guy tell me they avoid giving their female coworkers criticism—no matter how helpful feedback might be for the outcome of a project or situation—because they're afraid it will "make them cry." And unfortunately, sometimes they're right. If that's not a snapshot of perfection sabotaging us, I don't know what is.

Just like we're smart enough to know intellectually that perfection holds us back in all these ways and more, we're also wise enough to understand that just being aware of these myths doesn't mean the decades of training that went into them disappear overnight. As great as it would be to read a book and magically be free from the shackles of perfectionism, it doesn't work that way. The real key to breaking free is by retraining yourself to embrace bravery, which you'll learn how to do in Part Three. Then, and only then, does Perfect Girl 3.0 fade into the shadows, making way for the bold, confident woman to emerge.

The Truth about Perfection

Beyond all the myths about perfection lies one essential truth:
Perfect is boring.

We hold up the notion of "perfect" as the ultimate goal. No mistakes, no flaws, no rough edges. But the reality is that it's the messy, unfinished edges that make us interesting and our lives rich. Embracing our imperfection creates joy. Plus, if you're already perfect, where's the fun in learning or striving? I've always loved the stories about President Obama playing basketball. He wasn't great at it; he wasn't even technically that good. But he loved it, and so he practiced and practiced—and he got better at both getting the ball through the net, and at being okay with being less than perfect. Training a new part of his brain felt satisfying—and that quality was part of what made him a great leader.

The most interesting people I know have flaws and quirks that make them uniquely amazing. My friend Natalie is chronically late—but blows in every time with a thrilling story about where she's just come from. Daaruk leaves a mess all over our apartment whenever he comes to New York and stays with us—but has one of the most fascinating creative minds I've ever seen. Adita has absolutely no filter and will say whatever pops into her head; her observations may sting sometimes, but they are usually spot-on and helpful critiques. As for me, I know I love to be right and can be a little (okay, a lot) forceful about that, but that's what makes me such a stubborn champion for my ideals.

If you think about it, it's actually kind of funny that we even strive to be perfect in the first place, given how unfulfilling it is if and when you get there.

Bravery, on the other hand, is a pursuit that adds to your life everything perfection once threatened to take away: authentic joy; a sense of genuine accomplishment; ownership of your fears and the grit to face them down; an openness to new adventures and possibilities; acceptance of all the mistakes, gaffes, flubs, and flaws that make you interesting, and that make your life uniquely *yours*.

Part Two

Brave Is
the New Black

4

Redefining Bravery

As I write this, a watershed moment for women and bravery is playing out on the national stage. It began, of course, in the fall of 2017, when we witnessed just how awesome female bravery can be.

When the *New York Times* published a blistering exposé of Hollywood titan Harvey Weinstein revealing decades of sexual harassment, it unleashed a flood of personal stories. It felt like every day I'd get a fresh "Breaking News" alert on my phone about another powerful dude in entertainment, sports, academia, media, or politics who had used his status to harass, harm, and intimidate women into silence. Slowly at first, and then with shocking volume and speed, women joined the thunderous chorus of the #MeToo movement and freed themselves from years of shame. They came out from behind the fear and said: *No more.* No more silencing our voices. No more playing nice. No more trading in our self-worth or accepting patronizing bullshit and abuse because "that's just how it is." The results were historic, as the previously untouchable careers and reputations of these men instantaneously were reduced to smoldering ashes.

The #MeToo movement gave countless women their voices back, but it also showed the world what can happen when women band together and choose bravery. But it also gave us a different way to talk about bravery: why it matters, who has it (um, everyone), and, most of all, how we define what it means to be brave.

As of the writing of this book, we don't yet know if this movement will inspire the long-term, systemic changes in the lopsided power dynamic we desperately need. But the trends we are seeing give me real hope. I watched with pride as Serena Williams broke the unspoken genteel rules of her sport and dared to take an emotional and defiant stand at the U.S Open against the obvious bias levied at her, in an effort to clear her name and speak out for all female tennis players. I sat glued to the television with awe watching a terrified but determined Dr. Christine Blasey Ford testify before the Senate about her assault at the hands of Supreme Court Justice Brett Kavanaugh. This is how women will change the world, one brave voice at a time.

We are seeing more and more women displaying bravery in so many ways, including daring to defy entrenched stereotypes, claiming our voices and speaking out against injustice, shattering glass ceilings, and much more. It's time to redefine courage as a trait attainable by anyone and everyone, regardless of gender or biology.

Is Bravery a Male Trait?

Spoiler alert: No!

One of the most memorable responses I got to my TED talk about bravery was from a guy who posted a comment on the website Armed and Dangerous (its tagline: Sex, Software, Politics, and Firearms. Life's Simple Pleasures . . .) arguing that women are less brave because of our ovaries. Yes, you read that right: our ovaries.

He claimed that women are naturally more cautious and fearful because evolution has wired us that way. According to him, "women have only a limited number of ovulations in their lifetime and, in the EAA (environment of ancestral adaptation), pregnancy was a serious risk of death. Contrast this with men, who have an effectively unlimited supply of sperm—any individual male is far less critical to a human group's reproductive success than any individual female. Do the game theory. It would be crazy if women weren't *instinctively* far more risk-averse than men."

Well, listen up, sir: my ovaries have no say in how brave I choose to be. His reasoning may sound logical and elicit nods of approval from his male cronies, but his science is faulty at best. These kinds of arguments are sadly commonplace and need to be dismantled, *now*.

Bravery is not innate. Males are not biologically ordained to be the braver sex, and testosterone isn't the singular almighty ticket to courage. Unfortunately, this "men are hardwired to be braver" argument has been made many times in different shades. I'm sure you've heard any number of these variations: Our brains are wired differently when it comes to risk. Men are braver because they have more testosterone, or because they have been prehistorically programmed to woo reproductive partners with their bold prowess. I'm calling bullshit on all of it.

The evolutionary argument essentially comes down to reproductive success, or survival of the fittest. But this theory that male bravery is a trait that will enable the species to continue is also in need of a refresh. Today the whole Me Tarzan/You Jane notion of the big, burly caveman who fearlessly hunts down giant mastodons while his barefoot and pregnant wife hangs safely back at the cave ground nurturing the home and hearth is, to say the least, outdated. It may have taken millions of years, but we've evolved *way* past the days of a woman's job being restricted to gathering berries, or baking pies, or mixing a dry martini and acting as pleasant ornamentation.

Bravery in today's world is far more than just physical prowess, and we see hundreds of examples all around us of girls and women being brave as hell in myriad ways. From transgender soldier Chelsea Manning who exposed classified information about government corruption, to Australian senator Larissa Waters who boldly laid claim to working moms' rights and breastfed her daughter on the floor of Parliament, to the hundreds of women who risked their livelihood and reputations to blow the whistle on sexual assault at the hands of powerful men, we've amassed plenty of proof that the scope and definition of bravery has evolved mightily.

All this ends up being good news for us as women, because while we can't change biology, we sure as hell can change our environment—or at least how we respond to it. Just like we learned to be perfect girls, we teach ourselves how to be brave women.

A New View of Bravery

In 2013, I had two major life events. I lost my race for public advocate and I suffered my third miscarriage a few months later. I was a mess. All these bad things were happening to me and I didn't feel like I could stop them.

Not long after, my husband dragged me on a trip to New Zealand for our friend Jun's wedding. Jun is a little bit of an adventure nut, so the entire trip was centered on getting his wedding party to do semidangerous things. One of the activities on the agenda was bungee jumping. Now, I am terrified of heights. As in, I want to throw up when I am at the top of a building, so you can understand why I really didn't want to hurl my body off a bridge suspended only by an elastic band around my ankle. At the same time, my life felt out of control, and somehow I sensed that letting go of my fear of heights and going for it would allow me to let go of the lingering frustration and sadness I'd been carrying around, too.

So I jumped. Yes, in a tandem with my husband and with my eyes squeezed shut the whole time while I prayed to every Hindu god I knew, but I jumped. It was terrifying, but I'd be lying if I didn't say that flying through the air wasn't also thrilling and liberating. After that trip, I came back to the States, restarted my career, and tried yet again to have a baby—both of which worked out better than I ever dreamed.

Which of these acts was the bravest? If you go by the traditional (a.k.a. male) definition of brave, you'd probably say the bungee jump. But true bravery is more than being a daredevil. I consider *all three* of these choices—the jump, the career reboot after a humiliating loss, the pregnancy attempt after three devastating miscarriages—personal acts of bravery. Bravery takes so many different forms, and they're all important and valuable. *All bravery matters* because bravery feeds on itself. We build our bravery muscles one act at a time, big or small. This is what I mean when I say it's time for us to redefine bravery, on our terms.

In a World Full of Princesses, Dare to Be a Hot Dog

So how do I define bravery?

Bravery is my friend Carla who walked away from a massively successful company she'd built because her relationship with her cofounder had grown toxic. It took her a few years to work up the courage to leave because she'd given so much of herself to building the business and had banked so much on its success and didn't know who she would be if she was no longer a part of it.

Bravery is Sharon who gave up a comfortable twenty-five-year marriage and easy life because she knew deep down that she was gay and would regret it the rest of her life if she didn't follow her heart. It's my son's babysitter Audrey who battled and survived breast cancer. It's every woman who chose a life path or partner her family doesn't approve of, who had a baby on her own, or honored her inner voice that said motherhood *wasn't* the path for her. It's every woman who went back to school or to work after her kids were born, and every woman who chose not to. It's any woman who had the guts to shatter the illusion that she has it all together and ask for help.

Bravery is every woman who has spoken out against mistreatment, even if it meant risking her career or reputation. It's every woman who let herself off the hook for making a mistake, who gives herself a pass for feeding her kids pizza every once in a while instead of a home-cooked meal, who, when she knows she's wrong, says "I'm sorry" without being defensive or shifting blame.

It's brave to rock who you are, loud and proud and without apologies. We see examples of this all around us, and not only in the expected places. Not long ago, a photo of a five-year-old girl named Ainsley from North Carolina went viral after she showed up for "Princess Week" at her dance class dressed not as Cinderella or one of the sisters from *Frozen*—but as a hot dog. Her dance teacher was so wowed by Ainsley's gutsy choice that she posted a picture, and the Internet went nuts. Across the Twittersphere, people cheered for this little girl who unknowingly inspired every one of us who dream of letting our own freak flag fly. My favorite tweet: *In a world full of princesses, dare to be a hot dog.*

It just might be that today's youngest generation of girls could teach us a thing or two about bravery. My friend Valerie has a daughter who has known she was transgender from the time she was seven years old. Valerie helped her transition at that young age from James to Jasmine, and when Jasmine started a new school the following year, no one knew. She kept her birth identity a secret, unsure of whether she would be made fun of—or worse. In one of the most moving acts of bravery I can imagine, when her class was learning about gender identity, little Jasmine came out and told her classmates her secret. For a few short moments, they sat in surprised silence before gathering around to give Jasmine hugs of support and tell her they were proud to be her friend.

Bravery is taking an unpopular stand when everyone expects you to go along with the program—and then refusing to back down. In January 2017, a few days after President Trump was inaugurated, I received a phone call from Ivanka Trump's office inviting me to the White House to discuss a computer science education initiative she was spearheading. Then, a few days later, the president signed the executive order blocking the entry of citizens from seven predominantly Muslim countries. As the daughter of refugees myself I felt both sickened and a strong obligation to stand up for the many Muslim girls who participate in Girls Who Code. I declined Ms. Trump's invitation to partner with this administration.

Later that year, many big-name tech leaders gathered at an event in Detroit to celebrate the Education Department's commitment of $200 million for computer science education. Many were and still are my friends and industry colleagues. I did not attend, again feeling I had to take a stand against an administration that has inflicted such harm through its bigotry.

I felt so strongly about this that I decided to double-down

and agreed to write an op-ed for the *New York Times* explaining my position. I'll level with you: I was terrified the morning it was due to come out. I believed so deeply in what I was saying, and at the same time knew that some people in the tech industry would be very pissed off. It's very hard to stand up to powerful people, and I was acutely aware of the fact that there could be real fallout. I knew I could lose funding, because I called out some of Girls Who Code's biggest supporters, mostly tech giants and leaders who would not appreciate having their moral courage called into question. But I knew I had to brave my fear and do what I thought was right. I would rather have stood up to this issue than be silent in the face of a bully just because I was beholden to my funders.

Amazingly, the backlash I was braced for never came. Instead, donations for small amounts poured in from all over the country, along with notes of gratitude and support. Teachers who longed to see more diversity wrote to cheer me on, moms wrote to say "thank you" for my stance because, as one said, "There are things that should never be normalized." My point here isn't that I should be congratulated; it's that risky acts—like taking an unpopular stand—might be scary, but they often end up being the ones that are most appreciated and celebrated.

It takes guts to be the first one to do something, to break new ground. Take the brave women who called out Bill Cosby, Bill O'Reilly, Roger Ailes, then presidential candidate Donald Trump, investors in Silicon Valley, and many others, even knowing there was a strong likelihood that no one would believe their stories. This was before the Harvey Weinstein floodgates opened, unleashing the groundswell that became the #MeToo movement—which makes what these women did even braver. Their stories were largely discounted, their reputations were irreversibly smeared, and they were subjected to vicious threats and hateful attacks in the media, and yet, they refused to back down.

For a short while, it looked like all their pain was for nothing. But as we now know, it was anything but. Though they had no way of knowing it at the time, these women opened a tiny crack in the fault line, which grew into one of the biggest earthquakes in our modern social history. Without them, who knows if #MeToo ever would have happened? One thing I know for sure is that bravery is contagious, and when even one lone woman stands up, it inspires so many others to do the same.

Those are the big, public forms of bravery. Yet the quiet ones we tackle in our private moments are just as valuable. One of my Girls Who Code alums, Valentina, decided to grow out her natural curly hair in her junior year of high school. This may seem like an insignificant decision, but at her school, this just wasn't done; the standard of beauty was sleek, flattened hair. Did some kids make rude comments? Yes. But after so many girls told her privately that they wished they had the guts to do the same thing, Valentina decided to start a club at her school called Know Your Roots. "Society makes us feel like we need to straighten our hair just to fit in," she said. "I didn't know how many other girls felt insecure and struggle with feeling beautiful with their hair just as it is."

Bravery isn't always about doing the biggest, boldest, baddest thing. Sometimes it's braver to give yourself permission to be true to yourself by *not* doing something that is expected of you. When my son was born, for example, I assumed I would breastfeed him for as long as possible. That's what every book (and nurse in the hospital . . . and other mom I met . . .) told me I was supposed to do, and of course I wanted the very best for him, so I committed to it. I was going to be the best mom ever, damn it!

Once I went back to work, things got complicated. I found myself frantically searching every three hours for a private bathroom to pump, spilling breast milk down my blouse in tiny, smelly airplane bathrooms, and setting my alarm for 5 a.m. to get in a feeding before leaving for work. I was frustrated, exhausted, and miserable—not to mention pissed as hell at my husband for not having to deal with breastfeeding. Where was the joy of new motherhood I'd been promised? I turned to my friend Esther Perel, the renowned psychotherapist and relationship expert, for help. When I told her what was going on, she looked at me, and said plainly, "Just stop breastfeeding."

Bam! Her words hit me like a ton of bricks. I had literally *never even considered* that it was an option not to breastfeed. I stopped, and within days, I fell in love with being a mother. Finally, I could be the parent I wanted to be for my child, instead of continuing on as a pumping, crying, frustrated mess.

For every woman like the above-mentioned Sharon who bravely left a marriage, there's another woman who bravely chose to stay. For many years, it was believed that the bravest choice a woman can make when her spouse cheats is to leave and strike out on her own, not least because of the shame attached with getting a divorce. However, as Esther points out in her new book called *The State of Affairs: Rethinking Infidelity*, it isn't divorce that carries the stigma anymore. These days, choosing to *stay* if a partner has been unfaithful is looked down upon far more. And yet, for some, it may be the right choice. "Women have all kinds of reasons why they decide this one experience won't be the deciding factor in a decades-long relationship, and they should be able to do that without the fear of judgment of everyone around them," she says.

It's brave to respect yourself enough to say no to something you don't want to do, especially if it means disappointing a friend or loved one. It's nuts how hard this can be sometimes, isn't it? Our perfect-girl training that urges us to be helpful and accommodating at all costs is damn hard to shake. How many times have you agreed to go to a party, sit on a committee or board, volunteer at your kid's school, lend a family member money, or do a big favor for a friend that deep down you really didn't want to do? It takes guts to be able to say, "I'm sorry but I just don't have the time to take that on right now," and even more guts to say, "Thank you, but no," without the apology or excuse (I'm still working on that one . . .).

When you've got the "perfection or bust" conditioning, it's brave to put yourself out there and do something when you're not sure you'll succeed. Sue Lin worked for months on a treatment for a new comedy show and was terrified to send the pitch email to the content buyer at Netflix for fear she'd fall to pieces if it were rejected. But she prayed on it and hit send anyway. Marissa was terrified to start dating again after her divorce, but she wrote up a profile and joined an online dating site anyway. She knew, as we all do, that there are no guarantees, but she also knew that she was 100 percent more likely to meet someone by putting herself out there than by staying home binge watching *Downton Abbey*.

Bottom line here is that we need to recast bravery as far more than one-dimensional. It's broad, complex, and context-specific—that is, a person may be bold in one area but not another. You can be bold and fierce in your entrepreneurial spirit but skittish in dating, or perfectly comfortable investing in the stock market but wouldn't in a million years skydive. I've stood and given speeches in front of tens of thousands of people, but the thought of getting up to do karaoke at a friend's birthday party scares the hell out of me.

It's also deeply personal. For some, rappelling off a cliff is the bravest thing imaginable; for others, it's giving a speech in front of twenty people. Soldiers who fight on the battlefield are brave; so are the women who fight for the right to birth control and reproductive choice. First responders who step up to save lives are brave; so are the women who risk their livelihood to speak up about sexual assault at the hands of powerful men. Senator John McCain was brave in September 2017 when he crossed party lines to stand up for what he believes; so was Shonda Rhimes when she made interracial couples the norm on her groundbreaking hit television shows.

It's all bravery, and it all matters.

Brave like Women

It's no coincidence that our society has adopted the phrase "she's got balls" as a perverse compliment for when a woman does something bold or gutsy. The implication, of course, is that men's testicles are their seat of bravery and power. Well, just like we don't need to be like men to be brave, we definitely don't need to be like men to succeed. This is old, tired thinking that I'm so over.

It's not as though acting like a dude really gets us anywhere anyway. At work, even when women adopt the same career advancement strategies, they still get lower pay. We've heard again and again about the double bind we face: If we aren't nurturing, warm, and kind, we aren't liked—but we get shut out of leadership positions if we are. We're damned if we're confident, outspoken, and gutsy, and doomed if we aren't. Study after study shows that when women display stereotypically "masculine" traits such as toughness or nonverbal dominance (i.e., staring someone in the eye when speaking), they can come up against intense backlash. The receptivity to women displaying assertive behavior in the workplace just isn't there. I want to add, "For now." I am confident that if we reach back and start rewiring kids early, cutting out the gendered behaviors at the pass, we start changing this generationally.

But what about us here and now? To escape this double bind, we need to become brave not like men, but *brave like women*. We need to say, fuck the traditional rules and definitions, and do it our way, because we know that our contributions are just as valuable—if not more so. It's time to play to our strengths instead of hiding them, no matter how "masculine" or "feminine" we think they are. Women are more emotional than men? Awesome. I say that's an asset, not a liability, and the research backs that up. As just one of many examples, a report from PriceWaterhouseCooper and the Crowdfunding Center showed that women are 32 percent more successful at generating funds via crowdfunding than men. Why? Because they use more emotional and inclusive language in their pitches, which investors found more appealing than the clichéd sports and war metaphors and the typical dry business language.

It's the same with women and risk-taking. Yes, women are generally more risk averse than men. But where you might say timid, I say intelligently cautious and thoughtful. There's a reason why so many speculated that the economic crisis would never have happened if it were Lehman Sisters running the show.

We have spent so much time trying to figure out how to get into the game following the rules written by men. That makes about as much sense to me as trying to explore uncharted territory by following somebody else's path. We can't become unique by copying someone else's formula any more than we can become successful by striving for someone else's definition of success. And really, what's the point of succeeding by someone else's rules anyway?

We need to change our approach and do things authentically. Being brave like women is about making choices based on what we want and what makes us happy, not what others expect or want for us. If being a senator or a Fortune 500 CEO are your true goals, awesome! But they don't have to be. Just as there is no one "right" way to be brave, there is no one universal definition of success.

Look, we know the biases against women exist in the workplace, in politics, and elsewhere. There are real structural challenges against women. There's no denying that. Of the five hundred thousand elected officials in this country, 79 percent are still white men. Does that mean that if you're a brown-skinned woman you shouldn't run for office? Of course not. It means you should accept the challenges, recognize you might fail, and *do it anyway*.

I'm not telling you to just try harder to achieve your goals. What I am telling you is not to let fear stop you from going after them. I'm telling you not to give up before you try. If you succeed, the success will be even sweeter because it was fueled by courage and by genuine passion. If you don't, you may be disappointed but you will still feel proud, because it will be what Carol Dweck calls an "honest failure."

We've come a long way, but the reality is that it will still be a while before we see big changes in the gender equality landscape. That's the bad news. The good news is that how we respond and act in the face of these obstacles is up to us. I believe we need to stop trying to wrestle for power, respect, and opportunities from others and instead bravely make them for ourselves.

Don't misunderstand me: I think we need to keep pushing as hard as we can for cultural change. It's not okay for our girls to grow up in a world that tells them they have to starve themselves to meet some unrealistic standard of beauty, or that getting a degree in computer programming or speaking their minds is the exclusive domain of boys. We need to create a better world for them and for ourselves, and I believe we do this by defining bravery on our own terms one cause, one goal, one failure, one hot dog in a world of princesses at a time. We do it by cultivating the bravery that lives inside each and every one of us.

5

Why Be Brave?

*I*f you think about it, pretty much everything worth doing in life requires bravery. Bravery is why we try that twentieth cartwheel that we triumphantly nail after falling nineteen times. It's what sends us off to college or far from home where we don't know anyone, what encourages us to follow a passion into our first job. Bravery enables us to start a business, change careers, or ask for the salary we deserve. It allows us to be vulnerable enough to ask for help and helps us muster the strength to forgive someone who hurt us. It inspires us to be generous and support other women without fearing that it diminishes us. As Winston Churchill once said, "Courage is the first of human virtues because it makes all others possible."

Bravery makes falling in love possible. It takes courage to allow someone to see the real you, flaws and all, and to accept someone else who is equally imperfect. As Esther Perel told me, bravery allows us to be vulnerable and reciprocal, which in turn makes relationships robust. "People sometimes do the wrong things or hurt each other's feelings . . . being able to speak up about it or say 'I fucked up, I'm sorry' takes bravery," she says. "Bravery is the ability to see yourself as flawed and own it without plunging instantly into shame. It's also the ability to experience joy for the great things that happen to the other person, even if they have nothing to do with you."

Bravery transforms *all* our relationships from glossy and shellacked to honest, raw, and real. How often are we honest—truly honest—with our friends? Only by building your bravery muscles, does the veneer get melted and true heart-to-heart connections are forged. I have a crew of seven girlfriends from law school. Life got busy and we see each other now only once or twice a year, but when we do, it's like no time passed. We talk about the deeper stuff that's going on—the miscarriages, the bumps in our marriages, the fears we carry that no one else ever sees. It takes courage to open up like that to other human beings, but it's such a privilege to have this kind of safe space to be fully open and real.

Bravery makes us better parents. When we let go of the unrealistic expectations for ourselves, we then naturally ease up on our kids. When we stop obsessing about our kids' grades or college essays, we help them see the joy in learning. We show them by example how to pursue excellence without making it about perfection, and that the world won't end if they screw up or fail. It's brave to allow your kid to be exactly who they are and do what they love, *even if you don't agree with their choices*. They're happier and healthier for it, though, and so are you.

This may sound a little cheesy, but bravery helps us turn our dreams into reality. I don't care if your dream is to be in the C-suite, quit your job and start a business, be a hip-hop dancer, come out to your family, work at an animal sanctuary, run a marathon, go back to school, publish a novel, get married and have children, or make your mark on the world through activism—bravery will help get you from here to there.

Forget cultivating the perfectly polished exterior; that's just a flimsy façade that can come toppling down at any minute.

When we build our bravery muscles, we're safe for real because we know we can handle whatever comes our way. Bravery doesn't guarantee that everything will work out, just that we'll be okay if it doesn't. No matter what demons we face, bravery allows us to stand strong and *keep going*. Bravery—not perfection—is the only true armor there is.

Bravery keeps us afloat when we might otherwise sink. As we all know, shit happens in life that we can't control. We lose jobs, face health crises, lose loved ones—these are hard realities we can't avoid. When the really hard times hit, though, they are far easier to weather when our bravery muscles are strong. I'm not suggesting that the challenges we face won't sometimes feel cruel, unfair, and disheartening. But I am saying that we can acknowledge these feelings and (here's the brave part) persevere anyway.

Most of all, bravery sets us free. It gives us the power to claim our voice, and to leave behind what makes us unhappy and go for what sparks in our souls. It allows us to see that our gloriously messy, flawed, real selves are in fact the true definition of perfection.

Part Three

Kiss the
Perfect Girl Goodbye:
The Path
to Being Brave

Very early one morning, I was walking through JFK airport in New York, on my way to a speaking engagement in Atlanta. Because I'd gotten up so early to get to the airport—and because I had to go right to the event when we landed—I put my big curlers in my hair and left them there, planning to take them out right when we touched down. As I was going through security, I saw people staring at me and my head full of giant curlers, and I had to laugh. I must have looked a little ridiculous, but you know what? *I didn't care.* I had a moment of absolute giddiness realizing that not caring what other people think had gone from being something I deliberately practiced to being an automatic habit.

It's time we made bravery a permanent habit. And we're going to do it the way we train ourselves out of any bad habit into a better one: by first becoming aware of the behavior you need to change (chasing perfection), making a decision to change (opening this book), then consciously and repeatedly replacing the old behaviors and mindsets with better ones. Eventually, the new and better habits become so ingrained in you that they become a natural way of being.

The strategies in these chapters are here to help you do exactly that. They are a collection of tips, ideas, and practices I've gathered both from experts and from finding my own way from perfect to bravery (again and again and again . . .) to help you develop or reinforce your bravery habit. They aren't meant to be a prescription for "how to become brave"; there's no singular formula for that. What it means to be brave is personal for each of us, so I want you to pick, choose, and adapt the strategies that feel most relevant to you and that speak to what you need most. If saying no causes you anxiety, you may want to focus on the tips in Chapter Eight, "Nix the Need to Please." If fear of rejection is your thing, go right to Chapter Seven, "Get Caught Trying."

For those who want to learn how to build a sisterhood of strength by supporting other women in personal and meaningful ways, Chapter Nine is all about how we can band together to play for Team Brave. And for any of you who still aren't convinced that you'll survive a failure or serious mistake, take a look at the rebound plan in Chapter Ten, "Surviving a Big, Fat Failure."

Within each chapter you'll find several daily practices that you can use in any order, as often and whenever you can. Just like with any form of exercise, the more you practice them, the easier they get, and pretty soon you'll find the iron grip of perfection loosening and the bravery buzz taking hold. Don't worry, I won't ask you to walk through an airport with a head full of curlers (unless you want to), but I promise you, there's nothing more thrilling than the rush you'll get once you start practicing small acts of bravery!

6

Build a Bravery Mindset

I wasn't born brave. In fact, I was pretty timid and fearful when I was young—until the last day of eighth grade when a group of bigoted bitches pushed me too far.

The sun was shining brightly that day, and there was a warm breeze. (Isn't it always beautiful out just before something ugly happens?) Yearbooks were being passed around and the excitement of graduation was in the air. I was leaning up against the wall talking to my friend Phu when they surrounded me—the original mean girls—jeering and calling me a "haji." They were laughing hysterically, taunting me and inviting me to a fight. Yes, a real fistfight.

At first I rolled my eyes. As one of the only Indian families in my neighborhood, I was used to being harassed. Many mornings I stood outside the front of my house helping Mom and Dad clean up the remnants of the previous night's TP-ing or egging. Once, someone spray-painted "dot head go home" on the side of our house. As my dad and I picked the shards of eggshell off our lawn, I wondered if this was what he had imagined for us. My parents came to this country as refugees, fleeing a brutal dictator in Uganda. They were given ninety days to leave, or they would be shot on the spot. Somehow, though, in spite of all the violence they had witnessed, Mom and Dad always chose to show love and kindness.

They relished their freedom in America and assimilated. Dad changed his name from Mukund to Mike, and Mom quietly brushed off insults about her sari and bindi that she faced at the local Kmart. They silently endured such indignities, big and small, and constantly urged my sister and me to do the same.

Usually, I listened. Until finally, I'd had enough. I was tired of being obedient and quiet. So, when the girls told me to meet them that afternoon after school for a fight, I looked them straight in the eyes and said yes.

When the final bell rang, Phu grabbed me and tried to drag me toward the bus, "Let's just go, Resh, you don't need to do this." God, I wanted to get on that school bus so badly, but I couldn't. I knew I was going to get beat up. I knew I wasn't David against Goliath and this wasn't going to be a scene out of *Karate Kid*. I literally had no chance of winning that fight. I was just a small Indian girl, whose Hindu parents had taught her nonviolence. But I couldn't let those girls make me run and hide. So I walked back behind the school and there they were, armed with a Wilson tennis racket, a bat, and a plastic bag full of shaving cream.

Before I could even set down my backpack, the pack of mean girls was coming at me. All I heard were the screams and laughter from the crowd of spectators—that is, almost every eighth grader in our school—that had assembled behind them. Knuckles crashed into my eye, and I blacked out almost immediately. When I came to moments later, the kids were gone; just the cans of shaving cream and empty plastic bags were left behind.

I woke up the next morning in pain and terrified. I had

this beautiful black-and-blue lace dress that I planned to wear to my graduation that Sunday, and now I also had a big black eye to go with it. But the physical pain wasn't the worst part. I was embarrassed. To me, that black eye meant that I had failed at assimilating, at being accepted by my peers. I didn't know how I would walk into that ceremony with my head held high. But I did know that if I *didn't* show up, I would always cower. My graduation was a huge turning point for me. By showing up, I made a decision to be my whole self, even if that meant acknowledging that I had failed at fitting in.

So I pinned my hair in an updo and painted my lips pink and decided I was going to *rock* that black eye. My graduation turned out to be my first failure party. And, honestly, it was the best decision I could have made. I felt bolder and stronger and prouder that day than I ever had, knowing it was better to walk around with a black eye than with a heart full of regret.

The black eye eventually faded, and, sadly, for a long time, the memory of how I felt that graduation day faded, too. You'd think that girlhood experience would have fundamentally changed me, but over time, the memory got buried under the weight of everything I was working so hard to accomplish. It wasn't until that pivotal August day many years later when something in me snapped and said *Enough!* that I remembered how freeing facing my fears had felt. That was when something in me shifted for good and I decided to make a lifelong commitment to bravery.

I've learned that when it comes to being brave, your mindset determines everything. If I'd believed on those two fateful days that I simply wasn't capable of courage—that I just wasn't the type of girl who could stand up for herself against a pack of vicious mean girls, or that I wasn't the type of woman who could quit the life path she'd chosen to make her parents happy and go after what she really wanted—then I would have proven those things to be true. But somehow, I believed I could *grow into* the brave, confident person I wanted to be, and eventually, through lots of failures and rebounds, setbacks and small victories, I did.

Obviously, we can't simply will ourselves to be brave. There's no magic potion, no silver bullet. And it's not like we can do one courageous thing and then we're done. It's a process that we're called to, day after day, and it requires consistent practice. We'll always face new setbacks and bigger challenges, and to meet them requires strategies to cultivate the mindset out of which bravery can become a lifelong habit.

Strategy: Keep Your Tank Full

Every woman I know is exhausted. We do, and take on, so much—between working and being a mom, friend, daughter, mentor, keeper of the family's well-being, pet caretaker, travel planner, and master scheduler. Add to that the stress of trying to do all that perfectly and a deep-seated drive to put others' needs above our own and you've got a recipe for serious burnout.

But here's the good news: the era of burnout as a badge of honor is over. It used to be considered badass to juggle fifty things at once, to work twenty-four seven even if we were on vacation or had the flu, to subsist on caffeine and PowerBars. Not anymore. Now that we know the toll of these depleting habits, workaholism is out and wellness is in. After all, Arianna Huffington, arguably one of the biggest media moguls of our time, wrote a blockbuster bestseller about the power of sleep. That's right: the fifty-second-most-powerful woman in the world according to *Forbes* is on a mission to prove that one of the ultimate secrets to success is getting enough shut-eye. Good enough for me.

It's not just that fatigue costs us and the economy billions of dollars in lost productivity ($411 billion a year, to be exact), or that stress has been linked to serious ailments from obesity to heart conditions, or that we look and feel like crap when we're running on fumes. As Arianna pointed out when I told her I was writing about women and bravery, we can't be brave if we're burned out.

She's right, of course. There's no way you will have the stamina to take risks if you feel like you're out of gas. It's damn near impossible to muster the courage to say no or to try something scary and new when your energy is depleted and your brain is fried. I don't know about you, but when I'm wiped out, the last thing I want to think about is putting myself out there in any way. All I want to do is put on leggings and a sweatshirt, throw my hair up in a bun, swap out my contacts for my dorky glasses, collapse on the couch and escape into the oblivion of Netflix. Exhaustion and being overwhelmed are pretty much instantaneous bravery killers.

It demands emotional and even physical energy, stamina, and endurance to leave our comfort zone, which is why the first and most essential key to cultivating a bravery mindset is to put your wellness first.

Here are the basics:

- **Prioritize your health.** Lianna walked around with a painful sinus infection for four days because she didn't have time to go to the doctor. Yet when her dog got sick and started suddenly vomiting, she immediately dropped everything to run him over to the vet. Sound familiar? It's crazy how many of us shove our basic self-care aside—

and it's no wonder so many of us end up suffering from autoimmune diseases, back pain, depression, or worse. It's brave to say: *no more*. No more showing up for work or to meet a friend when you have the cold from hell just because you didn't want to let anyone down. No more sacrificing your workout plans or a doctor's appointment to accommodate someone else's schedule. You wouldn't ignore a troubling mole on your kid's shoulder, or let your best friend get away with postponing her mammogram because she's too busy, so take an equally powerful stance for your own well-being. Consider prioritizing your health as your first official act of radical bravery.

- **Take that "me time."** A 2012 national study done by the Family and Work Institute proved what we all intellectually know to be true: the women who make it a regular habit to set aside time for themselves are much more satisfied with their lives than those who put it off. But just because we know that relaxing and replenishing is good for us doesn't mean we actually do it. Saying yes to taking care of yourself usually means saying no to someone else in some form or another, and for those of us who are wired to think that prioritizing our needs is selfish, that's really, *really* hard. But that's also what makes it brave.

- **Get some sleep—seriously.** I'm going to go out on a limb and guess that you try to squeeze every last thing you can into your day, from waking up at dawn to work out and make your kids pancakes (even though cereal would be perfectly fine) to staying up late answering emails and cleaning every last dirty dish. Perfectionism compels us to burn the candle at both ends, but don't fool yourself into thinking that you can "get by" on only a few hours of sleep. Studies have shown that seven to nine hours a night is what you need to operate at your best. Being well rested won't automatically make you braver, but I can promise you that *not* being well rested will seriously get in your way.

- **Learn to meditate.** Scientific studies prove that meditation shrinks the amygdala, which is the part of the brain that is driving the bus when we feel threatened or scared. For a small time investment of ten to twenty minutes a day, you can literally rewire your brain to respond to everyday life situations from a place of calm rather than fear.

- **Schedule in gym time.** You knew this was coming. Sorry, but the stats are all true: Exercise has been proven to ward off everything from excess weight to stress to anxiety to disease—all of which influence whether we're feeling empowered or depleted. Besides, nothing makes you feel fiercer than looking in the mirror and seeing a strong, sexy warrior babe reflected back at you. (Just to be clear: we're talking about exercising to feel healthy, inspired, and accomplished . . . *not* to sculpt a perfect body! Keep it real; you know the difference.) As every fitness guru will tell you, the secret to making a fitness routine stick is to schedule it in advance, just like you would anything important.

Strategy: Claim the Power of "Yet"

I'm not brave.
I'm not the kind of person who takes risks.

I'm just not good at saying no.

Declarations like these are the very definition of what it means to be trapped in the fixed mindset I talked about earlier in the book. They leave no room for growth or progress; just a dead end. But look what happens when you add one small word to the end of those statements:

I'm not brave . . . yet.

I'm not the kind of person who takes risks . . . yet.

I'm just not good at saying no . . . yet.

Suddenly, you've gone from stuck to free. You're growing toward something, on your way from where you are to where you might go. Psychologist and motivational pioneer Carol Dweck referred to this as embracing the "power of yet" as opposed to "the tyranny of now."

This small mental shift can have a powerful impact, especially when it comes to reframing mistakes. You didn't "not succeed"—you just haven't succeeded *yet*. When you look at it that way, mistakes don't have to become glaring signs of permanent limitations or failures—they're just temporary setbacks. Less-than-perfect attempts don't have to put a hard stop to the story; instead, you can turn an "I blew it" into an "Okay, tried that, now I'll try something else."

Veronica Roth, author of the blockbuster *Divergent* series, told me that when she was growing up, there wasn't a single area of her life that wasn't touched by her desire to be perfect. Back then, if she wrote a draft that didn't come out so great, she would pronounce the whole thing "garbage." Now, she's trained herself to say, "This draft has potential and just needs to be fixed." In other words, "This draft isn't excellent . . . yet."

None of us is a finished product; we're all works in progress. Next time you catch yourself making a blanket declaration about your limitations, remind yourself of that by adding a "yet" onto the end and you'll immediately feel the difference.

Strategy: Do the "Drama vs. Wisdom" Test

Being thoughtful is smart. It's wise to survey the landscape and weigh the pros and cons before taking any action that involves risk. It's when we overthink, overprepare, and over-analyze that we veer out of cautious territory and into Stucks-ville.

The border between those two zones is marked by fear. The key to crossing it is learning to recognize when you're being wisely cautious and when you're talking yourself out of something just because you're afraid. When you pass on a challenge or an opportunity, ask yourself, *Does this really not make sense to do, or am I not doing it because I'm scared and out of my comfort zone?*

Or, as my brilliant executive coach, Rha Goddess, puts it, "Is that your drama or your wisdom talking?"

You'll know it's your wisdom when you feel at peace with your decision. The voice of wisdom is calm, with a sense of authority. Drama, on the other hand, tends to be a little whinier, more nervous, and more defensive (imagine a guilty Chihuahua and you'll get the picture). If you hear yourself making excuses, find yourself compelled to explain your choice to anyone who will listen, or just feel vaguely disappointed or unhappy, it's a sign that your drama is calling the shots.

I often think about this in weighing whether I want to run for public office again. Up until I started working on this book, I was absolutely sure the reason I wasn't going to run was because I felt like I was making a bigger impact doing what I'm currently doing with Girls Who Code. But after putting the question about drama versus wisdom to hundreds of women, I have to turn the lens on myself and ask, *Is it actually that I'm afraid to fail again?* (The jury is still out on this one.)

The next time you're about to take a pass on something, hit pause and ask yourself if it's your drama or your wisdom that's talking. It's a great way to practice calling bullshit on your automatic excuses and to get real with yourself instead.

Strategy: Look for Your Ledge

What's the one thing you're most afraid of doing? The thing that if you could do it, you know it would make a major difference for you in your life?

Rha Goddess calls that one thing your "ledge." She says all of us are being called to some ledge, whether we've wanted to consciously acknowledge it or not. I call that ledge "my scary thing." Whatever you call it, she's right that we all have at least one challenge, one change, one move, one dream quietly calling out to us that we're afraid to step up to. I've asked dozens of women the question of what's the one scary thing they could do that would shift things for them in a profound way, and the answers always came quickly. Jillian's one thing is telling her husband about her mountain of hidden debt. For Dawn, it's finding a job that pays more. For Lissette, the ledge is losing the seventy-five excess pounds that are impairing her happiness and mobility. Other women talked about ending toxic relationships, telling grown children they need to move out, taking care of legal issues, or changing their career or other life path. We may not be doing that one big thing (yet!), but deep down, we know what it is, and identifying it is the first step in seeing where we're stuck and what we can work toward tackling.

Where's your ledge that you're being invited to step out onto? If you're not sure, start looking where your comfort zone is; as Rha says, anyplace you're comfortable is a place to be a little bit suspicious. I'm not saying you have to go there just yet—or even at all—but training yourself to at least *look* for it channels your mindset in the right direction.

Strategy: Ask Yourself: What Scares Me More?

A highlight of the 2016 Women's March on Washington for me was the protesters' signs. There were so many smart, defiant, fierce, and funny ones (a personal favorite: "Hands too small, can't build a wall," but that's another conversation). Clever jabs aside, one in particular stood out for me, made by a quiet woman from New Hampshire named Mara. Mara is an introvert who hates big crowds, yet she showed up to bravely stand among the throngs of people filling the streets of D.C. that day. Her sign read, "Crowds scare me. Trump scares me more."

I love this so much more than just a political statement. It's a strategy we can use to put fears into perspective by shifting our focus from what scares us about taking action to what scares us about *not* doing something.

My friend Adam Grant, an organizational psychologist and *New York Times* bestselling author, says that the most brilliant, innovative people are very often procrastinators or afraid of taking risks. So what moves someone to go from just incubating a great idea to putting it out into the world? He says it's the moment when the fear of failure is overtaken by the fear of failing to try. It's when they realize that while they might fail, that's better than failing to matter. Just imagine what you might achieve once you make the shift from worrying about whether you'll make a fool of yourself to instead asking if you'll one day regret never taking the chance.

"A lot of it is doing mental time travel," Adam says. "Being able to mentally fast-forward ten years ahead is one of the most uniquely useful human skills. Maybe right now being told no or failing feels really uncomfortable, but even more uncomfortable might be someone staring back at you ten years from now who was unwilling to pursue that ambition. Mental time travel helps you detach from the immediate consequences of taking that risk and think about it with some perspective: *What will I weight more heavily, the sting of failing, or the pang of what might have been?*

For me the shift happened at age thirty-three. I'd always thought there was plenty of time to run for office, but I woke up one day and realized, *Oh shit . . . I'm not that young anymore.* The thought of running for office scared me, but the idea of running out of time to do so scared me more. Fear of regret can be a powerful motivator.

So can envy. I have a friend who is an amazing writer. She took a job as a journalism professor, but she hates it; all she wants to do is be an author. Anytime someone writes a book that she feels like she could have written, it's like a stab in the heart. While the torture she felt every weekend reading the Sunday *New York Times Book Review* certainly wasn't fun, it did provoke her to finally start working on her own book.

Author Veronica Roth, who suffered from lifelong anxiety and paralyzing self-doubt, eventually had to ask herself which was scarier: putting herself out there, or stifling her voice. "The scary thing about writing is opening yourself up to criticism and being vulnerable with strangers, but it was more important to me to grow as a writer than to avoid criticism," she told me.

I met a woman named Lauren who worried her daughters would grow up to avoid challenges just because they were afraid. So even though the idea of going white water rafting with them on a family trip scared the wits out of her, she went for it. The idea of modeling fear for her girls scared her more than putting on a wetsuit and getting into that boat.

When you smack up against a wall of fear, instead of focusing on what scares you, try taking a step back and asking yourself, *What might the cost be if I* don't *do this . . . and which option scares me more?*

Strategy: Take Your Own Advice

Here's another easy but highly useful tip from Adam Grant:

When you're faced with a "scary" challenge or opportunity and debating what to do, ask yourself what advice you would give someone else in that situation. "On average, we make better decisions for others than we do for ourselves," he explains. "All we need for ourselves is one or two reasons not to do it and we can give up. But if we're giving someone else advice, we can take a big step back and discuss the fundamental reasons why they should or shouldn't do it."

For instance, imagine you're asked to give a presentation at work that pushes you outside your normal comfort zone. Maybe the audience is much bigger than you're used to, or public speaking in front of clients makes you break out in a cold sweat. Left to your own rationalization, you might conclude it's just not worth it and say no.

Now imagine a good friend was the one who was asked to give the presentation and asked what you thought she should do. Chances are you wouldn't say, "Oh jeez, no way . . . forget that." You might point out to her what a great opportunity it is for her to try something new, to overcome her fear, or to get more visibility at work. You'd talk through the pros and cons, maybe even come up with some coping strategies to help her feel more confident.

Amazing how easy it is to encourage the people we love to be brave, isn't it? Even more amazing is what happens when we do the same for ourselves.

Strategy: Set Daily Bravery Challenges

One day, a Girl Scout from Washington, D.C., named Alice Paul Tapper noticed the boys in her fourth-grade class raised their hands much more often than the girls. It bothered her to see the girls staying quiet and she guessed it was because they were afraid their answers would be wrong and they would feel embarrassed, or that they worried they wouldn't be able to get the teacher's attention. Together with her troop, she created a "Raise Your Hand" patch to encourage girls to use their voices. Girls earn the patch by pledging to raise their hands in class and encouraging other girls to do the same. Since then the "Raise Your Hand" patch has caught on with Girl Scout troops all around the country.

If Alice and hundreds of other ten-year-old girls can practice bravery on a daily basis, so can we. I can't promise you a patch for your efforts, but I can promise that with every bravery challenge you take on, that muscle will grow stronger.

As Dr. Meredith Grossman explains, one of the best ways to change what we think and believe is by changing what we do—kind of like changing from the outside in. It's hard to believe something to be true without having the actual experience of it; seeing it in action gives you the proof. You can work hard to convince yourself that you won't forever lose the respect of your colleagues if you say something dumb in a meeting, but until you actually utter something less than brilliant and see that nothing terrible happens, you won't entirely believe it to be true.

There's no set path to "becoming brave" other than taking actions over and over again that reinforce bravery rather than fear. That's why I'm challenging you to choose one strategy each day from the chapters that follow and do it. I've said it before but it bears repeating; bravery is a muscle, the more you work it, the stronger it becomes. By practicing bravery on a daily basis when you're on stable ground, you set yourself up to survive the bigger, unexpected challenges that life will undoubtedly throw your way.

7

Get Caught Trying

Sometimes, the best way to become fearless is to walk straight into the fire of fear. I got my first taste of this on my final day of eighth grade, when I faced down that gang of vicious mean girls who wanted to kick my ass just for being brown, and again when I ignored the political elite who were telling me it wasn't my turn and I should get to the back of the line. I walked into that fire when I tried yet again to get pregnant after three miscarriages, when I launched Girls Who Code even though I knew nothing about coding, and in hundreds of little ways every day since. Practicing bravery in the small ways in my day-to-day life has allowed me to step up and face my larger fears when it counted.

Braving my fear enables me to go after what I want and do what I think is right, even when everything isn't perfectly aligned or guaranteed to work. As I said earlier, in the words of my mentor Hillary Clinton, I'd rather be caught trying than not at all. The strategies in this chapter will help you learn to get comfortable with your own imperfection—and yes, even failure—so you can stop being afraid of it. You've likely heard some version of the adage that bravery is not the absence of fear, but acting in the face of it. Because when you face your fear, you take away its power. That becomes your secret weapon that lets you escape the tyranny of perfection and go after what you really want.

Strategy: Ask for Feedback

For perfection-seeking girls and women, critical feedback is a bitch. If someone gives us anything less than a glowing review, we wither inside and immediately spiral into "I suck." We take it as a permanent indictment of our character. It's sickening, demoralizing, and altogether brutal.

The antidote to this is not to avoid criticism, but to actually invite it. Yes, you read that right: I want you to actively ask for cold, hard, unadulterated feedback. And *not* when you know you've aced something, but when you know you've got plenty of room for improvement. It's kind of like radical exposure therapy to desensitize yourself. It might feel like a swift kick in the gut for an instant, but the more you do it, I promise, you're going to discover really fast that critical feedback doesn't hurt nearly as much as you think it will. Eventually it becomes kind of like a positive addiction: I now actually love getting it because it points me to my next challenge.

Recently I spoke at a rally right after the woman to whom I lost my public advocate race, who happens to be an amazing speaker and knows how to fire up a crowd. It was pouring out, my son had been pulling on my coat to get my attention all day, and I was especially run-down from traveling; to be honest, I'd been doing so much public speaking that I hadn't really given much thought to what I was going to say. I figured, *It'll be fine. I've got this.* After I spoke, I got into the car with my husband and asked him how I did. He looked at me and said, "You kind of sucked."

Um, what?

"You were a two, maybe a three, out of ten," he said (as you can tell, we don't pull any punches in our relationship).

The tough love admittedly didn't feel great in that second—especially since it was an already serious sore spot to face the woman I'd lost my election to. Still, I was really grateful for his honesty. What good would it do me for him to sugarcoat and tell me I was great when I wasn't? For a few weeks after that, I thought long and hard about how I'd gotten into my comfort zone with public speaking and how I could get better in rally formats. I've now gotten excited about recognizing that even if I'm at the height of my game, I can (and should) still find ways to improve.

The key to this strategy is to not just endure feedback, but to actively seek it out all the time, everywhere, from everyone—*especially* when you don't want to hear it. I gave a speech recently in front of four thousand people and got a standing ovation. I was feeling really good about it and didn't really want anything to spoil that, but I still asked my staff to critique me. Why? Because even the best speeches can always be better. I even do this in my personal life; after my husband and I have an argument and the dust settles, I ask him how I could have communicated better.

Angela Duckworth, author of the bestselling book *Grit*, identified the courage to accept feedback as one of the four critical factors for building grit. Those who have grit are constantly looking to improve, so they ask, "How did I do?" Angela points to great athletes as examples. Think about someone like Michael Jordan or Michael Phelps; how did they get that good? First, they focused narrowly on the one thing they wanted to improve on. Then they practiced . . . and practiced . . . with 100 percent focus. But the other key component is that they solicited feedback. They had the courage to face the fact that they weren't perfect—to ask how and where they weren't great—so they could refine and get better. They were living at the cutting edge of their ability and were totally turned on by that.

When you're pushing yourself beyond where you're comfortable and striving for improvement, you're firing on all cylinders. That's when you enter that magical psychological state known as "flow." One secret to getting to that blissful state is to build up the courage to hear feedback, which points you to the next area of improvement, and the next, and the next. The more you do this, the easier it gets, and the faster you'll go from feeling kicked in the gut by criticism to feeling grateful and empowered by it.

Inviting criticism enables you to bear witness to your own imperfections and build a tolerance for them. First tolerance, then acceptance, and then, believe it or not, joy.

Strategy: Surround Yourself with Rejection

Boys and men aren't tyrannized by failure. Because they've been trained from a young age to shake it off and just keep going (a fall off the monkey bars, a science experiment that bombs, a date invitation that gets turned down . . .), mistakes and rejection tend to roll off them in a way that most women can only envy. Our perfect-girl training has kept us safely isolated from the sting of rejection and failure, but as you know, it also weakened our resilience in our adult life. One way we build back our resilience and take the sting out of rejection and failure is by normalizing it.

When Shaan was a baby, our pediatrician told us to skip the excessive use of hand sanitizer and expose him to as many germs as possible to build up his immunity. Much in the same way, we can all immunize ourselves against rejection by exposing ourselves to it. In other words, don't hide from rejection—own it!

Right now on my fridge I still have the original rejection letter from Yale Law School taped up right next to the rejection letter from my community board. Throwing them away gave them too much power over me. Staring them down, however, put me back into the driver's seat. They remind me every day to be brave and keep going.

The more I exposed myself to rejection, the less it terrorized me. I won't lie: there's always been a little undercurrent of a living-well-is-the-best-revenge fantasy there; I dreamed one day of showing these people what I could accomplish, which gave my motivation a little extra edge.

Display your rejections proudly; they're a mark of your bravery. Talk about your rejections, mistakes, and flubs, and invite your friends and colleagues to do the same. Read as many stories as you can about famous and accomplished people who lived through failures, like Stephenie Meyer, whose manuscript for *Twilight* was rejected by twenty publishers before it found a home, or Steve Jobs, who was long ago fired from Apple. Their setbacks didn't destroy them, and neither will yours. In fact, they'll set you free.

Strategy: Get Your Fear Signals Straight

The funny thing about feeling fear is that 99 percent of the time, it's a false alarm. Our nervous system was designed to keep us safe from predators, so anytime we feel afraid, our primitive brain believes we're about to be attacked and sends the signal to run like hell.

The problem, of course, is that your nervous system doesn't know the difference between perceived danger and real danger. Your heart may be hammering and your palms might get sweaty—clear signals from your body that you're in jeopardy—but realistically, standing up to your boss literally will not kill you. The doomsday we fear almost never happens. Your friend isn't likely to disown you forever if you forgot to call when her mom came home from the hospital. You probably won't lose your job if you show up late for a meeting. There's a slim chance your kid's future will be irrevocably destroyed if you accidentally send a snarky email about your kid's teacher to her, instead of sending it to your husband (yes, I did that, and no, Shaan didn't get blackballed).

When we're driven to be perfect, any small flaw or mistake will trigger the alarm and send us running. What we want to do is train ourselves to recognize that, most of the time, we should ignore the alarm because it's not a signal of genuine danger. It's not a tiger that's chasing you—it's your modern-day anxiety.

I love this advice Dr. Meredith Grossman gives her patients: Do the opposite of what your anxiety is telling you to do. Your anxiety will *always* scream at you to run, hide, bail. So don't! If it's telling you to skip that networking event because you'll feel too awkward, go. If it's urging you to spend hours scrubbing down your apartment before your mother-in-law comes over, do a light cleanup and leave it at that. If it's telling you to avoid making a public gaffe at all costs, type gibberish on your Facebook page and post it. It's so liberating to see that, honestly, no one cares. And if they do, really, does it even matter?

Look for whatever makes you feel uncomfortable and go there. Show up ten minutes late without apologizing profusely. Send an inconsequential email with a grammatical mistake in it. Wear a shirt with a stain on it. Leave the house not looking your best. Wear a skirt without shaving your legs that morning. Tell a friend that you're feeling insecure. Practicing imperfection doesn't have to be superhard or grandiose. You don't have to tell your boss to fuck off or become a hot mess in public. Do this in small, low-stakes ways so you can see that you can tolerate the stress. All the microactions we take to prove that our anxiety isn't a reliable narrator add up. This paves the way for bigger and more tolerance of imperfection and, in turn, opens the door for bravery.

Strategy: Start Before You're Ready

Here's what generally runs through our minds when we have a big idea:

> *Oh, wow . . . that could be great.*
> *I should do this.*
> *I'm definitely going to do this!*
> *Wait, but how about . . . ?*
> *I don't know how to. . . .*
> *I can't do . . .*
> *This is probably a dumb idea.*

Almost as soon as a brilliant idea arises, that annoying voice in your head starts yapping about all the reasons you shouldn't do it, what could go wrong, how you can fail, how arrogant you'll seem for trying, and how stupid you will look when you fall on your face. By the time you're done listening, you've talked yourself right out of trying.

The trick to shutting up that annoying voice is to *just start.*

It doesn't matter if you don't know absolutely everything you need to know right now to do a job—whether it's running a company or becoming a mom. Most people don't.

Honestly, I'm not kidding. They pick it up as they go along. Don't know how to change a diaper? You'll learn. Not sure how you'll manage thirty employees? You'll figure it out. You always do, don't you?

By all measures, I never should have started Girls Who Code. Remember, I had no idea how to code, I had never worked in the technology industry, and I had never started a nonprofit. But I couldn't get the image of all those missing female faces in the tech classes I'd visited on the campaign trail out of my head. So I made a few phone calls to solicit some advice from a few people I trust. Then a few more, and a few more. I spent a year meeting with anyone and everyone I could to learn about the tech industry and about teaching girls. Today, Girls Who Code is a global organization that has taught more than ninety thousand girls that they have what it takes to pursue a career in technology, but don't kid yourself that its founder knew what she was doing when she first started.

Cecile Richards, the formidable former president of Planned Parenthood, almost didn't apply for the position. She said her self-doubt kept reminding her how she'd never done anything that big before, and she had a long list of all the things she didn't know how to do. But, as she said, "I went ahead and tried it anyway. If you wait until everything lines up, it's over."

Next time you have that idea or project, instead of talking yourself out of it or putting it off for "someday," just start the process in some small way: make a phone call, buy the URL, write the first paragraph, set up a meeting to talk to some people you trust to get their thoughts. You don't have to tackle the whole thing all at once. Up until pretty recently, I used to be really afraid to ride my bike downhill. Every time I got to a big hill, I'd skip it, and then I'd feel bad. Then I checked myself and saw that my old perfection wiring was steering: if I was going to ride a bike, damn it, then I was going to do it perfectly! But really, why did I have to tackle the HUGE hill? Why couldn't I just start with a small slope, master that, and then go from there?

No more waiting until you're "ready." As Cecile Richards said, if you're waiting for the stars to all perfectly align, you'll be waiting forever. You'll never have the exact right résumé, experience, child-care arrangement, or wardrobe. There is no ideal moment to begin any more than there's the perfect version of you.

Just tackle the small hill first to get the energy moving in the right direction and see where it goes. The worst that can happen is that you fall. But so what? If you don't take those first steps, you'll always wonder what you missed out on. Far better to fall down trying than to never have tried at all.

Strategy: Choose Failure

Yes, you read that right. I want you to *choose* failure—or at least the potential for it.

In the start-up world, you're not taken seriously if you haven't had at least one colossal failure. The unofficial motto in Silicon Valley is "Fail early and often." Almost no one gets it right the first, second, or even third time. Failure is baked into the innovation process; it's how they learn what doesn't work so they can home in on what does. This is why the business world worships serial failures like those of billionaire and Tesla founder Elon Musk, who was ousted as CEO of his own company, fired from PayPal while on his honeymoon, and had to cop to multiple critical malfunctions (and explosions) of his SpaceX rockets. Failure shows you've got what it takes to execute, pivot, crash and burn, and rebound.

Most of us are experts at weighing the pros and cons of an opportunity. A woman I know who works freelance spends *days* debating whether she should take on a project (driving most of her friends nuts in the process). When our careful analysis shows that we could fail, we don't select that option; our perfection wiring urges us to look for a guarantee of success or forget it. Recently, I've gotten a lot of phone calls from women who are thinking about running for office and looking for advice. I always tell them to go for it, even if—*especially if*—their chances of winning are slim, because it's the value of the fight that matters.

Before she was a senator, Elizabeth Warren was a Harvard law professor and bankruptcy specialist turned activist. Beginning in 1995, she was involved in a monumental campaign to stop proposed legislation that intended to make it impossible for hardworking middle-class families in financial peril to file for bankruptcy. Despite her tremendous efforts in leading one of the biggest lobbies in history, they lost the decade-long battle when legislation was passed in 2005.

But, as Senator Warren has said, she's not sorry she jumped into that fight. Now leading the charge in the fight to fix the health-care system in our country, she credits that early loss as an invaluable training ground. Through that experience she learned how to effectively battle for what she believes, made powerful allies, and hatched important new ideas—one of which eventually became the Consumer Financial Protection Bureau. That failure helped her hone her voice and strengthen her bravery muscles—both of which I imagine came in pretty handy when she became a United States senator and famously stood up to the president.

So go ahead and do your risk calculus, same as you always do. Only next time, if it comes out seeming too high, do it anyway (as long, of course, as it's not putting you or anyone else in serious jeopardy). I promise, failure won't break you. Deep down, you know that. Here's your chance to prove it to yourself.

Strategy: Do Something You Suck At

I can remember the first time I tried something that didn't come easily to me. It was in sixth-grade gym class, and I attempted a cartwheel. All the other girls seemed to be able to easily launch their slender legs up in the air and execute a beautiful, graceful spin. But I wasn't a skinny kid, and my one clumsy attempt looked more like I was playing leapfrog than doing a cartwheel. When I stood up, I saw my classmates cracking up and heard one of the popular girls sneer, "That was pathetic." My cheeks burning with shame, I decided on the spot that that was my first and last cartwheel.

Even today, at age forty-two, I catch glimpses of that hot shame creeping in if I can't do something gracefully— especially when I'm comparing myself to others who look like they can. Just this morning I went to spin class and noticed I wasn't doing the moves as well as the woman on the bike next to me. Immediately I started judging myself, feeling bad, wanting to give up. But I didn't, mostly because I'm committed to building my bravery muscle every chance I get (and a little bit because I'm committed to keeping my rear end north of my knees). When I'm feeling over my head—whether in a fitness class or speaking in front of some of the most brilliant minds in technology—I don't fold. I don't pull back or hide, even if I want to.

Doing something that you kind of suck at is yet another way to build a tolerance for imperfection and, in turn, revive the joy that perfection may have strangled. A woman I met named Eva told me that for years, she labeled herself a notoriously bad cook. Nearly everything she tried to make came out burned or tasted awful. Frustrated and defeated, she gave it up. That is, until she became a mom and her five-year-old daughter asked if they could make homemade brownies for the school bake sale. The brownies came out kind of mushy and undercooked, but it was well worth it to Eva for the memory she made with her daughter that day giggling and licking the batter off the mixer.

Fumbling your way through something new isn't just about fun; it also changes your brain for the better. We can literally rewire our brains and what we're capable of, which in turn expands what we *believe* we're capable of. A famous study of London cabdrivers showed that learning the layout of twenty-five thousand city streets markedly increased the area of the brain that controlled their spatial memory. But you don't need to take on such a huge learning curve to benefit; research has shown that gray matter increases after practicing a new undertaking only two times.

If you're a lousy cook, make dinner (and I don't mean by dialing for takeout). If you're not the most coordinated person in the world, go to a CrossFit or dance class (see the next section, "Take on a Physical Challenge"). If you have two left thumbs, take a stab at painting or knitting. If you're still carrying around the "I'm bad at math" block, learn to code (go to www.khanacademy.com). Trust me, nothing will teach you to tolerate mistakes faster than coding!

It's probably time I give that whole cartwheel thing a try again.

Strategy: Take on a Physical Challenge

I was confused. Sitting with the seventh group of women I'd gathered together to talk about perfection and bravery, I found none of the things these women were saying jibed with all the other input I'd heard. When I brought up the topic of rejection, they said they were able to shrug it off by not taking it personally. Failure? Again, not a big deal for them; win some, lose some. Fear of taking risks? Not really, because the worst that can happen is you screw up and just try again.

Then it hit me. This particular group of women all worked in the fitness industry in one capacity or another, from trainer to fitness model to CEO of a national sports club chain and every single one of them had grown up as athletes. I asked about the impact of that and without hesitating, they all said playing a sport as a kid gave them a resilience they draw upon in their everyday adult life.

It turns out that empowering your body empowers your bravery. Sports have been shown to be an invaluable way for girls to build their self-esteem—and sidestep the perfect-girl wiring. On the field or court, there's no room for being nice, polite, sweet, accommodating, neat, and clean. That's where they get to be assertive, competitive, loud; where they get dirty, don't have to hold back or apologize for their talent, and communicate directly and honestly in the interest of building a united team. It turns out that even mastering a physical activity is a *huge* bravery boost. This past summer, my fifteen-year-old niece Maya came to visit us and wanted us to take a surfing lesson together. I hate cold water (anything less than 85 degrees is cold to me), and did I mention I can't swim? But because I hadn't done anything outside my comfort zone in a long time, I said sure, let's do it. I needed to shake things up.

I woke up that morning still pretty excited about doing something new and scary. When we got to the beach, I put on the wetsuit and felt kind of fierce. I loved the superchill energy of the surfer dudes, since I'm normally pretty uptight. We had a brief lesson on the beach and everything was going fine until I had to get in the water. Suddenly I got scared out of my mind and started asking John, my instructor, to tell me all the ways a person could die while surfing, which led to him eventually begging him to take me back to the beach. He was having none of it.

So I got myself into the water and paddled out a bit, finally. The next challenge was jumping up to get on my board, which meant falling into the water over and over. I was annoyed, frustrated, and drenched with saltwater up my nose and stinging my eyes . . . but I kept going. The waves kept crashing on me but I held on, and John kept telling me I was doing, "Awesome!" Trust me, I didn't feel awesome. I *really* wanted to give up.

At one point, I looked to my left at my niece, who is an athlete, so of course she was a total natural at riding the waves. Then I looked to my right and saw—I kid you not—an eight-year-old doing a handstand on his board. I felt like an idiot shaking and swearing like a sailor, clutching my board for dear life. *Come on, Reshma*, I thought. *This is ridiculous. You've tackled harder things than this!* I'd come this far and wasn't going to leave that ocean until I'd gotten up on that board one way or another.

When the next wave came, I hopped up on my two feet and stayed up for about ten seconds before I fell off. It was *thrilling!* I tried five more times, never staying up for more than ten seconds, but I didn't care.

Would I do it again? For sure. I loved the challenge and

the fact that it didn't come easy for me. In fact, I *want* to go back and learn how to get past the fear barriers in my mind. It was an amazing experience, not because I managed to get up on that board (because I didn't, really), but because I didn't give up. I can't remember a day where I felt so free and joyful.

You don't have to try surfing to get this same boost—any physical act of bravery will get you there, as long as it's something that's both challenging and outside your comfort zone. Sign up for a 5K run, take a bike trip, hike a big mountain, chop wood, learn to ice-skate, try indoor rock climbing, take a Zumba class . . . whatever scares you most, that's your ticket. Even if you spent your time as a kid reading instead of running, lack any semblance of hand-eye coordination (guilty on both counts), it's not too late.

Trust me, if I can get myself on a surfboard, anything is possible.

Strategy: Use Your Hands

Anytime Shaan gets a new toy that has to be put together, my first instinct is to tell my husband to do it. Even if I open the box and start the process, almost immediately I get frustrated by how long it takes to figure it out. Hello, perfect-girl training . . . if I can't get it right immediately, I'm outta there.

Same goes for Dimitra. She works in the tech industry, but if her laptop goes down, she immediately turns to her boyfriend for tech support instead of taking the steps to fix it herself. Kate, a wholly capable and competent single mom, told me she has a helpless meltdown anytime an appliance breaks in her apartment. "It's like I turn into a 1950s housewife," she said.

These kinds of tasks have become the territory of men

partially because of old, outdated attitudes about what women can and should do, and partially because as women, we've never been taught to sit with the frustration and challenge that the majority of mechanical tasks require. After all, our society encourages boys to go for it and keep trying even if it's complicated but lets girls off the hook, so we've never really been put into situations where we're told to figure it out. This is the same phenomenon we see in our coding classes; when society is telling girls they aren't good at something, there's no motivation for them to stick with it and work through the problem. Later it colors everything from putting together an IKEA dresser to driving a stick-shift car. So ingrained is our aversion to frustration that not only do we believe we *can't* do these things—we don't want to try!

Don't be a damsel in distress. Building or fixing something with your own two hands gives you power. Computer or phone freezes? Instead of immediately asking someone else to figure it out for you, call tech support and (calmly, with patience) go through the steps to fix the problem. Need to install your toddler's new car seat but are confounded by the instructions? Find a YouTube tutorial and set up that sucker yourself (tip: you can find an instructional video on there for pretty much any task). Empower yourself with the basics to prevent yourself from slipping into old, helpless behaviors: make sure you've got the number for roadside assistance in your phone in case your car breaks down (no, your husband's or dad's phone number doesn't count); take a walk around your house and check the batteries on the smoke detectors; gather up the instruction manuals for appliances and put them all in one place so you can find them when something goes on the fritz.

Learn how to check the air pressure in your tires (*before*

you get a flat); check out a makerspace or sign up for a wood-working class; learn to operate a power drill and put up a shelf in your home; set up that coffee maker that's been sitting in the box since you bought it.

If you get frustrated in the process, remind yourself that you're not aiming to get the gold star here. It's the doing that counts.

8

Nix the Need to Please

*L*ast year, I was invited to speak at a big tech industry conference. This was shortly after a now-infamous (and hideously inaccurate) memo from a Google employee about why women are biologically unsuited to work in technology was leaked, and just around the time that the first wave of accusations that sparked the #MeToo movement were emerging, so the feminist in me was extra charged up. I guess the guys who ran the conference expected me to give a nice, cheerful talk about girls and coding, but I felt we were in too important a moment to ignore what was happening around us. So instead, I got up onstage and talked about how it wasn't enough for us to teach girls to code, that to level the playing field, Silicon Valley needed to fundamentally change its sexist culture and approach.

When I finished speaking, I didn't exactly hear crickets, but there definitely was no thunderous applause, either; and then my Q&A that was supposed to follow was mysteriously canceled. Behind the scenes it was made clear that the organizers of the event were not happy with me. They thought my talk was inappropriate and that I came across as angry (well, duh). Let's just say there's a more-than-good chance I won't be invited back next year.

In the days after, I was upset. It really irked me how I'd been pressured to fall into line, and I resented the passive-aggressive blackballing that I sensed would be my punishment for daring to be an angry woman. Even more enraging was the thought that they would never slap down a dude for going rogue or being outspoken (in fact, they would probably have applauded it). But mostly, if I'm being honest, I was upset because they didn't like me.

I talked to my executive coach about what had happened, and she said something that really struck home. "The work here isn't to figure out why they didn't like you, or who's right and who's wrong," Rha told me. "It's to practice being okay with the idea that there are some people who will get you and some people who won't . . . *and that's fine.*"

Whoaaa.

It had literally never occurred to me that it's perfectly okay if I'm not liked or understood by some; those just aren't my people. There are plenty of others who do get me, and who are aligned with who I am and what I'm here to do.

The more comfortable you get with doing, saying, and being in your truth, the less you'll get caught up in what others think of you. The strategies in this chapter are powerful tools to help you nix the need to please. The irony is that once you free yourself from the need to always be liked, you clear a path for "your people"—the ones who get you—to like you that much more, for all the right reasons.

Strategy: Trust Yourself

Our perfect-girl training has taught us that being accommodating means we agree to go along with what someone else suggests we do, even if deep down we know it's not what we want. We take advice that we aren't really sure feels right, buy the expensive shoes that our friend says we *have to* get (even though we can't really afford them and kind of know we'll never wear them), say the thing our boss thinks we should say to a client even though it doesn't feel entirely genuine to us—often because it's just so much easier to agree than to hurt someone's feelings by saying no.

Early in her career, actress Bridget Moynahan was auditioning for a big role that a guy in her acting class offered to help her with. Every bit of feedback he gave her felt wrong to her, but he'd had success getting work, so she figured he knew what he was doing. She followed his lead—and didn't get the role. "That was a turning point for me about trusting myself," Bridget says. "For me, that's a key element of bravery. You have to trust yourself, whether it's how to play a role or falling in love again even if you've gotten burned. You have to trust that you're going to be okay, that you have something to offer. You need to be brave enough to trust yourself, knowing you'll survive even if it fails."

This strategy is a subtle but crucial one. It requires that you really pay attention to what your gut is telling you, ask yourself whether you're saying yes just to be agreeable, and become aware of when you give away your decision-making power to someone else. Tuning out the urgings of others and listening to our instincts is an important act of bravery.

Strategy: No Fucks Given

Caring about what other people think of us is a habit. It's so deeply ingrained in us to crave the approval of others that we often don't even realize how many of our choices and actions are tied up in that need. One way to break this habit is to be on the lookout for stories of women who do and say what they want, regardless of what others think.

In other words: we need to consciously look for fierce and fabulous examples of *no fucks given*.

I look for stories like these every chance I get—in the news, in stories friends or colleagues tell me, in books I read. I literally collect them and keep both mental and actual files as inspiration. It isn't that hard, really, because if you look around, you'll see plenty of examples everywhere, every day. I will never forget the awe I felt in the 1980s watching Madonna unapologetically break every taboo by writhing around onstage wearing religious ornaments, or the amazement I felt in 2016 witnessing Beyoncé command dancers in Black Panther berets into formation and giving a Black Power salute at the Super Bowl halftime show. Stand-up comic Amy Schumer routinely says whatever she wants, no matter how shocking. Frances McDormand blew off the norm of Hollywood polished glam and accepted the 2018 Golden Globe for Best Actress with zero makeup and tousled hair, then gave a wild and fierce Oscar acceptance speech in support of women in her industry. During a House Financial Services Committee hearing, Congresswoman Maxine Waters refused to let Treasury secretary Steve Mnuchin derail her line of questioning with flattery, pressing for answers and pointedly declaring she was "reclaiming her time." Kiran Gandhi shocked the world when she ran the 2015 London Marathon while "free flowing" on her period to make a statement about the shaming of the processes of women's bodies. Caitlin Jenner blew up the legend of decathlon winner Bruce Jenner to proudly claim her authentic gender identity, right on the cover of *Vanity Fair*. Like I said, no fucks given.

Then, there's the indomitable Dame Helen Mirren. Though

she's famous today for her fierce candor, that wasn't always the case. When a reporter asked her what advice she would give to her younger self, she replied that it would be to not be so "bloody polite" and say "fuck off" more often.

You don't have to agree with these women, or even like them (they don't care if you do, anyway). But you do have to admire them for caring more about what matters to them than what other people think.

Start making it a habit to find examples of women who don't give a fuck what anyone thinks. It's a powerful way to train your brain to focus less on what others think and more on who and what you want to be.

Strategy: Ask "And Then What?"

Our deep longing to be liked is utterly human, a relic of prehistoric days when being accepted (and therefore protected) by your clan literally meant the difference between life and death. Here in the twenty-first century, though, your survival is rarely if ever at stake just because someone thinks you're a bitch. So why, exactly, do we as women so desperately need to be liked?

Each one of us has our own individual reasons why we need others to like us—all of which are driven by what we're afraid will happen if they don't. Think about one specific area in your life where you care most if you're liked (hint: it's usually the space in which you twist yourself into a pretzel to be nice/funny/accommodating, or smile when you really want to scream). Maybe it's at work, or in your mommy and me playgroup, with your in-laws or stepkids, with employees or authority figures, in romantic relationships or friendships.

Got one in mind? Good. Now ask yourself: *What exactly am I afraid will happen if this person/these people don't like me?* For instance, "I'm afraid if the moms at my kid's school don't like me, my son won't be invited on playdates," or "If my employees don't think I'm supercool and amazing, they won't work as hard for me."

Now go deeper. Take it to the absolute worst-case scenario by continually asking, "And then what?" For instance:

> *I'm afraid my boyfriend will be annoyed if I tell him I'm pissed off.*
> And then what are you afraid will happen?
> *He'll break up with me.*
> And then what?
> *I'll be alone.*
> And then what?
> *I may never meet anyone else and end up alone forever.*

Ouch. See how fast we take it from zero to sixty, casting ourselves out into the dark void of shame, ruin, and eternal solitude?

Here are some other real-life mental spirals women have shared with me:

> *I'm afraid if the moms at my son's school don't like me, they won't invite him on playdates.*
> And then what?
> *He'll have no friends.*
> And then what?
> *He'll have a sad childhood.*
> And then what?
> *He'll end up on drugs or depressed as a teenager.*

*If I call out my colleagues for making sexist jokes, I'll be
    "that woman."*
And then what?
No one will want to work with me.
And then what?
I'd lose my job.
And then what?
I'll have no money and lose my house.

It's pretty powerful to see for yourself how deep that "be liked or be damned to hell" hardwiring goes—and, more importantly, how preposterous your worst-case scenario really is. Honestly, is he *really* going to dump you if you tell him you're angry? And even if he does (besides him being an ass not worth your time), does that *really* mean you're going to die alone? Is your son *really* going to be ostracized if the other moms don't like you, and even so, is he *really* going to become a heroin addict because he didn't go on playdates with the alpha moms' kids?

We've sold ourselves on the narratives we've created around what it means if we're not liked, but we need to question if those are true. Playing through these scenarios helps you shrink the overblown fear and look at them through the lens of what might actually happen, instead of what you're terrified of.

Look, I'm not saying that there are never consequences. If your boyfriend is an ass, then indeed he might dump you. If your work atmosphere is truly sexist, then it's not impossible you could be asked to leave if you call them out on it. For all these worst-case scenarios, though, ask yourself again, *And then what?*

You'll survive and move on to people who get you, that's what.

Strategy: Just Say No

I really have a problem saying no. I don't want people to think that I'm too big for my britches, or that I'm mean or ungrateful in any way. When I first started Girls Who Code, a high-powered woman in the industry was such a bitch to me, and so I vowed that from that day forward, I would never behave like that toward anyone else.

So now I say yes all the time—at work, to favors, to anyone who asks for a few minutes of my time for advice. I say yes to speaking events halfway across the globe even it means I'll be exhausted and to exploratory meetings with friends of friends that I could delegate to someone on my team. Like you, probably, this is something that drains my time and energy and leaves me depleted. It's also something I'm working hard on changing.

It takes courage to say no—especially when others want or expect you to say yes. Rha Goddess says it's the bravest thing a woman can do, and I'd have to agree. All our perfect-girl tendencies are tied up in saying yes or no to requests: the pressure to be accommodating, to be helpful, to be nice, to be selfless and put others' needs above our own.

I've learned to look at saying no as a value calculation. I ask myself: *What are the things that are the highest value for me? What aligns with my purpose?* This helps me find the line between supporting others but not to my own detriment. Remember back in Chapter Six when we talked about asking "What scares me more?" That's a value question. Only here, the question is, "What am I giving up/not doing by saying yes? What matters more?"

My two highest priorities in my life are my family and making a difference in the world. So I try—and I stress *try*, because this is a work in progress—to make choices that serve those priorities and say no to the things that don't. Turns out it's pretty easy to tell the difference; when I say yes to activities that are aligned with my purpose of being a loving mom and wife or to meetings that move my company's agenda forward, I feel excited, energized, and joyful. But when an entire day goes by and most of that time was spent on what mattered only for someone else, I'm exhausted and grumpy. We've all had the feeling of coming home after a long day feeling like we've been run over by everyone else's agendas, and pissed off that we've ignored our own. At the very least, we can all use days like these to make better choices about what we'll say yes or no to the next day, and how and to whom we'll devote our time and energy.

Recently I got an email from a woman inviting me to an event she had organized. I don't know her personally; she got my name through a professional organization we both belong to. Her email had come in during a moment when I was seriously up to my eyeballs in work and other commitments, and I didn't have a chance to respond. Then I got her follow-up email, in which she informed me, in all caps (i.e., yelling), how disappointed she was that I didn't attend, and she inferred that I broke some unspoken code of conduct of the group we belong to. As I read it, all I could think about was how sick to my stomach with shame and guilt I would have been if I'd gotten that kind of admonishment five years ago. Not that I love being bitched out now, but after working damn hard on becoming brave enough to put my agenda first, I don't take that kind of thing too personally anymore.

Saying no is hard at first; I won't lie. It's one of the biggest challenges we face on our path to becoming brave, but it's also the most gratifying. It's remarkably empowering to claim your right to put you and your life priorities above the mandate of making nice for the sake of everyone else.

Strategy: Make the Ask

If the idea of asking for what you want is painful for you, you're not alone. We perfect girls tend to feel horrified by the idea of seeming pushy, needy, demanding, obnoxious, entitled, or aggressive. Those are not "pleasing" qualities. But you're not here to please everyone else; you're here to build your bravery muscles. So it's time to get in the habit of asking.

Start small by asking for one thing each day that's a little bit outside your comfort zone. If your food arrived cold, ask your waitperson to take it back to the kitchen and have it reheated. Ask a colleague to take a few minutes to read over something you're working on and offer some thoughts. Ask a friend (who reasonably can do so) to drive you to the airport. Invite someone you want to get to know better to have a cup of coffee with you. If you're worried about coming across as pushy, don't. Research has shown that people routinely see themselves as far more assertive than others do. So your version of "pushy" is really probably just normal to everyone else.

Then go bigger. Negotiate for a better price on a car. Request the plum assignment. Ask your significant other to stop doing something that's driving you nuts. Request a meeting with someone you'd like to mentor you. Petition for the flexibility you need at your job.

Here are a few tips I've learned to make asking easier and more effective:

- **Start with "I."** For instance, "I would appreciate if you could take a look at this report" or "I was wondering if you might like to get coffee sometime." This puts you in the driver's seat.

- **Be direct and clear about what you're asking for.** No beating around the bush or making the person guess what you're asking.

- **Be respectful.** This is a sign of strength, not weakness. Saying "please" and "thank you" shows grace and class.

- **If you tend to get nervous, practice** what you want to say in advance so you're not fumbling for words.

- **Don't automatically offer an out.** I can't tell you how often employees will ask me for something and then immediately backpedal by saying, "But if it's not possible, that's okay." Just ask and then be quiet; let the person answer for themselves.

- **Don't apologize for asking.** No request should start with "I'm sorry, but would you mind . . . ?"

Strategy: Nevertheless, Persist

Who knew Mitch McConnell, of all people, would hand women such an empowering rally cry when he disparaged Senator Elizabeth Warren for pressing her line of questioning in a hearing after being told to sit down and be quiet? It's not all in our heads that men try to bulldoze women out of their voices. As an article in the *New York Times* reported, "Academic studies and countless anecdotes make it clear that being interrupted, talked over, shut down or penalized for speaking out is nearly a universal experience for women when they are outnumbered by men."

To that I say: The bulldozers have had their day; now it's our time.

For every time you've ever been silenced or interrupted, it's time.

For every time you've felt too intimidated or scared of being not liked if you spoke up, it's time.

For every accomplishment you've glossed over out of modesty, it's time.

For every moment you've played nice and swallowed your truth, it's time.

For every time you've stayed quiet when you knew with every fiber of your being you should have spoken up, it's time.

It's time to claim your voice in any and all of these ways:

- **If you have something to say, say it.** If interrupted, *keep talking*. If they tell you to be quiet, *keep talking*. If they call you a "Nasty Woman," say "thank you" and *keep talking*. After being released from spending seven years in a military prison for leaking classified documents, Chelsea Manning faced an onslaught of pressure to shut up and go away. She refused. For her, the fact that everyone was telling her not to speak up was exactly the reason why she believed she should. Amen, sister.

- **Reclaim your time.** I realized recently that I often hurry through my speech when giving a keynote or speaking on a panel because I don't want to take up too much of people's time. None of the men I've ever seen up on a podium or stage do this. They spread out their papers, stand or sit with a more open posture without worrying about taking up too much space, take a long, slow drink of water, and then once they finally start speaking, they take their sweet time. So I'm working on slowing down when I speak. In honor of Congresswoman Maxine Waters, let's all reclaim our voice, our space, *and* our time.

- **Promote yourself.** Studies show that women who are most proactive about making their achievements broadly known get ahead faster, make more money, and are happier overall with their careers. In Silicon Valley, for example, visibility was shown to be a top criterion for promotion to senior levels. Sadly, other studies tell us that women are highly reluctant to talk about their own accomplishments because of that deeply seeded modesty and that voice constantly whispering in our ear, "Don't brag . . . it's not becoming." Here's where we need to take a page from the playbook of men, who have no problem broadcasting their achievements. Close a big deal? Tweet it out. Get a promotion? Send an email to let people know and submit it to your main industry newsfeed so they can publish it. And don't stop there: ask other people to share your good news, too. Anytime someone I admire and respect asks me to shout out the great things that happen to them, I'm happy to do it, and I'm guessing the people in your life will be, too.

- **Spit out the salty lemonade.** Remember the study from Chapter One, where girls choked down salted lemonade because they didn't want to make the researchers feel bad by telling them it was gross? Well, here we are as grown-up women and it's time to spit that lemonade out. In other words, when someone tells you something that you know is wrong, call them out on it. If someone tries to intimidate you into seeing something their way, stand strong. When the cross-examining attorney tried to discredit Taylor Swift during her trial against a radio host who had grabbed her ass during a photo op, she was having none of it. Fielding insulting question after question, she shut him down like a boss. My favorite: When he pointed out, as though it was proof of his client's innocence, that her skirt didn't look as if it was disrupted in any way in the photo, she calmly replied, "That's because my ass is located in the back of my body."

- **Articulate your agency.** Like so many others, when I read the blog post accusing actor Aziz Ansari of sexual harassment for not picking up on his date's "nonverbal cues," I was upset and conflicted. Nearly every woman I know, myself included, has had an experience where someone said or did something that made us feel uncomfortable and we didn't speak up. From the rude and inappropriate to the physically threatening, too many of us, like the woman who wrote the story, have found ourselves in a situation with a guy pressuring us to do something we didn't want to do but didn't overtly say no. Why didn't she—or we—just get up and leave? Why didn't we—or she—speak up? Because we'd never been taught how. No one told us it was okay to have the agency to say *no, get off me, that was inappropriate*, or *fuck off*. So I'm here to tell you it's more than okay. It's your right. The "me too" rage that's been unleashed is the product of decades of pent-up frustration and buried shame from these moments. We're marching with pitchforks to reclaim that power, and now we need to do it by bravely claiming our voice each and every time something like this happens. Time's up, indeed.

9

Play for Team Brave

When Shalene Flanagan blazed past the finish line in 2017 to become the first American woman to win the New York City Marathon in forty years, she did more than just set a record. Her achievement brought to light what the *New York Times* dubbed the "Shalene Flanagan effect," which broke the every-woman-for-herself mold that was pervasive in the professional running world. Instead, she banded female athletes together to push, support, and inspire one another to win. As a result of her efforts, Flanagan and her teammates are now ranked as some of the world's best long-distance runners, winning everything from marathons to Olympic medals.

This is what it means to play for Team Brave. I believe so strongly that the way to change the global landscape for all women is by supporting and pushing one another in personal and meaningful ways. When we encourage each other to be brave and share the results—both the good and the bad—we build a sisterhood of strength that supports us to take on even more courageous acts.

Being brave is a powerful form of activism. When you break ground and become the first to do anything, whether it's winning a marathon or telling someone that the sexist comment he just made wasn't appropriate, it opens the door for other women to do the same. That's how we all get stronger, one brave act at a time.

Strategy: Show the Mess Behind the Scenes

Hanging on the wall in the offices of popular media company theSkimm is a framed copy of a *Vanity Fair* article featuring its two founders, Danielle Weisberg and Carly Zakin. The powerhouse millennial duo are smiling broadly in the photo, looking casually professional, calm, and confident. I was visiting Danielle and Carly to talk about the perfection trap women face, and Danielle immediately pointed to the article on the wall and started to laugh. It turns out that while the women in the picture were projecting an air of effortless success, they were still in hard-core fight-for-your-life start-up mode and had actually had their credit card declined less than an hour earlier.

"I met a female tech entrepreneur recently who said she wanted to hate us, because we make it look easy," Danielle said. "I was stunned by that, because of course it's not true. I feel bad if we've put that image out there because it's equally important to show every Advil-inducing moment along the way. Glamour jobs are never quite what they seem."

There is no such thing as effortless perfection. No one wakes up looking flawless. No couple "never fights," no one's child is a perfect angel, no one landed in the C-suite or at the top of the masthead without breaking a sweat or clawing through some serious setbacks along the way. Instagram filters go a long way toward making us believe that every perfect picture is a snapshot of an equally perfect life, but we know better. Everyone—and I mean *everyone*—is imperfect. Everyone struggles. Everyone screws up. Everyone says stupid things or yells at their kid or forgets to send in their quarterly taxes. Everyone has little secrets they squirrel away shamefully; whether it's that we're in therapy, or that we sometimes stress-eat excessively or that we cry sometimes in the bathroom at work.

We already know the energy and effort it takes to maintain the illusion of perfection—and how empty that struggle ultimately is. The braver step is to let others see that we're human: we struggle; we make mistakes; we fail. What if we could finally let down our "perfect" veneer and allow people to see the messiness behind the scenes?

First, it would relieve us of the heavy armor we've been dragging around with us. That casing weighs a ton. It's a giant relief just to be real.

It would allow us to connect with people authentically, rather than in a hollow and superficial way. If you think about the relationships that make you feel energized, happy, and inspired, they are the ones where there's no bullshit or pretense. No one is *trying* to be anything or look any particular way. No one is looking to impress anyone or be anything other than exactly as silly and human as we all are.

And showing the mess behind the scenes allows everyone else around you to relax and do the same. I know a woman who throws the most amazing political fund-raising parties. Everything always looks impeccable, from the flowers to the food to her hair and makeup. But if you compliment her and marvel at how perfect everything is, she's quick to laugh and tell you that the cat threw up on the rug just before everyone got there or that her gorgeous dress is on loan from Rent the Runway. She's utterly real and maintains a sense of humor about the hard work it takes to make everything look fabulous. In my mind, that humility, that realness—not the impeccable decor or the mouthwatering menu or the expensive china—is what makes her the perfect host.

Don't hide your mistakes in shame—display them with pride! It's brave to reach for something out of your comfort zone, and even braver to let the world see (and commiserate or laugh along with you) when you fall flat on your face. By all means, share your successes, but also share the embarrassing *oops* and *oh shit* moments that got you there. Remember Carly and Danielle's tradition at theSkimm of passing around the "Fail So Hard" hat at their weekly staff meetings for people to put on and share their messiest moment of the week; borrow that tradition and make it your own. My staff and I have started posting #failurefriday moments on social media to get this started . . . come join us.

The point is to just take a deep breath and let people see the real you. You're being brave by letting yourself be vulnerable and, because authenticity inspires authenticity in others, you're paving the way for other women to be, too.

Strategy: Support the Sisterhood

I hate to say this, but bitch culture is never more vicious than when it's woman against woman. Even though it's been proven anecdotally and in research that mentoring one another benefits everyone, we still compete like she-gladiators and craftily tear each other down—usually behind the scenes, through snide comments, gossip, maneuvering, and manipulating. It's death by a thousand cuts, executed through whispers in the ladies' room, passive-aggressive emails, backhanded compliments, icy snubs, and withering comments disguised as "constructive criticism."

I remember so clearly when *The Devil Wears Prada* came out. Pretty much every woman I know had a story to tell about her own Miranda Priestly who tortured her in one way or another. A friend with one of those coveted jobs as an assistant at a talent agency had (on more than one occasion) a cell phone thrown at her by her frustrated female boss. Another who worked in retail stood stunned and speechless as her manager reamed her out for a mistake that the manager herself had made to cover her own ass, in front of an important customer. It's no wonder that the majority of women report that they'd rather work for men than for other women.

There are lots of theories about why we undermine and sabotage each other like this. Some rightly point to the very real obstacles to gender equality that still exist in the workplace. We live in a culture where women need to work twice as hard to earn half the same respect (and less than three-fourths of the same pay), so perhaps we try to hold each other back because every inch of advantage matters. Maybe it's the undercurrent of that double bind of needing to be assertive and bold to get ahead, but then reviled and criticized for being so. Some claim that women are biologically programmed to compete with one another, just as we did back in primitive times when winning the affection of the alpha male—and the protection and resources that came along with that—was paramount for survival.

But underneath all those theories is one unifying truth: we're scared of being outshone, outranked, outdone, or knocked down by another woman, so we strike first. Scared that others will see our imperfections, we make sure to shine a big spotlight on others' flaws. Scared to trust and collaborate with other women, we stick to the every-woman-for-herself style of combat. Feeling vulnerable, we lash out, abuse, and sabotage, doing the very things that we most fear other women will do to us.

What if we looked at this a different way? What if we

viewed supporting other women as a show of strength rather than weakness? What if we worried less about our imperfections and instead focused on enhancing our skills, and helping other women do the same? What if, instead of feeling intimidated by an assertive woman and bitching about her behind her back, we talked about how we admire her instead? What if, instead of worrying there isn't enough room at the top for all of us (and by the way, there is), we went out of our way to help a female colleague or friend get there? What if, instead of feeling "less than" some other woman, we reminded ourselves that we are equally smart/talented/valuable and asked her to collaborate with us instead?

Generosity and bravery are intertwined—especially when it comes to women supporting other women. As many of us know all too well, the drive to be perfect can also drive us to want to be "the best." Giving your time or energy to support other women is brave because it calls you to put aside your quest to be better than everyone else and help make another woman's experience better instead.

In your everyday life, look for opportunities to lift up, mentor, applaud, promote, and support other women. Here are a few ideas to get you started:

- **Brag about each other.** Any time a friend or colleague does something amazing, be their cheerleader and let the world know. If your assistant gets into grad school, post a note on her Facebook wall singing her praises. When a coworker gets promoted, send an email to everyone you work with and invite them for after-work drinks to celebrate. If a woman in your industry wins an award, tweet out a congratulatory note. This kind of support is contagious and will undoubtedly spread, hopefully far and wide until we all get it that we're playing for Team Brave together.

- **Share your random acts of bravery.** The fastest way to inspire other women to be brave is by example. If they can see it in you, they can be it themselves. So share your acts of bravery with your friends, family, and colleagues and let them be *your* cheerleader.

- **Be a bravery mentor.** If you see a woman struggling to speak up or be assertive, reach out and offer to help. If you can tell she's nervous about giving a speech, ask if she'd like you to look over her notes or to be a practice audience. If a friend tells you she would love to take a dance class but is afraid to make a fool of herself, offer to go with her and make fools of yourselves together. Or if she tells you she's been putting off making an important doctor's appointment because she's scared, make her promise to do it *today*, and hold her to it.

- **Give honest feedback.** If a woman asks you what you think, tell her the truth. Don't tell her a white lie to protect her feelings—that compromises both of you and helps no one. You don't need to be harsh to tell the truth; just be direct, calm, fully honest, and respectful.

- **Take her seriously.** If a woman asks you a question, or asks for your advice or input, don't blow her off—you never know how scary it may have been for her to ask in the first place. Whether you agree to her request or not, don't ignore it; none of us is too busy or important to give another woman that level of respect.

- **Form a bravery club.** Just like ten-year-old Alice Paul Tapper, who launched a Girl Scout patch to encourage other girls across the country to raise their hands in class, pull together women you know and launch a bravery initiative. Make a pact to do one brave act every day, and set up a chat group to share your daily acts of bravery.

- **Be a connector.** Know someone who could help out with a project that a colleague is working on? Make the introduction. Have some research that could help make a colleague's work better? Offer it to her. Be generous with your resources and your network by sharing not just what you know, but who you know. The old boys' network encourages men to be abundant with their networks, and we need to be, too.

10

Surviving a Big, Fat Failure

So you went down in flames. Welcome to the Big Fat Failure Club! It's a club no one ever hopes to be a member of but almost inevitably gets invited to join at some point. We will all experience crushing disappointment at one time or another, whether it's losing an election or a job, bombing an interview or presentation, not getting into the school of our dreams, or seeing our relationship, business, or big plans go up in smoke.

When you're in the midst of despair, it can feel like you'll never recover. But just like that first crushing heartbreak back in middle school that you swore you'd never survive, somehow, you do. Everything you're doing now to strengthen your bravery muscles will go a long way toward getting you through and out the other side.

This step-by-step guide will help you find your way through when things don't go quite as you'd hoped or planned.

Step One: Throw a (Short) Pity Party

The morning after I lost my big race for Congress, I woke up in a hotel room alone, still in the "victory dress" I'd worn the day before, surrounded by the debris of what was supposed to be a celebratory party. My head throbbing and heart heavy as a stone, I somehow managed to get myself up and back to my apartment, where I immediately tossed my crumpled clothes on the floor, put on sweats, and climbed into bed. I pretty much stayed under the covers for the next three days nursing my bruised ego, only crawling out of my hole long enough to consume some Wheat Thins and Diet Coke before getting right back in and resumed mindlessly staring at the television. I felt like complete and utter crap, and probably looked like it, too.

Eventually, I got myself up, turned off the TV, and washed my hair. After a last round of fresh tears and a good strong cup of coffee, I slowly started making the necessary calls to thank my supporters and donors—and you know the rest of the story from there.

Looking back, I absolutely believe that those days I spent wallowing in pity were every bit as essential for my rebound as all the other steps I took next. So I say go ahead and throw yourself a pity party. Allow yourself a finite amount of time to really mourn what you lost (for big painful setbacks I usually go with three days). Put on your comfiest sweats, call your best girlfriends to cry or scream, binge-watch *The Crown*, crack open a bottle of wine, eat Ben & Jerry's right out of the pint—whatever your creature comforts are, go there.

Then, and only when you're good and ready, get up, toss away the empty ice cream containers, and move on to Step Two.

Step Two: Celebrate Your Failure

In the world of scientific research, much like in Silicon Valley, repeated failure is a given. Sometimes, the studies and trials pan out, resulting in millions of lives helped or saved and even more dollars earned; more often than not, they don't.

Yet those failures are still celebrated. Why? Because as Merck's director of neuroscience said, "You celebrate the achievement of getting an answer." Even if that answer isn't the one you'd hoped for.

In 2013, the outlook was promising for Biogen's new drug to treat ALS (amyotrophic lateral sclerosis; also called Lou Gehrig's disease). Early study results were encouraging—a rare ray of hope for sufferers of this debilitating disease—so the company launched a final-stage clinical trial. Patients and doctors around the world hoped and prayed that this would finally be the breakthrough they had been waiting for. When the eagerly anticipated trial failed, the devastated scientists broke down in tears.

Then they went out for drinks.

I wasn't there, of course, but I can just picture these brilliant men and women raising their glasses with heavy hearts, not just to commiserate in their disappointment but also to honor the victories they'd had along the way. I'll give cheers to this team myself, because I know all too well how vitally important this kind of closure can be. Celebrating small accomplishments—even in the face of big failures—is what enables us to press on and hold on to hope that eventually our efforts will result in a breakthrough success.

If you failed, it means you tried. If you tried, it means you took a risk. Celebrate the fact that you put yourself out there and dared to go for it. That's damn brave, woman! Take time to honor that. Celebrate the fact that you got a result, even if it wasn't the result you'd hoped for, because it means you saw something through to its conclusion and can now pivot to your next move.

Step Three: Shake It Off (literally)

In the weeks following the leaked memo by Google employee (now former employee) James Damore that claimed women were biologically unsuited for careers in tech, a tornado of responses hit airwaves and newsfeeds. Like so many women in my industry, I was outraged, so I channeled my disgust into an op-ed for the *New York Times* that took on the memo, point by point. The editors at the paper were superexcited about the piece, as was I, and planned to run it on Sunday, August 13.

The afternoon of Saturday, August 12, our country watched horrified as a white supremacist at a rally in Charlottesville, North Carolina, mowed down protesters, killing one woman and injuring dozens more. Needless to say, the op-ed pages quickly (and appropriately) shifted their focus to the deeply troubling race relations in America, and my piece got pulled. Of course I completely understood—I was as sickened by the events as the rest of our country. Still, I was disappointed that something I'd worked really hard on and felt so passionate about would never see the light of day.

I sat on my couch feeling bad for about a half hour (a very brief pity party), then got up and laced up my sneakers to go out for a run to shake it off.

When I say, "shake it off," I mean *literally* shake off the disappointment, shame, or regret that's clinging to you and preventing you from moving forward. Research has shown that physical activity after an emotional blow is key for promoting resilience, so get moving. Go for a run or a long walk, hit the gym, do yoga; even better, do it with friends (strong social connections are another proven resilience booster). If exercise isn't your jam, go do anything that gets you out of your head and back into self-care. Make or bake something. Read an inspiring book. Meditate. Spend an afternoon in the park with your kid. Go to a museum, a movie, a concert.

Will doing these things suddenly make everything peachy again? No, of course not. But it will jolt you out of the funk you're mired in. It'll help refuel your tank and give you the energy and strength to move ahead to Step Four.

Step Four: Review, Reassess, Realign

It's go time. Here's where you make like Beyoncé and turn that proverbial lemon into lemonade.

First, review. The key to this step is to tell or write your story of what happened with as little editorializing as possible. Include just the objective facts, with no blame, or interpretation—as though you were a journalist doing the reporting in the most objective terms. Ask yourself:

- What happened?
- Where, when, how did it happen?
- Who was involved?
- What are the (real, actual) consequences?
- What needs to be changed, repaired, or put back on track?

Second, reassess. This requires what psychologists call "cognitive flexibility," which is a fancy way of saying having the ability to see the situation through a different lens. Psychotherapist Esther Perel refers to it as "reframing your narrative." It's easy to fixate on a single narrative, replaying it over and over in our mind. But when we get stuck on a single, black-and-white version of events—especially one distorted by shame or self-doubt—it limits our ability to see the shades of gray around us. That's when we need to reframe it by taking a step back and asking some broader questions:

- You know what went wrong. But what also went right?
- You didn't achieve what you set out to. What did you learn or gain in its place?
- You've beaten yourself up enough by this point, I'm sure; now it's time to show compassion and let yourself off the hook, same as you would a friend. What worthy efforts and actions did you take that need to be acknowledged? What are you proud of having done? The key to self-forgiveness is focusing on what you did right and remembering that *no one*—not even you—is perfect.
- You got crushed, screwed over, rejected; this is the disempowering blame game. Shift out of blame and into responsibility and ask: What could you have done differently, and what will you do differently next time?
- The walls came crashing down, but what's still standing? What can you salvage?
- You didn't get what you wanted. Is there any upside to it not working out?
- This is the end of one chapter, not the end of the whole story. What could the next chapters be?

Last, realign. Three factors that have been proven to help us bounce back from setbacks are having a sense of purpose, gratitude, and altruism. We realign with our purpose by remembering *why* we took on this challenge in the first place. When I lost my election, I went back to what drove me to run for office, which was a deep desire to serve others and make a difference. Then I redirected my efforts in another direction that allowed me to serve, only in a very different way. In an inspiring TED talk, bestselling author Elizabeth Gilbert shares how she rebounded after her second book bombed. She said, "I will always be safe from the random hurricanes of outcome as long as I remember where I rightfully live." Her love of writing is her "home"—her purpose—her reason for trying. What's yours?

Gratitude is a potent and proven way to shift your mood and energy, because it's not possible to feel bummed out and grateful at the same time. After the painful and public flop of her movie *Beloved*, Oprah Winfrey fell into a depression. But when she eventually pulled herself out, the tether she tied herself to was gratitude. "That's when the gratitude practice became really strong for me," she said, "because it's hard to remain sad if you're focused on what you have instead of what you don't have."

The best way to practice gratitude is to make a daily list. I started doing this every morning about a year ago and I can tell you it has 100 percent made a difference in how I launch into my day. Every morning or evening, write down three things you are most grateful for—and I mean *truly* grateful for. It's easy to just tick off, "my health, my family, my job," and if those are your top three, fantastic. But it's even better to dig a little deeper into specifics. What is it about your family that you are grateful for? (i.e., how they make you laugh, their support, coming home to them every night . . .) What aspect of your job do you appreciate? (the satisfaction of the work, your colleagues, the snacks in the break room . . .) What experience had a positive impact on you? (a book you loved, conversation you had, food you enjoyed, a trip you took . . .) Which elements of your health do you most value? (not being ill or injured, being physically able to do the things you love, feeling energized . . .) What circumstances do you have and hold as personally meaningful? (the unconditional love of your partner, the support of your friends, your comfortable home . . .)

I often put the screwups and setbacks of my day on that list, too, because while I might not be feeling particularly grateful for them at the time, I've learned that every one of them ends up shaping who I am and who I become. I picked up this tip from Ralph Waldo Emerson, who once said, "Cultivate the habit of being grateful for every good thing that comes to you, and to give thanks continuously. And because all things have contributed to your advancement, you should include all things in your gratitude."

Last, altruism is a guaranteed ticket out of a negative headspace. You don't have to donate a ton of money or volunteer in a soup kitchen to activate the positive energy flow of altruism; there's plenty of research that shows that *any* form of giving and being kind to others has a major impact on our health, longevity, happiness, and overall well-being. Since you're already invested in empowering Team Brave, how about aiming your efforts in the direction of a fellow woman? Might as well boost the sisterhood while you're getting yourself back on track! Offer your assistance to a colleague who is working on a big project. Reach out to a new mom in your kid's school and invite her for coffee. Send a personal note of thanks to a friend who supported or inspired you in some way. Visit the elderly woman who lives alone next door. Like gratitude, generosity pretty much vaporizes any lingering feelings of bitterness, shame, or disappointment and lifts you up, while at the same time bringing light and joy to someone else—so really, it's a win-win for everyone. When we realign with our generosity of spirit, we realign with our sense of purpose and bravery and can get back on track with what we want to do or accomplish.

Step Five: Try Again

You will falter. You will fuck up. You will have setbacks, flops, and failures. And yet . . .

Each time you screw up, you learn what not to do.

Each time you falter, you prove that you can right yourself.

Each time you fail, you get to try again.

Ultimately, your failures give you your edge. They make you stronger, wiser, more empathetic, more valuable, more real. And when you stop demanding perfection of yourself, they become your personal bravery badges of honor. Wear them with pride, and then get back out there and do it all over again.

I want every single one of us who have lived at the mercy of our perfect-girl training to know that no failure will break you. Will you make mistakes, maybe even fail? Absolutely. Will it break you? No way, sister. No mistake or setback will take you down once you become a die-hard member of Team Brave. Every setback is just another chance to further strengthen those fierce bravery muscles you're building by getting back up and trying again.

We are all in this together, and I believe with every fiber of my being that by practicing bravery every chance we get, we can create a powerful movement of strong, happy, fulfilled, and formidable women who can and will change the world.

So kiss that perfect girl goodbye and go be brave. It's your power to claim.

Acknowledgments

This book is a result of a lot of support from so many people in my sisterhood who inspire me on a daily basis. It started with the girls at Girls Who Code who inspired my TED talk and continued on with the many women who bravely shared their deepest fears and dreams with me.

I want to thank my writing partner Debra Goldstein. One of the best parts of writing this book was taking this journey with you. As a writer, it's a joy to find someone you can collaborate with—someone who pushes you to go deeper. I found that in Debra. Thank you for encouraging me to find my truth.

Thank you to Richard Pine, my incredible agent. You pushed me to write this book and have believed in this movement from the moment you saw me deliver that TED talk on stage. Thanks to Eliza Rothstein and the amazing team at Inkwell. I am happy to call you family!

Thank you to Tina Constable and the incredible team at Crown. To Candice from my publishing team, who made *Brave, Not Perfect* a permanent part of her life with a bnp tattoo, thank you for living this book every day. To my editor Talia Krohn, your brilliant editing and sage advice made this book come to life.

Thank you to Charlotte Stone for taking on this book and helping me create a bravery movement. You have put your heart and soul into elevating leadership for women and girls since you graduated college and I am grateful you took this journey with me.

Thank you, Priya Fielding-Singh, for your research and brilliant analytical mind. I am so grateful for the time and care you showed this book. Thank you, Sarah Beckoff, for your contribution and your support on this book.

Thank you to all the brilliant thinkers, authors, and change-makers who contributed their valuable insights and stories to this book: Dr. Catherine Steiner-Adair, Rachel Simmons, Dr. Andrew Shatte, Dr. Meredith Grossman, Adam Grant, Rha Goddess, Veronica Roth, Tiffany Dufu, Esther Perel, Bridget Moynahan, Danielle Weisberg, and Carly Zakin.

Thank you, Debbie Hanney, and Brad Brockmueller, for contributing your invaluable perspective as educators to this book.

Thanks to all the women and girls who participated in our brave not perfect focus groups and shared their stories with us. Writing this book taught me the obvious—that a mix of wine, sushi, and pizza can inspire honest sharing and lots of laughs.

Thank you to my Girls Who Code family and friends: Deborah Singer, Ben Yarrow, Trina Dasgupta, Rha Goddess, Tania Zaparaniuk, Ashley Gramby, and Emily Schienvar.

To the male allies in my life: my husband Nihal, my son Shaan, and my dad, thank you for inspiring me to always show up as my bravest self. And to my sister Keshma, my niece Maya, and my mom, thank you for teaching me so many life lessons.

Notes

Chapter One: Sugar and Spice and Everything Nice

19 **ascribe certain expectations** Sharon Begley, "Why Parents May Cause Gender Differences in Kids," *Newsweek*, September 2, 2009, http://www.newsweek.com/why-parents-may-cause-gender-differences-kids-79501

31 **women who earn B's** Claire Gorden, "Why Women Are Afraid of Failure," *Elle*, June 6, 2016, https://www.elle.com/life-love/a36828/why-women-are-afraid-of-failure/

36 **Mansplaining and dominance** Eddie Wrenn, "The Great Gender Debate: Men Will Dominate 75% of the Conversation During Conference Meetings, Study Suggests," Daily Mail.com, September 12, 2012, http://www.dailymail.co.uk/sciencetech/article-2205502/The-great-gender-debate-Men-dominate-75-conversation-conference-meetings-study-suggests.html

37 **We undervalue our contribution** Michelle C. Haynes and Madeline E. Heilman, "It Had to Be You (Not Me)! Women's Attributional Rationalization of Their Contribution to Successful Joint Work Outcomes," *Personality and Psychology Bulletin*, May 7, 2013, http://journals.sagepub.com/doi/full/10.1177/0146167213486358

Chapter Two: The Cult of Perfection

44 **the gender marketing of toys** Elizabeth Sweet, "Toys Are More Divided by Gender Now Than They Were 50 Years Ago," *The Atlantic*, December 9, 2014, https://www.theatlantic.com/business/archive/2014/12/toys-are-more-divided-by-gender-now-than-they-were-50-years-ago/383556/

44 **Professor Sarah M. Coyne observed** Sarah M. Coyne, et al., "Pretty as a Princess: Longitudinal Effects of Engagement with Disney Princesses on Gender Stereotypes, Body Esteem, and Prosocial Behavior in Children," *Child Development*, June 18, 2016, https://onlinelibrary.wiley.com/doi/abs/10.1111/cdev.12569

47 **twice as likely to take leading roles** Donna Ferguson, "Must Monsters Always Be Male? Huge Gender Bias Revealed in Children's Books," *The Guardian*, January 20, 2018, https://www.theguardian.com/books/2018/jan/21/childrens-books-sexism-monster-in-your-kids-book-is-male

Chapter Three: Perfection 3.0: When the Perfect Girl Grows Up

62 **On average, a woman spends 127 hours** Martha De Lacey, "Women spend ALMOST A YEAR counting calories and worrying about their weight during lifetime . . . but men aren't far behind!," Daily Mail.com, June 26, 2013, http://www.dailymail.co.uk/femail/article-2348972/Women-spend-year-counting-calories-worrying-weight-lifetime—men-arent-far-behind.html

62 **National Eating Disorders Association reports** UNC School of Medicine, "Statistics," accessed May 31, 2018, https://www.med.unc.edu/psych/eatingdisorders/Learn%20More/about-eating-disorders/statistics

66 **A seminal study done** Ross Douthat, "Liberated and Unhappy," May 25, 2009, https://www.nytimes.com/2009/05/26/opinion/26douthat.html

71 **A national survey** Kelly Sakai, "Work Is Not to Blame for Women's Lack of Free Time; Time-pressure Is Often Self-imposed, According to Real Simple/Families and Work Institute Survey," January 11, 2014, http://www.familiesandwork.org/the-results-of-a-new-groundbreaking-national-survey-women-and-time-setting-a-new-agenda-commissioned-by-real-simple-and-designed-by-families-and-work-institute-released/

75   **psychologist Thomas Greenspan** Melissa Dahl, "The Alarming New Research on Perfectionism," September 30, 2014, https://www.thecut.com/2014/09/alarming-new-research-on-perfectionism.html

78   **A study released in** McKinsey & Company, "Women in the Workplace," September 2015, https://www.mckinsey.com/business-functions/organization/our-insights/women-in-the-workplace

80   **Jennifer Lawrence discovered** Jennifer Lawrence, "Jennifer Lawrence: 'Why Do I Make Less Than My Male Co-Stars?'" October 13, 2015, https://www.lennyletter.com/story/jennifer-lawrence-why-do-i-make-less-than-my-male-costars

Chapter Four: Redefining Bravery

99   **the Crowdfunding Center** PWC, "Women Outperform Men in Seed Crowdfunding, According to Analysis by PwC and The Crowdfunding Centre," July 11, 2017, https://press.pwc.com/News-releases/women-outperform-men-in-seed-crowdfunding—according-to-analysis-by-pwc-and-the-crowdfunding-centre/s/ad6ee60a-c3be-478b-9e51-9a7ac4692cd3

Chapter Six: Build a Bravery Mindset

117   **It's not just that fatigue** Rand Corporation, "Lack of Sleep Costing U.S. Economy Up to $411 Billion a Year," November 30, 2016, https://www.rand.org/news/press/2016/11/30.html

119   **seven to nine hours a night** Ibid.

120   **the "power of yet"** Carol Dweck, "The Power of Believing That You Can Improve," TED Talk, November 2014, https://www.ted.com/talks/carol_dweck_the_power_of_believing_that_you_can_improve

126   **Alice Paul Tapper noticed** Alice Paul Tapper, "I'm 10, and I Want Girls to Raise Their Hands," *New York Times*, October 31, 2017, https://www.nytimes.com/2017/10/31/opinion/im-10-and-i-want-girls-to-raise-their-hands.html?_r=0

Chapter Seven: Get Caught Trying

136   **Cecile Richards, the formidable former president of Planned Parenthood** Dayna Evans, "Cecile Richards: If You're Not Pissing People Off, You're Probably Not Doing Your Job," *The Cut,* July 19, 2017, https://www.thecut.com/2017/07/cecile-richards-planned-parenthood-interview-92y.html

140   **famous study of London cabdrivers** Eleanor A. Maguire, Katherine Woollett, and Hugo J. Spiers, "London Taxi Drivers and Bus Drivers: A Structural MRI and Neuropsychological Analysis," *Hippocampus*, October 5, 2006, https://www.psychologytoday.com/files/u81/Maguire__Woollett__and_Spiers__2006_.pdf

140   **research has shown that gray matter increases** David Marchese, et al., "Why You Suck at Stuff and How to Get Better," *The Cut,* November 17, 2016, http://nymag.com/scienceofus/2016/11/why-you-suck-at-stuff-and-how-to-get-better.html

Chapter Eight: Nix the Need to Please

150   **Helen Mirren** Michelle Lee, "Why Helen Mirren Wishes She'd Said 'Fuck Off' More as a Young Woman," *Allure*, August 14, 2017, https://www.allure.com/story/helen-mirren-cover-story-september-2017

156   **see themselves as far more assertive than others do** Daniel Ames and Abbie Wazlewek, "Pushing in the Dark: Causes and Consequences of Limited Self-Awareness for Interpersonal Assertiveness," *Personality and Social Psychology Bulletin*, February 28, 2014, http://www.columbia.edu/~da358/publications/Pushing_in_the_dark.pdf

157   **being interrupted, talked over, shut down** Susan Chira, "The Universal Phenomenon of Men Interrupting Women," *New York Times,* June 14, 2017, https://www.nytimes.com/2017/06/14/business/women-sexism-work-huffington-kamala-harris.html?_r=0

158   **Chelsea Manning faced an onslaught of pressure** Jennifer McDermott, "Chelsea Manning: 'I Believe I Did the Best I

Could,'" *Daily Herald*, September 17, 2017, http://www.daily herald.com/article/20170917/news/309179906

159 **discredit Taylor Swift** Christopher Rosa, "Taylor Swift's 10 Most Powerful Statements from Her Sexual Assault Trial Cross-Examination," *Glamour*, August 10, 2017, https://www .glamour.com/story/taylor-swift-sexual-assault-trial-cross -examination?mbid=social_facebook_fanpage

Chapter Nine: Play for Team Brave

165 **very real obstacles to gender equality** Olga Kahzan, "Why Do Women Bully Each Other at Work?," *The Atlantic*, September 2017, https://www.theatlantic.com/magazine/archive /2017/09/the-queen-bee-in-the-corner-office/534213/

Chapter Ten: Surviving a Big, Fat Failure

171 **In 2013, the outlook was promising** Damian Garde, "How to Fail Well in Biotech: Shed a Tear, Grab a Trophy, and Move On," STAT, August 17, 2016, https://www.statnews .com/2016/08/17/biotech-drug-development-failure/

172 **When I say, "shake it off,"** Brian Iacoviello and Dennis Charney, "Psychosocial Facets of Resilience: Implications for Preventing Posttrauma Psychopathology, Treating Trauma Survivors, and Enhancing Community Resilience," *European Journal of Psychotraumatology*, October 1, 2014, https://www .ncbi.nlm.nih.gov/pmc/articles/PMC4185137/

175 **Elizabeth Gilbert shares how** Elizabeth Gilbert, "Success, Failure, and the Drive to Keep Creating," TED talk, March 2014, https://www.ted.com/talks/elizabeth_gilbert_success _failure_and_the_drive_to_keep_creating#t-415147

175 **Gratitude is a potent and proven** J. Vieselmeyer, J. Holguin, and A. Mezulis, "The Role of Resilience and Gratitude in Posttraumatic Stress and Growth Following a Campus Shooting," January 9, 2017, https://www.ncbi.nlm.nih.gov/ pubmed/27548470

175 **Oprah Winfrey fell into a depression** Jonathan Van Meter, "Oprah Is on a Roll (Again)," *Vogue*, August 15, 2017, https://

www.vogue.com/article/oprah-winfrey-vogue-september
-issue-2017

176   **altruism is a guaranteed ticket** Stephen G. Post, "Altruism,
Happiness, and Health: It's Good to Be Good," *International
Journal of Behavioral Medicine*, 2005, https://greatergood.berkeley
.edu/images/uploads/Post-AltruismHappinessHealth.pdf

176   **generosity pretty much vaporizes** Alex Dixon, "Kindness Makes You Happy . . . and Happiness Makes You Kind,"
Greater Good Magazine, September 6, 2011, https://greatergood
.berkeley.edu/article/item/kindness_makes_you_happy_and
_happiness_makes_you_kind

Index

Discussion Questions

1. Which part of *Brave, Not Perfect* resonated the most with you? Did you recognize yourself in any of the stories?

2. Do you ever feel like you are putting too much pressure on yourself to be perfect? To win gold stars at work? To "do it all" as a mom? To be nice and polite, at all times? Do you think this pressure is holding you back in any area of your life?

3. Do you ever feel like you're living the life others expect from you rather than the one you authentically want? If you could change anything without worrying about "letting someone down," what would it be?

4. In the opening chapter, Reshma talks about how running for Congress was the first time she did anything that she wasn't positive she could succeed at. Have you ever shied away from challenges or opportunities because you feared you would fail, look silly, or that it would take you outside your comfort zone?

5. Do you ever worry about seeming too aggressive, or about "not being liked," at work? Do you think the men in your position feel the same way? How can you tell?

6. Reshma writes about how "today, social media feeds the expectation of polished perfection perhaps more than any other influence out there." Does looking at photos of

people's "perfect" family or "perfect" vacation or "perfect" lives on social media make you feel inadequate? Do you refuse to post something that's any less polished for fear of what others might think? If you have a daughter, is she experiencing social media the same way?

7. In the book, Reshma talks about how as women we tend to treat our appearance as our armor. Do you ever think that if you look polished and flawless—thin, full face of makeup, not a hair out of place—people can't judge you? That you'll somehow be "safe"?

8. One of the myths debunked in the book is this idea of "perfection is the same as excellence." Even when we know that we can be excellent without being perfect, it's often hard to find the line. Where is that line for you?

9. If you are a parent of both boys and girls, do you notice any ways in which you might inadvertently be treating them differently when it comes to perfection and bravery?

10. If you have girls, what are some ways you might model bravery for your daughter(s)? How can you teach her that it's okay to fail?

11. Count how many times you apologize in one day. Can you try going one day without making a single apology and see how that feels?

12. Have you ever gotten stuck in a cycle of rumination, worrying that you offended someone, or said the wrong thing? What would be the worst that could happen, even if you did?

13. In chapter six, Reshma talks about the idea of finding our "ledge," the one thing that scares us the most. What is your

"ledge"? And how would your life improve if you faced that fear?

14. Part two of the book is full of stories of courageous women of all ages who are changing the world, one brave act at a time. We all need more (realistic) brave role models like these. Who is yours?

15. In chapter seven, Reshma explains how "getting caught trying" helps us build a resilience to failure. What's one thing you can try—and maybe fail at—today?

16. At the very end of the book, Reshma talks about the importance of sisterhood—or what she calls "playing for team brave." What's one thing you can do tomorrow to support another woman's bravery?

17. How else will you use the insights and tools in this book to jump-start your brave, not perfect life?

Want to
Jump-start Your

Brave,
Not
Perfect

life?

Take the
Brave, Not Perfect
Challenge

visit reshmasaujani.com

ADVANCE PRAISE FOR

Meet the Sky

"*Meet the Sky* is a heartfelt, heart-pounding look at weathering all of life's many storms—a story about strength, difficult choices, second chances, and the power of forgiveness. Sophie is highly relatable and deeply honest, and her beloved—yet treacherous—North Carolina barrier islands are beautifully evoked."

Kelly Loy Gilbert, author of *Picture Us in the Light*

"In every hurricane, there is an eye, and in every McCall Hoyle book, there is a core of deep emotion. With effervescent prose and vivid characters, *Meet the Sky* is a sweeping tale of unwavering hope in the face of a relentless storm."

Pintip Dunn, *New York Times* bestselling author of YA fiction, 2016 RWA RITA winner for Best First Book, and 2018 RITA finalist for Best Young Adult Romance

"*Meet the Sky* is an endearing story about how love can help us weather the storms of life."

Katie McGarry, acclaimed author of *Breathe*

"Sophie and Finn will take your heart by storm! A suspenseful story about the power of nature and two teens learning to live and love in an uncertain world."

Amy Fellner Dominy, award-winning author of *The Fall of Grace*

"McCall Hoyle's *Meet the Sky* is a story of survival, courage, and love. Compelling and wonderfully written, it will resonate with readers seeking a protagonist who is selfless and resourceful, forced to battle a setting both beautiful and brutal. This book is not to be missed!"

Katy Upperman, author of *Kissing Max Holden* and *The Impossibility of Us*

"Against the stunning backdrop of the Outer Banks mid-hurricane, complete with wild horses and even wilder winds, McCall Hoyle turns grief into something beautiful. *Meet the Sky* is a story about broken families trying to put the pieces of their fractured lives back together. Sophie and Finn prove what it means to forge ahead against all odds, even in the eye of a storm."

Stephanie Elliot, author of *Sad Perfect*

"*Meet the Sky* is a beautifully crafted story about grief, love, and the power of tragedy to shift our perspective on life. The character's realistic struggle through a deadly hurricane will have you devouring the pages! A perfect summer read."

Lorie Langdon, bestselling author of *Olivia Twist*, *Gilt Hollow*, and the Doon Series

"A riveting story about the quest to find safety and survival, and also the things we stay alive for: friendship, family, and love."

Katie Nelson, YA author of *The Duke of Bannerman Prep*

"A turbulent and emotionally-charged tale of survival, hope, and second chances. *Meet the Sky* is a beautiful testament to the only thing more powerful than nature—the resilience of the human spirit."

Darcy Woods, award-winning author of *Summer of Supernovas*

"In *Meet the Sky*, McCall Hoyle weaves a lyrical tapestry of beauty in the midst of devastation. A moving reminder of the importance of seizing every moment with the people we love."

"McCall Hoyle does it again! She weaves a tale that leaves us clinging to hope, courage, perseverance, family, and love. *Meet the Sky* is a beautiful story of standing strong in the path of extremes—in the eye of the hurricane, in the eye of the human condition."

"With tension splashed on every page, Hoyle takes her readers—and characters—on an emotional journey that will keep them up all night, turning pages."

"*Meet the Sky* is a wonderful story that dares to ask the question, 'Is it *really* better to have loved and lost than to have never loved at all?' Written with honesty, yet also full of sweetness and hope, this is a story that will touch readers' hearts and linger with them long after they have finished the book."

"A whirlwind of a story full of hope and second chances. Hoyle stuns with *Meet the Sky* and leaves us in raptures with her beautifully crafted tale."

"*Meet the Sky* was a hurricane I wanted to stay stranded within! I was hooked in the first few pages and swept away until the end."

Other books by McCall Hoyle

The Thing with Feathers

Meet the Sky

McCall Hoyle

BLINK

BLINK

Meet the Sky
Copyright © 2018 by McCall Hoyle

Requests for information should be addressed to:
Blink, 3900 Sparks Dr. SE, Grand Rapids, Michigan 49546

Hardcover ISBN 978-0-310-76570-7

Audio download ISBN 978-0-310-76568-4

Ebook ISBN 978-0-310-76565-3

33614080747156

Cover design: Brand Navigation
Interior design: Denise Froehlich

Printed in the United States of America

18 19 20 21 22 / LSC / 10 9 8 7 6 5 4 3 2 1

To Dusty, who believes I can meet the sky, even when I don't always believe it myself.

On either side the river lie
Long fields of barley and of rye,
That clothe the wold and meet the sky;
And thro' the field the road runs by
    To many-tower'd Camelot;
And up and down the people go,
Gazing where the lilies blow
Round an island there below,
    The island of Shalott.

"The Lady of Shalott"
—Alfred, Lord Tennyson

CHAPTER ONE

*So many worlds, so much to do,
so little done, such things to be.*

ALFRED, LORD TENNYSON

Once upon a time, I believed in fairy tales. Not anymore. If Prince Charmings and happily-ever-afters were real, I'd have a godmother and a fancy dress. Instead, I've got a pitchfork and a pile of horse manure.

Don't get me wrong. I'm thankful for what I have. I'm thankful for the rumble of the incoming tide in the distance. I'm thankful to live on the barrier islands of North Carolina, which might be as close to heaven as anyone on earth will ever get. But I'm also realistic. I overslept this morning and have a tight schedule and five more stalls to clean before school. The smallest complication can knock my entire day out of whack, and when that happens, it affects the horses and what's left of my family. That's why I'm sprinting behind the bouncy wheelbarrow like I'm competing in some kind of *American Ninja* manure challenge.

"You okay, Mere?" I call over my shoulder as I dump the wheelbarrow full of dirty wood shavings on the manure pile.

"Yes," she answers from inside the barn. Her voice sounds the same as it always has. It's about the only thing in our lives that's still the same, though. This time last year, Meredith was applying to Ivy League colleges, helping me with the barn, and dancing her heart out. Since the accident, she's content binge watching *Full House* episodes and sitting alone in her room. Whether or not she believes it, she needs me. Mom needs me too.

And I will not complain. Ever.

Pushing my shoulders back, I drop the pitchfork into the empty wheelbarrow and march back up the little hill to the barn. Jack, the old sorrel gelding in the first stall, whinnies when I reach the concrete pad in front of the double doors. I need to keep moving. Any minute now Mere will have had enough. She'll be too hot or too tired and need to head back to the house. But I can't resist the old guy. He's been part of this family longer than I have.

Leaving the wheelbarrow in the middle of the aisle, I head to his stall. His ears perk up as I pull two carrots from the back pocket of my faded jeans. For just a second, his whiskered muzzle tickles my palm, and I forget the chores I need to finish before school. But not for long. When I glance out the opening at the back of his stall, the morning sun reflects off the dunes. It's going to be brutally hot in another hour. With a sigh, I give Jack a quick scratch under his forelock and return to the wheelbarrow.

I peek in at Mere each time I pass the tack room. She sits in a straight-back chair in front of a row of saddles and bridles. Her hands lie motionless in her lap as she stares at the blank wall in front of her. When I finish the fifth stall, I stand the wheelbarrow beside the pile of wood shavings at the back of the barn, then hang the pitchfork on the wall. Brushing my hands on my jeans, I head to Mere in the tack room and run through my mental checklist of assignments due today at school—an illustrated timeline for US History, annotations for English, and a translated paragraph for Spanish.

When my boots hit the hardwood floor, Mere blinks but doesn't move. "You okay?" I ask.

She shrugs.

I reach for her blonde braid to give it a gentle tug, but she slouches lower in her chair. I let my hand fall back to my side. Her thick hair reminds me of Dad's. She got his movie star good looks, complete with square white teeth and defined cheekbones. I, on the other hand, inherited more of Mom's girl-next-door vibe—pretty on a good day, but not startlingly so like Mere.

"Who colored that?" She points to a page torn from a coloring book that's pinned to the corkboard on the wall above the saddles.

"You did, with one of the tourist kids last year. Remember?" I shouldn't have said the *remember* part. She's sensitive about being forgetful.

Shaking my head, I try not to stare at the colorful picture. A little over a year ago, Mere colored every speck of the princess's skin neon green and her long hair violet. Pinned up beside the princess is a coloring page of a castle. I colored that one with the same little girl.

It had been raining that day, and Mere and I were supposed to entertain the kids of the family waiting to ride horses on the beach. The girl had painted the sky above the castle rosy pink. I'd colored the individual stones a bland gray and had never once gone outside the lines.

"I don't remember," Mere says, closing her eyes and resting her head against the back of the chair.

It's best just to let it go, so I don't say anything. I reach for her Pop-Tarts wrapper. "Let's pick up, okay?"

Mere nods and brushes a few crumbs from the table at her side to the floor. I double-check the latch on the feed cabinet before we head out. We can't afford a repeat of the mutant-mouse infiltration we experienced a few months ago—not with Mere's physical and occupational therapy bills stacking up on the kitchen counter. As I turn back to Mere, a cat brushes my leg and meows.

"Oh, Jim—" He stares up at me with pitiful eyes, balancing on his three good legs. His fourth leg hangs awkwardly above the floor. I doubt we'll ever figure out what took his paw. He waves the knobby leg at me when I don't move, clearly hoping I'll acknowledge his cuteness and whip out the cat treats.

Meow. "Come on, sweet boy." I lift the lightweight cat into the crook of one arm and scratch him under his orange chin. Mere finally gets up and walks over to nuzzle her cheek against Jim's. When he purrs, his whole body vibrates. He reaches toward Mere with his nub of an arm, and she and I both giggle.

I set him on the counter, then grab an empty bowl and the plastic tub of cat food from the overhead cabinet. When the first bit clinks the bottom of the metal bowl, he digs in.

"Okay, Mere, let's get you back to the house." I squeeze her hand and lead her toward the sandy hill that separates our house from the barn.

As we climb the steps to our cottage on stilts, I'm careful

to position myself behind her in case she misses a step. She holds on to the stair rail, carefully planting one foot and then the other on each step. It's hard to believe this is the same girl who literally pirouetted and plié-ed her way through life, that all that muscle coordination and grace could be ripped away in an instant.

I sigh as the sun rises off to the east over the Atlantic. Swirls of pink and orange mingle with the occasional wispy cloud, kissing the gray-blue water where they meet on the horizon. The brushstrokes of color take my breath away. They're almost beautiful enough to make me believe in fairy tales again.

Almost.

I wipe a bead of sweat from my forehead as I reach for the doorknob. Despite the colors whirling in the sky and the grumble of the distant surf, the air has been oddly still the last couple of days. There is no rustling of sea oats today, not even a hint of a breeze. And it's hot. And humid—unnaturally so, more like July than October.

"That was quick," Mom says as we enter the kitchen. She turns down the volume on the weather radio she's been listening to 24/7 since a tropical depression formed out in the Atlantic three days ago. As the screen door bangs shut behind us, I realize a wave of bacon-y goodness fills the kitchen.

"I used my super manure powers." I swoosh my arms back and forth, ninja style.

A faint smile lights her face as she stands perfectly still, her metal tongs hovering above the frying pan. Her small frame and light-brown ponytail are identical to mine. In fact, people used to confuse us for sisters. But now her skin has lost its healthy and youthful glow. My chest tightens at the sight of the furrows in her forehead, deep enough to grip a pencil.

"You're working too hard, Sophie. I wish we could afford to hire someone."

If Dad hadn't left, she wouldn't have to worry about me. Before the accident, Mom ran the business side of things— answered the phone, paid the pills, advertised on social media, even dealt with finicky customers looking to purchase once-in-a-lifetime memories for themselves and their children. With Dad gone, the place was going downhill—fast. I might be a manure master, even a veterinary technician in a pinch, but I wasn't that great with hammers or handiwork. Last year, we had tourists lined up months in advance. Now, people could show up unannounced and pretty much be guaranteed a ride.

When the grease in the pan pops, Mom and I both jump.

"I told you it's not a big deal. I've got it." Mere and I wash our hands at the sink, then I hand Mere a pillow from the nearby couch as I guide her toward the breakfast table. She grips it against her chest. Somehow squeezing an object against her core improves Mere's balance—something to do with centering or activating one side of her frontal lobe. Plus I think the velvety texture soothes her somehow.

Mom has good intentions with the whole let's-find-someone-to-help-around-the-barn project, but she's living in a dream world if she thinks anyone would shovel horse poop and haul hay bales for what we could afford to pay anytime in the near future.

"Someone moved into the cottage near the dunes," she says as she flips a piece of bacon.

"Mmm hmmm." I grab three plastic cups and a carton of OJ from the fridge and head back to the table.

Mere smiles when I approach. I unfold the cardboard spout and fill her cup.

"I'm pretty sure it's the same family that used to live there. What was their name?"

My hand jerks. Juice splashes Mere's arm, and she gasps. Mom turns around to see what happened.

"You okay?" she asks.

"Uh, yeah."

I scurry toward the sink for a towel. I'm being silly. First, it's probably not the same family. Second, even if it is, it's not a big deal. So what if I had the crush-to-end-all-crushes on Finn Sanders. So what if he said he'd meet me at homecoming and didn't show. It was freshman year. It was a crush. It wasn't like we were together or anything. It wasn't even a real date. But it was still humiliating. Yesenia and a couple of other girls came over to my house ahead of time. Mere did our hair and makeup. They were as excited as I was. Then he didn't show, and I spent the night acting like I didn't care.

Even if it is Finn, he and I have no reason to interact or cross paths now. We became friends in middle school when we were dumped into the morning chess club together; the school had to do something with us since our moms dropped us off so early. Finn and I became obsessed with beating each other and with putting our heads together to beat Mr. Jackson and his Dutch Defense. It was surprisingly fun. But that was years ago. I can't even remember the last time I played chess or thought about Finn.

"I just drew a blank. What was the boy's name? Jeff?" Mom lays the last slice of bacon on a paper plate to drain.

"Finn. His name's Finn." I dab Mere's placemat and arm with the towel while she hums a piece of music she danced to a couple of years ago.

"That's right—Finn. Maybe he'd like to earn a few dollars helping around the barn." She brings the bacon and a plate of blackened toast to the table, and I do my best not to sigh.

"I've got it, Mom. I promise." I try not to sound concerned as I slide into my seat and reach for a piece of toast. I really don't want her asking me why I'm not eating, but suddenly a flock of seagulls is swarming in my belly.

"Something will work out. It has to. You can't keep going like this." She pushes the plate of bacon toward me.

She's the one who can't keep going like this. But instead of arguing with her, I bite into my dry toast and try to swallow my feelings.

"I bet you'll see Finn today. You could ask him about it."

Or not.

My throat tightens around the single bite of toast as I twist my lips into a smile and check the time on my phone. I have precisely twelve minutes if I'm going to leave on time.

I may not be able to leave home a year early for college like we'd planned. I may not be able to follow my dreams of veterinary medicine. But I can control one thing. I can control whether I talk to Finn Sanders.

And let me assure you, there won't be conversation or anything else going on between us.

CHAPTER TWO

My mind is clouded with a doubt.

ALFRED, LORD TENNYSON

I make it to seventh period without any drama and without any run-ins with Finn, so the optimistic part of me, the part I've squashed down recently, starts to believe maybe Mom was wrong about the whole Finn thing. Besides, I love seventh period. It's technically a study hall, but it's the one hour in the day that's completely mine. No chores. Nobody counting on me. It's pretty much my hour to do whatever I want, and I normally spend it in the media center with Yesenia. She and I have been best friends for as long as I can remember. We're perfect together. I'm a good listener. She's a good talker. It's a win-win.

Mrs. Hampson, the librarian, nods as I pass, but her eyes remain locked on the TV mounted above the checkout desk. Even with the sound muted, it's obvious the meteorologist is taking the weather seriously. His face is grim as he points to the kaleidoscope of green, blue, and yellow on the radar map that's starting to resemble a spiral of colorful soft-serve ice cream.

I head to the overstuffed leather chairs near a big wall of windows to wait for Yesenia and check my phone to make sure I don't miss any notifications about my schedule, or

Mom's, or Mere's. The view of the dunes out back calms my nerves even though they remind me of Dad. He loved those dunes. Mere and I spent much of our childhood exploring them with him.

"Scout," he'd call to me over the wind, "chart your own course." He loved that I was brave enough to charge up one side of a dune and down the other without him.

As the waves of heat shimmer and bake the sand, I wonder what happened to that gutsy little Sophie. It's like she died in the accident. Or is she still inside me somewhere, like the mountains of sand in the distance that constantly shift and change but never actually blow away? I don't know anymore. Right this minute, though, I'm content to admire the dunes in the distance.

For the first time today, I breathe—really breathe—and open my tattered collection of Alfred, Lord Tennyson poems we're reading for English. Yesenia's familiar footsteps interrupt me on page three. When I look up, she huffs and plops her army-green bag on the floor beside the chair facing me. Her favorite patch—*half Mexican, half American, completely Awesome*—dangles from a few loose threads.

"You heard, right?" She leans toward me, her eyes wide. Locks of thick black hair bounce around her face.

I fold down my page and play dumb as my earlier optimism fades. "Heard what?"

"He's back," she hisses, trying to avoid the wrath of Mrs. Hampson. "And he starts classes tomorrow."

"Who's back?" I ask, but the rocks in my stomach tell me I already know.

"Finn Sanders." She pauses, waiting for the news to settle.

"He's supposed to be hot and some kind of supersurfer now. And he's in all advanced classes."

I force down the lump in my throat. If he's in all advanced classes, we're going to have almost the same exact schedule. "It's not a big deal—really. He and I never had anything in common."

She lifts a finger and points teasingly at my face. Her brown eyes reflect the sunlight streaming in through the bank of windows. "What about chess?"

I smirk and tilt my head. "Haven't played in months."

She narrows her eyes. "Science fair?"

I swipe at a strand of hair that defiantly refuses to remain braided and cross my arms. "Didn't compete last year."

She switches tactics. "I think it's romantic, like a reunion. You know what I always say about fate—"

"Yes." Yesenia has a saying for everything, and I adore her. But sometimes her glass-is-always-overflowing outlook gets us both in trouble. In sixth grade, when I still believed in imaginary lands and magical creatures, she talked me into writing a play and spending all our Christmas money on props and costumes. We didn't sell any tickets and had nothing to show for our Christmas cash. In eighth grade, her school spirit ended up getting us sent home for the day to wash our neon green Cindy Lou Who hair. And if I remember correctly, she was the one who encouraged me in ninth grade to "go after Finn Sanders."

She barrels on anyway. "And you *did* have a lot in common. You two were always competing."

"We weren't."

"Ummm, yes, you were. There was the Humane Society fund-raising contest—"

21

Thankfully, she's interrupted by Emilie, a relatively new member of our junior class who also managed to score a free seventh period. She has a seizure response dog because of her epilepsy, and she hangs out with him in the media center most afternoons. He's gorgeous, with a big, blocky golden retriever head and sheets of feathery blond hair on his chest, legs, and tail. The moment I met him, I loved him—though to be fair, I love pretty much every dog I meet. Okay, I pretty much like all the cats and guinea pigs and baby goats too.

"Hey, Hitch." I pat my leg in invitation.

He glances up at Emilie, hopeful.

"Free," she says, and he ambles over to rest his head on my lap.

I give him a good scratch behind the ears and lean down to rub my face against his. Before my family fell to pieces, I had a plan. I'd graduate a year early and head to State for my veterinary degree. Even though vet school is extremely competitive, I knew I would almost certainly get in. I've been around animals since the day I was born, and other than Yesenia, animals tend to be my best friends. Doc Wiggins, the vet who cares for our horses, graduated from State and promised me a great reference, and my parents are known for their work protecting and rescuing wild horses on the Outer Banks. They even built a fence that spans the entire island and keeps the wild horses safe from the people and buildings that continue to encroach on their habitat. I dreamed of working with animals like Hitch and little Jim every day and of living happily ever after.

Then everything changed with one tick of the second hand, and I learned an important lesson. Actually, I learned several important lessons—be alert, protect what you love, and maintain control of what you can at all costs.

That's what I do. And it's working.

"Do y'all think we'll have to evacuate?" Emilie asks, interrupting my thoughts.

I snap to attention, my hands freezing on Hitch's ears. "Evacuate?"

"Yeah, the weather service announced that the tropical depression is now officially Hurricane Harry." She touches her leg. Without a second's hesitation, Hitch pads to her side. "My mom will want to leave tomorrow to beat any rush."

"We won't go unless there's a mandatory evacuation," Yesenia says with a shrug. Like most people living on the Outer Banks, she's no stranger to storms. But I get why Emilie and her mom have to be careful—Emilie has to have access to 911 and the hospital across the bridge if she seizes.

I miss what they say next. I'm thinking about Mom, Mere, the horses, and Jim, and how this could be a false alarm. We won't evacuate unless it's a mandatory evacuation either. It takes a tremendous amount of time and work to get the horses off the island, and it's expensive to board them on the mainland until the storm dies down. We have to be careful because of money—or the lack of it. That's why I've had to put college on hold—unless I get a full ride to State, we can't afford it, and even if I did get a scholarship, Mom and Mere couldn't keep the barn going without me. That barn is what keeps the roof over our heads and dinner on the table.

The librarian gives us the stink eye, so Emilie and Hitch head toward their standard spot near the biographies. Yesenia spends the rest of the period working on her math homework, though I can feel her glancing at me from time to time like she wants to say more about Finn. I manage to read a few more pages of Tennyson.

When the bell rings, releasing us from seventh period, I've put the Finn conversation behind me. Yesenia and I swing by my locker on our way out of the building, and I grab the poetry anthology Mr. Richards has required for next semester. If I have any time before bed, I might get a jumpstart on annotating. I'll be lucky to scrounge up enough time and money in the next year and a half to sneak away to the community college a few days a week, but that doesn't mean I'll let my grades slip.

"Really?" Yesenia asks with a laugh when she sees me put the book in my bag. "We don't have to read that until January."

"I know," I tell her, sheepish. "I can't help myself."

As we push through the double doors and step outside, the heat smacks us in the face. Our sandals scuff the sandy sidewalk as we stroll toward the parking lot. There's no reason to hurry. One thing all Southerners know is how to match their pace to the ninety-plus degrees and one hundred percent humidity without breaking a sweat.

Yesenia points at a dance banner tied to the chain-link fence by the parking lot. "Don't forget about the dance next week."

Shifting my heavy backpack from one shoulder to the other, I nod and keep moving.

"What?" she asks.

"Nothing."

She grabs the sleeve of my T-shirt, stopping me in my tracks and leveling her eyes on me. "Don't you dare think about bailing on me."

I scan the parking lot for my battered truck, avoiding her gaze. "I'm not bailing on you. Promise." I force a half smile.

"Okay." She doesn't sound convinced. "Because you promised. This is supposed to be our year to live. Have fun being in high school before next year, when we'll be totally stressed about college applications. We're upperclassmen now. Remember?"

"I remember," I say, scrolling through the mental list of things I need to do after school.

"Good. You also remember our motto, right?" she asks when we reach the truck.

I open the driver's door and step up onto the running board. "Yeah, shoot for the moon. Even if you miss, you'll—"

"No, not that one." She tosses her bag on the floor and climbs into the passenger seat in one fluid movement. "The Tennyson quote."

We snap on our seat belts, and, holding my breath, I turn the key in the ignition. One day my family will have dependable vehicles with new tires and engines that don't leak oil. Not today. Today it's just me and Mom, still trying to recover from the accident that wrecked my parents' marriage and ruined Mere's future. When the engine roars to life, I exhale, thankful to have dodged a possible crisis. Then we turn out of the parking lot, and I tighten my grip on the wheel. Ever since Mere and Dad's accident, I see danger around every turn and around every vehicle within a quarter mile radius of my bumper.

"You know," Yesenia says when I don't respond. "*'Tis better to have loved and lost than never to have loved at all.*"

I study oncoming traffic as I try not to roll my eyes. There's no point in arguing with her. She's never lost anything, not even a pet, and certainly not half of her family. She believes Tennyson.

I happen to know better.

It's way worse to love and lose than to play it safe and miss the heartbreak altogether. Yesenia can have Tennyson's pretty words. Personally, I'm more of a don't-count-your-chickens-before-they-hatch kind of girl.

As we creep along the beach road, Yesenia unzips her bag and pulls out a battered composition book. I know what's inside—the high school bucket list she's been working on since freshman year.

"The love doesn't just have to do with guys, you know," Yesenia reminds me as she flips the pages. "It's about loving *life*, or at least taking an occasional risk."

"Uh-huh," I reply. We've had this conversation a million times, but I remain unconvinced that taking a risk—any risk—is a good thing. When a gust of wind rocks the truck, I ease my foot off the brake and tighten my grip on the steering wheel. The cedar-sided shacks to our right balance on wisps of sand too small to be called actual dunes. It's a wonder the breeze doesn't wash them out to sea.

"Which is why we have a lot to accomplish in the next two years." Yesenia starts reading from her list. "Hang glide, go on a cruise, skinny-dip, invite dates to the Sadie Hawkins dance—"

"Invite dates?"

"What? That's been on there for ages. You don't listen, Sophie."

"I always listen. It's just the list is always growing. It's hard to keep track. You said, 'go to dance.' I don't remember anything about *inviting* someone." I mean, I know the whole purpose of a Sadie Hawkins dance is that girls do the inviting, but still. I try to formulate an argument about living in a feminist society where we don't need Sadie Hawkins dances in the first place, but Yesenia is still reading.

"Build a snowman—I know it's impractical at the beach, but still—enter hot dog eating contest, learn to play the ukulele, eat caviar—"

"I don't remember any of those." I glance in my side and rearview mirrors as I prepare to flick my turn signal. A blob of green barrels up behind me, practically kissing my bumper.

"A few of those might be new, but . . ." She trails off as I tap my brakes and looks behind us. "What is that guy doing?"

A vomit-green Chevy Blazer whips around us despite the double yellow line and flies past my driver's side window. The car or truck or whatever it is has larger rust patches than mine. I hold the steering wheel tight and train my eyes straight ahead, braking as quickly as I can. My heart pounds in my chest, a rapid, harsh rhythm that makes me feel faint.

Yesenia jabs my shoulder, laughing.

"Stop," I squeal. "We're about to die."

"No, we're not. That was Finn. And he looks good—really good." She fans herself as he drives on, leaving us in a cloud of exhaust and sand.

I pull over to the edge of the road to rest my head on the steering wheel and make sure I'm not really having a heart attack. "I . . . I . . . That jerk. He's going to kill someone. He shouldn't be allowed to drive."

"But he looks good behind the wheel."

"Stop, Yesenia. It's not funny. He could have hurt us. My brakes aren't all that reliable, and I really need new tires." As if to prove my point, my back tire spins, kicking up sand before gaining enough traction to move back onto the road.

"I doubt they're that bad," she says. "Your mom wouldn't let you drive if the truck wasn't safe."

"She doesn't know. She's got too many bills to worry about already. And if a storm is really coming, shutting down business this weekend won't help either. For some reason, people don't want to horseback ride on the beach with a hurricane coming."

"You should tell her if the truck is that bad." For once, Yesenia sounds serious.

"No. I'll have enough tip money in a week or two—if some idiot reckless driver doesn't kill me first."

When we pull into her driveway a few minutes later, she smiles and reaches for the door handle.

"Be safe. Call me later," she says, then hops out of the truck.

I wave. Yesenia blows me a kiss and races up the steps of her house two at a time with her backpack thrown over one shoulder. Despite her never-ending desire to push me out of my comfort zone, she really is the best kind of friend. I know all that bucket-list stuff is more for me than for her, that it's Yesenia's way of wanting to help me get past all the crap that happened last year. Even though it's never going to work, I love her for trying.

Heading north with the ocean on my right, I catch an occasional glimpse of the rising tide between gaps in the dunes. I tell myself the waves are no higher than usual. Even if they are, that proves absolutely nothing. Higher waves could mean a tropical storm, a nor'easter, a false alarm, or even just a full moon. Nine times out of ten, all the hurricane hype is for nothing.

The hardware stores sell out of plywood and batteries. The gas stations might even run out of gas before an evacuation. Then more often than not, the hurricane turns back out to sea or just dissipates to a bad thunderstorm.

As I get closer to home, I ignore the cottage on the dunes near our house and the green Blazer in front of it. I flick my turn signal and pull into my driveway.

When I cut the engine, I tilt my head back and pray Finn will stay away.

CHAPTER THREE

O earth, what changes hast thou seen!

ALFRED, LORD TENNYSON

Mom and I have an after-dinner dishwashing routine. She scrapes plates and washes. I dry and put away. Mere and Jim cuddle on the couch under an old quilt as I slip the last chipped plate into a cabinet. Outside the window, the sea oats swish and swirl, signaling a break in the fierce heat, or at least a break in the eerie stillness of the last few days. The early evening sun casts rays of golden light on the trembling seed heads.

Mom's bare feet pad the wood floor as she heads to her spot at the end of the couch. I give the counters a quick wipe, trying to remember if she's wearing the same clothes she had on yesterday. I add laundry to my to-do list.

"You want to play checkers?" Mom asks as she settles into the worn cushions. I can see the exhaustion on her face, but I also know she'll do anything to draw Mere out of herself and into the world with us.

Glancing at the clock, I realize we have over an hour until dark. "I have a better idea," I say.

"Better than checkers?" Mom looks skeptical. Checkers

is one of the few activities that draws Mere out of her shell. Something about the rhythm of the game and the consistency of the red and black squares seems to organize her thinking. Sometimes she seems almost herself when we play checkers.

"We're going for a ride on the beach." I nod confidently as if it's a well-thought-out idea as opposed to a spur-of-the-moment plan to give Mom a break for an hour or so.

Mere tosses off the quilt, stands up, and grins, showing more emotion than I've seen from her in days. Poor Jim barely gets his three good legs under him before he slips to the floor, tangled in the quilt. But when Mom taps her thigh, he jumps into her lap, completely unfazed. He seems to smile and purrs as she runs her hand down his arched back. She smiles too as he kneads her faded leggings with his one good paw and his little nub.

Then Mom looks at me. "I thought you had homework." Her smile falters.

"It wasn't as much as I thought." I step around the table and pull Mere gently toward the hall leading to our bedrooms.

"Give me two minutes to grab my boots," Mere says, proving she's interested in the ride.

I duck into my room for my soft Justin Ropers, glad I suggested getting out of the house and onto the beach. Even though Mere may not think about it consciously, I believe the dancer in her likes the movement of the horse beneath her.

In a few minutes, we're out the door and almost to the barn. Mere walks ahead of me, then pauses to turn around with her arms spread wide. It's not exactly a *croisé devant*, but it's something. A light wind lifts her hair, and I smile. As we approach the breezeway of the barn, Jack nickers a soft greeting.

"I want to ride Roxie," Mere says as we step onto the concrete aisle. Hay particles hang suspended in slanted rays of sunlight—gold and amber with the occasional speck of ruby.

"But Jack will get his feelings hurt. And he didn't get out today." Roxie was Mere's before the accident, but she'll never ride her again. The mare's high-strung. If Jack has the even temper of a master yogi, Roxie is his polar opposite—whatever that might be. Her moods change like the wind.

"You ride Jack. I'll ride Dolly. They like to be together," I say. They're also guaranteed not to shy away from anything or cause any uncertain movement that might unseat Mere.

Jack and Dolly are Mom and Dad's original pair of trail horses. They're both mixed breeds, combining the intelligence and athleticism of their quarter horse dams with the calm nature and immense strength of their Clydesdale sires. The Clydesdale genes make them sturdy enough to carry even the most out-of-shape tourists through soft sand. They also have wider ribs and broader backs, perfect for riders like Mere who don't have good balance.

"Whatever." Mere's jaw twitches like she's contemplating arguing. Dolly shakes her mane, distracting her, and Mere seems to forget which horse she wanted to ride. She turns back to Dolly, humming quietly as she brushes her long gray neck while I saddle and bridle Jack. In no time, we're moving along the marked path over the dunes. The horses know the drill. Their hooves *shish-shish* rhythmically through the sand. The receding tide whispers to us—*whish, thump, whoosh*—as the low waves approach, break, and then recede.

With my lungs full of warm, salty air, there's less room for stress or worry.

"Look! Look!" Mere stands up in her saddle, pointing out to sea. Jack's ears flick back and forth between the flock of screaming, dive-bombing seagulls up ahead to the excited girl on his back.

"Easy, Jack," I soothe. His ears flick in my direction, his head dropping back to a more relaxed position. On autopilot, the horses plod toward the firmer sand near the water.

"Whoa, girl," I say to Dolly when a dolphin erupts from the frothy water beneath the gulls. Jack stops without instruction from Mere.

The dolphins have multiplied, and they're showing off like they know they have an audience. They take turns breaching, jumping clear of the water, then diving. They disappear for a minute, then emerge in perfect unison nose-first ahead of an incoming wave. They wear smiles beneath their bottlenoses as they head south, whistling and squeaking. Their enthusiasm is contagious.

I click my tongue on the roof of my mouth, instructing Dolly and Jack to move along. The temperature drops a degree or two, and the wind picks up half a notch as the horses clomp into the shallow surf. Even old Jack and Dolly seem to have a bit more spring in their steps.

"You want to race?" I ask.

Mere looks at me as if I've been inhabited by an alien.

"Really?" she asks.

"Really." I bounce my heels against Dolly's sides. She picks up the pace. Jack breaks into a bouncy trot.

"Use one leg," I call over the rush of wind and waves, hoping Jack will lope for Mere. We've been riding since we were three, but Mere's lack of coordination makes even the most natural commands difficult to carry out. Jack's trot is so jarring, there's no way she can stay balanced for long, but his lope is like sitting in a rocking chair. She could probably handle that for hours.

I lift my right heel into Dolly's ribs. She immediately leads off with her left foreleg, transitioning smoothly from a walk to the rolling one-two-three, one-two-three loping rhythm I could sit all day. Dolly takes the bit in her mouth and pulls steadily on the reins, clearly ready to show old Jack what she's got. I apply just enough pressure to ensure her nose stays behind Mere's thigh.

"I'm going to get you!" I say, teasing as we near the pier. Out here with the dolphins, and the wind, and the horses, I feel a tiny glimmer of my old self and tilt my face to the sky to soak up every last morsel of this feeling, wishing it could last forever.

"No way!" Mere pushes Jack harder.

He lumbers on ahead of me. Sitting deep in the saddle, I drop my heel, lengthen my calf, and ask Dolly to walk with my seat. She slows without any verbal command.

"You win, Mere. Jack, walk—easy," I command. He obeys.

"A little farther?" Mere twists in her saddle, her cheeks rosy.

"It's time to head back." And it is. I'd love to ride with Mere forever, but I need to study for an AP US History quiz. And Mere's moodiness is aggravated when she stays up too late.

I let her lead the way home. We ride in silence. The sea lulls my senses; it's the one constant in my life, despite all the changes of the last year. A year ago, Mere was the real leader, the role model, the big sister.

Then everything changed.

Now we pretend.

CHAPTER FOUR

*I must lose myself in action,
lest I wither in despair.*

ALFRED, LORD TENNYSON

Somehow, I don't pass out when I see Finn on the way into school the next morning. It helps that he's distracted by whatever's playing through his earbuds. When our eyes meet, he opens his mouth like he's about to speak. His chin lifts, and his eyelids drop a bit, masking what I seem to remember are green eyes.

Okay, I totally remember. They're precisely the same shade of dark green as the pine trees on the mainland. His hair is still jet black. But I forgot how big his nose is and how the hook of it is somehow attractive. A nose that prominent would make most guys self-conscious, but he wears it like a symbol of greatness.

I give a quick nod and pick up the pace so he can't see my face or the red splotches of heat I feel traveling from my neck to my ears. His flip-flops slap the concrete as we approach the breezeway. I keep moving, silently cursing Yesenia for catching the bus and leaving me to navigate this situation alone.

"Long time, no see, Bookworm." He bumps my arm with his elbow, forcing me to slow down and acknowledge him and his favorite nickname for me in eighth grade.

"Yeah. Long time." I shrug, sounding way cooler than I feel. "Sorry. I'm kind of in a hurry."

"After school, then?"

I glance at the time on my phone, scrambling for an excuse. "I have a tutoring session for math."

Unable to meet his eyes, I stare at the stubble on his chin, a reminder of how much older we are now.

"I just thought you might want to play." He wiggles his eyebrows and reaches in the back pocket of the jeans that hang at a perfect angle around his narrow hips. His long fingers conceal whatever he retrieved from his pocket. My face goes from warm to blazing. He's toying with me, I know, but I'm two steps behind and don't know where this is headed.

"I don't have time to . . . uh . . . *play*." I nod and scurry forward to open the door for a girl on crutches.

"I'll let you be white." He waves a small metal box in front of my face.

"What are you—" I'm thankful for my firm grip on the heavy door.

"I promise not to open with the Sicilian Defense. I remember how you hate that." He braces his hand on the door above my head and motions for me to enter ahead of him.

I blink at him. The fog in my head clears as I pass under his arm. He's talking about chess. The small box he was waving in my face is the same magnetic travel chess set he carried in his pocket in middle school. I almost laugh, but I don't want to encourage him.

"I don't play anymore." I glance at my phone again. This time I see a text from Mom, telling me to check the weather forecast.

"But you—"

"I've gotta go." I point at my phone and duck toward the science hall.

"Okay . . ."

I can't be certain, but I'm pretty sure his goofy I'm-too-cool-to-care grin wavers for a second. Without pausing to verify, I lift my hand in a weak farewell and scurry to safety. Halfway down the hall, I risk a quick glance over my shoulder. Finn's gone. I exhale slowly and detour to the girls' bathroom to catch my breath.

I make it through math without talking to Finn again. Even in fourth period, when Mr. Richards assigns him the seat directly behind me, I don't turn around to ask him how the past two years have been. I touch my finger to the jagged initials carved in the top of my desk, willing myself to focus on the day's lecture. But the part of my brain that's supposed to be analyzing the poem on the board constantly jumps to the barn and home.

The National Weather Service alert about the approaching storm doesn't scare me. Mom, on the other hand, has worked herself into a frenzy. She's texted me three times, asking me to check myself out for the day and come home. She doesn't care if I miss my Physics test. She says the horses are acting weird, and she trusts them way more than meteorologists or Doppler radar.

Mr. Richards doesn't seem to share my concerns, because his Robert Frost lecture has gone on without ceasing.

"Why does Frost say, 'Nature's first green is gold'?" he asks.

No one volunteers. No one moves. Maybe I wasn't the only one not paying attention.

Mr. Richards's eyes meet mine. He lifts one sparse eyebrow hopefully. "Sophie?"

I don't look away fast enough. He knows I'll have a decent answer, and he knows he can count on me to be respectful. I'm his go-to girl in a teaching pinch.

"Yeah, Sophie. Let's hear some scholarly analysis." Warm air brushes the back of my neck.

My teeth grate as I concentrate on not turning around. I know from middle school that acknowledging Finn will only encourage him, and I do not want to encourage him. The conversation this morning was enough interaction for the month. I swallow, lock eyes with Mr. Richards, and ignore the stare of the girl beside us who is obviously wondering why Finn is egging me on.

"Frost is using the metaphor to emphasize the precious nature of spring's first hint of green—of rebirth and renewal." I scoot to the front of my seat, trying to distance myself from Finn.

Mr. Richards nods, looking like he wants me to say more.

"You could say it's hyperbole and imagery too, and maybe even alliteration if you focus on the *green* and *gold*," I continue. It can't hurt to be nice to Mr. Richards. Maybe he'll remember my efforts on the essay portion of our next test.

A yawn breaks the stillness. Mr. Richards squints at someone in the back of the room. Then he does that teacher thing when he randomly calls on another unsuspecting soul to see if they're paying attention.

"What do you think, Mr. Sanders?"

Twenty-something heads swivel in Finn's direction. His presence may annoy me, but the rest of the class seems fascinated by his return. By the way everyone was laughing with him before the bell rang, he has slipped back into life at North Ridge without missing a beat. Finn may be smart, but he also loves to play class clown.

"Einstein here pretty much said it all." He flicks my ponytail with his pencil, clearly oblivious to the chilly vibes I've been sending his way all morning.

The people sitting near us chuckle. Not me. Finn starts to say more, but the intercom crackles overhead, and I breathe a sigh of relief, thanking God for the interruption.

The room goes silent. There's nothing like the threat of an oncoming hurricane, even a Category 1 storm, to get the attention of anyone who lives or works on the Outer Banks of North Carolina.

"Dare County Emergency Management has issued a mandatory evacuation to begin at nine o'clock tomorrow morning," our principal says. Even he sounds a little excited. Or nervous— it's hard to tell. "School will be canceled tomorrow and until the advisory expires."

Crap. Crap. Crap.

That means loading up the horses, locking up the barn and house, and racing to beat the evacuation madness. No one else in the room seems to care. When the room erupts in cheers, even Mr. Richards's face relaxes a bit.

"Sweet!" The kid at the front of my row fist pumps the air.

Someone mumbles something about a hurricane party and hunch punch. I don't want to care, but I can't help myself. Finn is less predictable than the weather. I'm curious to see how he will react, so I glance over my shoulder. I've heard rumors about his extreme surfing life in Virginia Beach, and some part of me wants to know how the fearless risk taker will react to the imminent threat of a hurricane.

Shockingly, Finn's bent over his notebook, his pencil clamped in his bright white teeth, deep in thought. I twist further in my seat, angling for a better view of the numbers he's studying, and my hoodie catches on the edge of his binder. He glances up at me, smiling.

Lifting my eyebrows, I try to sound cool as I point at the equations on his paper. "Math homework? No hurricane parties for you?"

He plucks the pencil from his mouth and taps his eraser on the tip of my nose. For the life of me, I can't understand why he's acting like we're friends.

We're not friends.

We haven't been in a very long time.

"Close, Bookworm," he says. The corners of his mischievous green eyes crinkle like he's laughing at me. "I'm calculating wave heights for tonight."

My mouth drops. "What? You can't surf with a hurricane coming."

"I can. I've got it all worked out." He points down at the numbers on his paper.

Ugh. I turn back around. It's none of my business if he wants to kill himself.

"Loosen up, Bookworm. Life's short." His pencil returns to *scritch-scratching* across his paper as I shake my head.

Clamping my teeth shut and willing myself not to respond, I wait for Mr. Richards to continue. My pulse pounds behind my forehead. That boy has a lot of nerve. If I thought for an instant we could ever be friends again, those thoughts died when he told me to *loosen up*. He might be able to loosen up. He might be able to surf in a hurricane. He might not have to take care of anyone or anything but himself.

If anyone—*anyone*—in this school knows how short life is, how quickly things can change, it's me.

CHAPTER FIVE

Shape your heart to front the hour,
but dream not that the hours will last.

ALFRED, LORD TENNYSON

After school, I drop Yesenia off at her house, and I can see her parents and siblings already getting ready to evacuate. I envy them—without horses to worry about, they'll be out of here in no time. I hurry home as quickly as I dare, knowing that in the twenty minutes since I pulled out of the parking lot, Mom has texted me probably thirteen times. I don't blame her. She can't help that she's gone from zero to full-out-natural-disaster mode since I said good-bye to her after breakfast, and there's a lot to get done before we can leave.

Taking a steadying breath, I climb the steps to the front door. The sky presses down, heavier than usual, and I realize there's no breeze. It's as if Mother Nature is holding her breath too. I count to ten before opening the screen door and crossing the threshold into the chaos that's our home.

"Oh, Sophie! Thank goodness." Mom pours what's left of the milk into the sink, then tosses the empty container into the recycling tub. "I've hooked up the truck and trailer. Can you start packing Mere's things while I finish cleaning out the fridge?"

"Sure." I glance at Mere, asleep on the sofa with an afghan pulled up to her chin. A *Full House* rerun plays quietly on TV.

The wall above her head that's normally lined with family photos is all but bare. My mother is a force to be reckoned with when she puts her mind to something. And she's totally put her mind to evacuating and protecting and saving what she can.

"I guess we're leaving tonight," I say as she tosses a bag of lettuce into the trash.

"The sooner the better. Aunt Mae's expecting us, and I've called the mainland stable about the horses. Do you have gas?"

"I'm taking my truck?"

"Yes." She adjusts the dial on the weather radio. "I'd rather be in one vehicle, but we can't risk losing your truck. This one's going to be bad."

I know better than to ask where she got her information. The weather service may be predicting a direct hit farther south, they may be predicting a Category 1 storm, but clearly the horses or the seagulls or some other more accurate information source has told my mother otherwise. And for better or for worse, the horses and the gulls are usually right.

"Do you have gas, Sophie?" she asks a second time.

I nod, trying not to think about us traveling in separate vehicles. It's not ideal, but losing the truck to saltwater damage or flooding isn't an option either. "I have over half a tank. And I can find my way to Williamston with my eyes closed."

She pauses to smile at me. "Stop in Manteo and fill up, okay?"

"Okay." The lines will be ridiculously long, but I don't argue.

"Promise," she says, reading my mind.

"I promise."

"We won't try to stick together. It's too stressful—too dangerous. Go at your own pace. By the time we get to Columbia, traffic should be thinning. Let's meet at Dunkin' Donuts, then head to Williamston together." She tosses a bag of chips and a box of graham crackers into the canvas tote bag at her feet for road snacks.

"Now you're speaking my language." I grab the apples she forgot from the basket beside the toaster and drop them into her bag. "The horses can have them while we're pounding down Strawberry Frosteds and Boston Kremes."

Mom takes a moment to smile at me. "I don't know what I'd do without you, sweetheart. I know you'll be careful."

My chest expands a little. Our life has not turned out the way I expected, and I never would have asked for the heartache or the financial stress that came from the accident. But I like that Mom can count on me—that I can alleviate a bit of her anxiety. "Careful's my middle name," I tell her.

Her smile widens as she points to the cat carrier by the front door. "After you pack Mere's stuff, can you put Jim in his crate?"

"Yes, ma'am. On it." I salute and head down the short hall to Mere's room, determined to do everything I can to get us out of here on Mom's schedule. Mere's wardrobe is beyond simple—flannel pajamas, jeans, T-shirts, and hoodies. She gave away all her dance stuff months ago. I have the basics packed—including her toothpaste, toothbrush, and tear-free shampoo—in less than ten minutes. Packing my stuff doesn't take much longer. I pull the three hundred and forty-seven dollars I've been saving for tires from my sock drawer and carefully zip it in the inside pocket, then throw in some extra red pens and highlighters for annotating. A minute later, I carry our bags to the kitchen.

Mom ties a knot in the trash bag as I pass. "While you get Jim, I'll put the trash out and grab my bag. Everything else should be in the truck. Let's try to be on the road before five, okay?"

"What about Mere?" I ask and lift our bags to carry down to the truck.

"Let her rest. I'll wake her when we're ready to walk out." She double-checks the fridge for anything that might spoil as I slip out the door.

The truck and trailer are parked beside the barn, facing out, ready to go. As soon as Mom finishes in the house, we'll load the horses and hit the road. I sling our duffle bags into the backseat of the cab, then quickly survey the bed of the truck. Clear plastic tubs contain extra halters and lead ropes. Bales of hay and a couple of fifty-pound bags of sweet feed and oats hold the buckets and other odds and ends in place. I lift my chin with pride. My friends and teachers think I work hard, but they should see my mom. Sometimes I think she's Wonder Woman.

"Hey, guys! It's me," I call as I turn toward the barn. Jack whinnies. The other horses shuffle around in their stalls. They know something's up, from the change in barometric pressure or the change in my routine or maybe both. And they're restless.

If I'm honest, I have to admit I'm on edge too, so I pick up the pace as I head to the tack room for Jim. "Kitty. Kitty. Jim-bo!" I call. He's not around, so I grab the can of cat treats and shake it. Jim usually doesn't go far. I use the time to inventory the tack room and make sure Mom packed a couple of saddles and bridles and basic first aid supplies. Of course, she has.

Shaking the cat treats again, I step down the center aisle of the barn toward the paddocks and ring out back. When the familiar rumble of Doc Wiggins's diesel truck breaks the quiet, I smile and head back to the parking area in front of the barn. He tips his straw Stetson as the vehicle grinds to a halt. I'm not sure I'd recognize him without the signature hat.

"You evacuating?" I ask as he wrestles the heavy door open and steps down to the driveway.

"After I finish checking on my favorite patients." He winks.

Everyone knows Doc doesn't have favorites. He loves all the animals he cares for . . . and their families too.

"We're all good," I tell him.

"I can see that." He surveys the truck and trailer, then lifts his eyebrows when his gaze settles on the cat treats.

"Just have to find Jim, then we're ready to hit the road."

"Good deal." He nods. "I know you can take care of yourself, and Jim's smart—he'll show up."

I smile, wishing my insides felt more confident than the fake smile on my face. Doc Wiggins is right. I can take care of myself. It's everyone else I'm worried about.

Determined to be efficient and get this show on the road on schedule, I head back through the barn to search for Jim before Doc's truck reaches the end of the driveway.

But there's no sign of Jim anywhere, so I set the treats on the ground and cup my hands around my mouth. Scanning the dunes and horizon behind the barn, I call for Jim and pray for a splotch of orange . . . but find nothing.

When I swallow, my throat feels tight. Jim is a survivor. He's also kind of our family mascot.

He was the first animal I rescued all by myself. The first time I saw him, he was a four-legged kitten on the side of the road. I tried to coax him to the house with food and a soft voice. I left tuna on the front porch, but he had no interest in humans. At that point, he'd rather scavenge than accept hand-outs, and I knew he'd either take up residence or disappear. Feral cats are funny like that. He finally started sleeping in the barn but kept his distance, always bolting when any of us approached. Then he disappeared for a week or so. The next time we saw him, he was limping—hobbling on three legs. He couldn't move as fast. When I tried to approach, he scuttled off to the scraggly trees at the edge of our property, but not fast enough to hide the bloody stump that had replaced his paw.

I finally caught up with him, and stayed in surgery with the little guy as Doc Wiggins fixed him up. Ever since then, Jim has been part of the family.

The wind picks up, startling me and rustling the seagrass out near the dunes. I grab the cat treats, ready to investigate the gnarled maritime trees behind the manure pile. Movement beside the barn stops me in my tracks.

"Jim?" I call, my voice cracking.

My heart sinks when I see it's a piece of a feed bag blowing in the wind. I glance back at the trees. I don't want Mom to freak if we miss our five o'clock deadline, but there's no way I'm leaving without Jim.

I have to find him.

Now.

CHAPTER SIX

The old order changeth,
yielding place to new.

ALFRED, LORD TENNYSON

After an hour of searching, I'm about to give up. It took a lot of persuading to convince Mom to wait this long for Jim to return. But Jim's lucky. If most cats have nine lives, I'm pretty sure he has nineteen. He survived in the wild as an orphan and is still an excellent mouser despite his missing paw.

But even as I tell myself that, I can't help but worry.

"Sophie, we have to go." My mom sounds upset at the thought of leaving Jim behind, but we're already half an hour past our scheduled departure. I can tell each minute is stressing her out more, and I know we're pushing our luck.

"Where are you, Jim?" I whisper, scanning the area around our house one last time. Nothing.

Finally, Mom fires up the big truck. With no other choice, I walk toward my own truck, trying to convince myself Jim will be all right. And then, just as I'm about to climb into the driver's seat, I see a flash of orange.

"You smart boy!" I croon as I pick up Jim and hug him tight.

Of course he would have perfect timing—just like Doc said. Instead of roughing it out in a hurricane, he shows up just in time to take a mini vacation to Aunt Mae's, where he'll be spoiled with lots and lots of salmon and tuna treats.

With a few more compliments, I place him in the crate on the backseat of Mom's truck. He circles a few times, curls up in a ball, and closes his eyes like he doesn't have a care in the world. I smile at his whiskered face as I close the truck door. Mom blows me a quick kiss. The diesel engine groans as she changes gears and eases forward down the sandy driveway and toward the main road.

I just need to grab my backpack. Then I can focus on the road and Strawberry Frosteds and Boston Kremes, and maybe if we're feeling really adventurous, a couple of Butter Pecan Macchiatos. I find my pack right where I left it on the floor beside the front door. As I hoist it onto my shoulder, a large black trash bag in the kitchen catches my eye. Cleaning out the fridge is kind of a waste if you leave the food to spoil.

I grab the bag, wondering how Mom could have walked past the trash and forgotten it. That's not like her at all. Clearly, she's beyond stressed. For the thousandth time, I wish Mom had a reliable partner—a spouse who didn't bolt when life got too hard. I'm pulling the back door closed behind me when the bottom of the trash bag falls out. My stomach twists at the mound of cottage cheese mixed with leftover taco meat and a couple of other unidentifiable mystery foods.

Great.

I shoot Mom a text, letting her know I'll be a little bit

behind because of the mess. It takes a good ten minutes to re-bag the trash and pour a cup of water over the icky residue on the deck. By the time I finally toss the bag in the back of the truck and hit the road, I feel like Mom and Mere are hours away. I tell myself I'm being silly and focus on navigating the already deserted roads. The safety-conscious residents, like Mom, packed up and left immediately. The less cautious will leave in one final rush. And by this time of the year, the tourists are gone. That leaves the road all to me. As I drive, I try to avoid looking at the angry white caps of the Atlantic churning out past the dunes or listening to the doom-and-gloom radio announcer narrating the progress of the storm. Lost in my thoughts of Mom and Mere, I don't see the boards in the road until it's almost too late. Gripping the steering wheel, I grit my teeth and swerve to avoid the wood. Who knows how many nails the stuff is riddled with. My right front tire clicks when I clip the edge of one board. Thankfully, I manage to avoid swerving off the road or running over the boards head-on.

My hands unclench a little when the radio switches back to its regular programming—some sappy love song. I relax but keep my eyes peeled for more debris in the road.

Then the truck jerks. A *thwump-thwump* ignites a new spark of fear in my gut. Clicking off the radio, I ease my foot from the accelerator and lean forward, listening. My heart sinks when I recognize the sound.

I've blown one of my bald tires. I should have told Mom they were in bad shape, even though I know it wouldn't have helped. She doesn't have four hundred dollars lying around to buy tires. Plus, I was so very, very close. Between the discount the tire guy promised me and the three hundred and forty-seven bucks now zipped in the duffle in Mom's truck, I was only seventy-three dollars from a new set of tires.

I look around on the road for another car that could help, but I'm totally alone, and the screech of metal scraping pavement can't be good. I'm about to cause more than tire damage to Dad's old truck, so I pull off the side of the road. Tapping my forehead on the steering wheel, I pray for a miracle, or better yet, a way to turn back time. When I step out of the truck, the temperature has dropped several degrees. The wind rakes at my hair, and I shiver as I go to check the damage.

My front tire is gone, shredded and left in a trail on the road behind me. The rim, or whatever it's called, has sunk several inches into the sand on the side of the road. Dad taught me how to change a tire a million years ago, but I'm not so sure I remember how to do it on my own. And I'm definitely sure I don't want to be caught trying to wrestle a spare tire onto my ancient truck during a hurricane.

As I survey my surroundings, the rumble of a large engine growls over the moaning wind. Maybe it's an answer to my prayers in the form of a police officer or one of those giant trucks that hauls cars on the highway. I squint down the road. As the approaching vehicle comes into focus, my stomach feels like it dropped to my knees. Holding my breath, I grip the tail of my OBX T-shirt in my fists.

I'd recognize that vomit-green, rusted-out deathtrap anywhere. The surfboards and rack on top are probably worth more than the actual car. Before I have time to formulate a plan or run screaming over the dunes, the vehicle screeches to a stop beside me, and out pops my rescuer. No Prince Charmings or white knights for this girl—I get Finn Sanders.

As he's all I've got at this point, I squinch my face into what's supposed to be a smile.

"What's up, Bookworm?" He screws the cap back on a bottle of Dr Pepper and sets it on the hood of his car.

Heat prickles my chest as I bite my tongue.

"Changing a flat not on the syllabus?" He cocks one eyebrow and flashes the smile that earned him extensions on incomplete homework assignments in eighth grade.

"I'm sure I can figure it out." I lift my chin, not wanting to ask him for help.

His face goes serious, but I'm pretty sure a smile still tugs at the corner of his mouth. "I don't mind changing a flat. I'm good with my hands." One of his eyebrows lifts mischievously.

"Thanks." I ignore his attempt at humor. Sea oats rustle and swish as a rush of wind flattens them to the sand out on the dunes. I want to argue. I could totally change a tire if I had time to figure it out, but time is the one thing I don't have much of today.

"So where's the spare?" He shoves his hands into his front pockets. Something about the tilt of his head and the quirk of his mouth says he's testing me. And if there's one thing I don't like, it's failing tests. You don't earn a perfect score on the pre-SAT if you can't think fast and use the process of elimination. I point to the back of the truck. "It's under the bed."

He props himself against the side of the truck like we have all day. "Where's the jack?"

Crap. I have no idea, and it could be anywhere. I open my mouth but can't think of anything to say.

Smirking, he heads around the front of the truck. "It's behind the passenger seat."

I could live without the attitude, but in all fairness, I wasn't exactly a ball of sunshine when he approached me at school this morning. At least he seems to know what he's doing. He extracts a plastic box with several crowbar-looking tools and what I assume is the jack, then carries them to the back of the truck, where he lays them on the edge of the road. When he shimmies under the truck on his back, his T-shirt rises, revealing a sliver of his toned abs. Thank God he can't see my face or see me staring in the general vicinity of his waistband. His ego is big enough already. I'd light my hair on fire before I'd give him the satisfaction of thinking I was checking him out.

"Uh . . . Einstein . . ."

My body stiffens at the way he says *Einstein*—half confused, half concerned. "Yes?"

"I hate to break the bad news, but your spare's gone."

"What do you mean *gone*? That can't be."

"You want to look for yourself?"

"Yes. Yes, I do, actually." Squatting, I twist my neck, trying to glimpse the underneath of the truck. It's pointless, though. He has no reason to lie, and from what I can see, there isn't a spare.

He slides out from under the truck, stands next to me, and slaps me on the back. "Guess you're stuck with me, Bookworm."

My shoulders tense. My legs tense. I think maybe my toenails tense. I don't want to be alone with Finn, even if it's to flee to safety in the face of a storm.

But on the other hand, I'm not about to wait for someone else to come along and help me. "Could you take me to the forest ranger station in Manteo? I have friends there."

Well, Mom has a friend there—Carla, who's one of the

rangers. She's about the only person I can think of who would still be around and willing to give me a ride to Williamston with an evacuation in progress and a hurricane bearing down. By now, Yesenia and her family will be across the bridge, and there's no way I can ask Mom to turn around and get me.

"Sure." He steps toward his Blazer, opening the passenger door for me.

I turn back to the truck to grab my belongings, leaving the bag of trash where it is. As I reach into the backseat, I spot Mere's compass—one of the few trinkets she still cares about—and grab it too. Finn raises an eyebrow at the device.

"It's my sister's." I don't explain how Dad bought each of us our own compass before our last big family vacation to Yellowstone, or why Mere still keeps hers around. Thankfully, he doesn't ask.

"I just have to run supplies up to a relative in Corolla first," he says.

"You do know high tide is coming. Right? And that Collington Road washes out on a windy day. Parts of the beach road could wash out long before a storm hits."

"I don't have a choice. My uncle's going to ride it out. He needs fuel, batteries, water." He points to supplies piled in the backseat beside a massive plastic tub overflowing with what appears to be several wetsuits.

I want to argue, to ask him what kind of stupid relative would *ride out* a mandatory evacuation, but I keep my mouth shut. It's his car, and he's the only person to come along since I pulled over.

As much as I hate to admit it, I'm no longer the one in control.

CHAPTER SEVEN

We cannot be kind to each other here for even an hour.

ALFRED, LORD TENNYSON

We ride north in silence. I send a quick text to Carla, who says she can get me to Williamston. Then I draft a longer one to Mom, telling her about the flat, not to worry, and that Carla's taking me to her. But now my dumb phone refuses to cooperate. The delivery receipt won't load.

Come on. Come on. I hold my breath. This message has to go through or Mom will freak. I exhale when it finally sends. But the farther north we drive, the more my service bars dwindle. Signals are always a bit spotty up here but not this bad. The approaching storm must already be taking its toll. I feel like I'm letting go of a lifeline to my family, at least until we head south to Manteo.

I sit still, staring out the passenger window and trying not to touch any of Finn's stuff. The inside of his car isn't exactly dirty, but it definitely falls on the sloppy side of the cleanliness spectrum. Think several beef jerky wrappers, a couple empty Dr Pepper bottles, and at least one empty Doritos bag, not to mention surfing magazines and what looks like some kind of textbook on homeopathic healing.

The boy's an oxymoron. What kind of person eats this much junk, drinks this much high-fructose corn syrup, and owns a book on natural remedies? I shift sideways, trying to get comfortable in the cramped space. But my foot brushes an empty donut box, causing a tattered book to slide to the floor. At least I think it's a book. The thing is more duct tape than actual cardboard and paper. Clearly, it's been read about eighty-bazillion times. I lift it to read the title—*Don't Sweat the Small Stuff . . . and It's All Small Stuff*. It's heavy from all the tape and looks like it would hold meaty information despite the silly title.

"Uh, sorry," I say, apologizing when I realize Finn looks uncomfortable with me handling his raggedy book. Studying the minefield of crackling papers and plastic bottles surrounding my feet, I bend over to return the book to its special place atop the donut box.

"No. I'm sorry. I really need to clean my car," he says, looking relieved when I return the book to its rightful place.

"You weren't expecting a passenger." I can tell he's trying to be nice, and he did help me. My foot rustles an unidentifiable bag. We make eye contact, and I smile, a little peace offering. "But maybe you should cut back a bit on the junk food."

"A guy's gotta eat." He shrugs and turns back to the road.

I should keep my mouth shut. Of course, I don't. "That's not actually food, you know? It'll kill you," I say, pointing at a beef jerky wrapper.

"But it tastes so good. I'll die happy." He rubs his stomach area.

I shoot a fleeting look at the big white textbook with the

herbs and vegetables on the cover. He follows my gaze, then turns back to the road. His knuckles whiten a shade, like he's uncomfortable again. I don't understand why this boy, who doesn't seem concerned about an oncoming hurricane, gets all nervous when I draw attention to his books, which can't be all that important if they live in the landfill that is his vehicle.

"Hey, it's protein," he says, reverting to his class-clown demeanor. When a gust of wind threatens to blow us off the road, he appears completely unfazed.

Humph. I cross my arms, telling myself to bite my tongue. I'm not the healthiest person on the face of the planet, but calling beef jerky protein is a bit generous. "It's sort of protein. In an artificial-chemical-mystery-meat kind of way."

"Are you a dietician or something?"

"No, just trying to help. Speaking of which, we should really be heading south while we still can. Have you listened to the news?" Somehow, he manages to bring out the snippy verbal side of me that normally spends most of its time in hibernation. Unless it involves a class participation grade, I'm generally pretty good at keeping my mouth shut and my sarcastic comments inside my head.

"I don't listen to the news. Way too bad for my health."

I twist to look at him, ready to crack a joke of my own, but his face is . . . serious? I catch a glimpse of my open mouth in the rearview mirror. *Way too bad for his health?* Is he kidding? Is he crazy? I can't even formulate words.

As we near the end of the paved road north of the last lighthouse, I close my eyes to the count of three, breathe deeply, and try a new tactic. "Maybe we could listen to the radio for a minute. You know? Just in case."

He reaches for a knob on the old radio. "Sure. But it won't change anything. I have to get this stuff to Zeke."

I don't respond. I strain to hear what the radio guy says between bursts of crackling static.

". . . Repeat: the Emergency Management System has moved the mandatory evacuation to eleven o'clock tonight. Hurricane Harry is now a Category 2 storm. Based on the currently increasing wind speeds, it has the potential to reach Category 3 by the time it makes landfall. The forecast now predicts the storm will hit the Northern Outer Banks near high tide, creating an unpredictable storm surge. Please take all precautions to evacuate tonight. Expected road outages will prevent emergency personnel from reaching residents after that time."

I have to stifle a gasp and clench the armrest tightly at the thought of a storm that bad. But paradox-boy seems completely unworried as he continues in the opposite direction of safety.

He taps out a happy rhythm on the steering wheel with his thumbs as if he didn't just hear the same warning I did. Chewing my lower lip and sitting on my hands, I search for a more persuasive argument than the weather forecast we just heard. But I come up blank.

"What time is it?" I ask, nodding at the cracked leather watchband circling his wrist. Maybe drawing his attention to the passing hours will spark some sense of urgency.

He shrugs without checking his watch.

"Um, I'm pretty sure the thing on your wrist will tell you."

"Oh, this?" He glances down and jiggles his watch.

"Yeah, that." I try not to sound sarcastic. I really do.

"It hasn't worked in months."

I don't want to ask. I know the answer will be something ridiculous, but I can't help myself. The boy's an enigma begging to be solved. "Then why are you wearing it?"

"It's symbolic." He continues his sporadic drum solo on the steering wheel.

I press my lips together.

Don't ask, Sophie.

Don't ask.

"Of what?" *Crap.*

"Of time." He glances over at me, like I'm purposely being stupid. When I don't say anything, he continues. "It really does fly, you know? I want to make sure I get the most out of it. Plus, it's still correct twice a day."

I have no response to that, so I check my phone despite its dwindling battery power and see it's almost seven o'clock. We continue in silence until we reach the ramp to the four-wheel-drive beach road, where Finn pulls over to let air out of his tires. At least he has some knowledge of where and how to drive on the beach. But his experience with the upper reaches of the four-wheel-drive area isn't helping the nerves simmering in my belly.

It's not just the storm now. I haven't been north of the sound-to-sea fence Mom and Dad fought so hard to build since before Dad left. It's the best thing I remember them doing together before the accident ruined our lives—before he walked out on us.

Finn glances at me when we reach the packed sand near the shoreline. "You okay, Bookworm? You look carsick."

"I'm fine." I'd rather swallow mouthfuls of sand than disclose to Finn Sanders all my family drama.

"Whoa." He points at the dune line to our left. Several wild horses huddle together near a line of weathered utility poles. Heavy-duty wire cable links the poles one to the other, forming an almost indestructible fence. The gray poles resemble weary soldiers, marching inland as far as the eye can see and out into the choppy Atlantic in the opposite direction.

The horses could be statues in iron, copper, and marble except for their long manes and tails gliding on the northerly wind. They look like Jack and Roxie and Dolly with a few glaring exceptions. They're more compact than the typical domesticated horse. Their backs are shorter, making them more square and less rectangular. And if you look closely, their tails are set lower on their hindquarters, evidence of their Spanish Mustang heritage.

Finn eases his foot off the brake as he studies the horses. "I haven't seen them this far south since . . . I don't think I've seen them this close to the fence since they were penned in."

My heart constricts. I'm not sure if it's a wave of grief or the way his voice drops on the word *penned* as though it disgusts him. Probably, it's a combination of the two.

"They're not penned in. That fence saves their lives from . . ." I want to say *reckless drivers like you*. Instead I grip the door handle as we bounce over an uneven patch of sand.

"That fence is a cage—keeping them from expanding their habitat. They're no better off than if they were in a zoo." He shrugs like he doesn't care enough to argue, but I'm pretty sure the arch of his eyebrow confirms my gut instinct—he's challenging me, like he thinks he scored a point in this debate that's not really a debate.

I level my eyes on his profile, trying to sound confident and casual at the same time. "They have seventy-five-hundred acres to roam. My parents organized the fundraising and building of that fence. They love those horses. They'd be extinct if it weren't for people like my parents. Even with the fence, they're critically endangered."

For once, he shuts up.

I scan the beach for more horses, determined to keep my mouth closed, but I can't. "My mom says the horses migrate ahead of the storms. They've moved the evacuation up ten hours. Surely if your friend Zeke or whatever his name is—"

"He's my uncle."

"If your *uncle* lives up here year-round, he must know the risks. He must be prepared in case of emergency, especially if he plans to stay put. If you won't turn back, will you at least hurry? Please."

Mom's the superstitious one. Not me. Logically, I don't think the horses can predict weather that far off. Maybe they sense the dropping barometric pressure or something, but they can't possibly know where the storm will make landfall when the weather service isn't even certain. But Mom's been right so often when it comes to the weather and her animals, I can't help but consider the possibility she might be right again. The horses might be pushed up against their southern boundary in an attempt to dodge the oncoming storm.

"Relax, Worrywart. We've got hours—more than enough time to get you to Manteo and a dependable ride." His biceps twitch beneath his short sleeves when he jerks left to avoid a wave rushing in farther than the previous ones.

Refusing to be baited, I clamp down on my lower lip with my teeth and contemplate the absence of sea birds. I pray they're floating to safety on the winds ahead of the storm or that their automatically clenching toe muscles will keep them safely perched in a sturdy tree somewhere. I try not to think about Doc Wiggins telling me about the birds that seek refuge in the eye of the hurricane, then die of fatigue or starvation if the storm outlasts their stamina.

Marker signs count off every quarter mile as we head farther north. We've traveled several miles when Finn veers left and stomps the gas pedal. He thrusts us over the dune line and into a grove of gnarled trees, heading for a shack that blends in with the maritime forest around it.

"How did you know where to turn?" I ask, marveling at his sense of direction. We passed the last vacation rental a ways back. Since then it's been nothing but a stretch of dunes and sea oats that all look pretty much alike.

He lifts his shoulders, like he's never thought about it before. "Instinct, I guess."

At the sound of Finn's Blazer, a hunched figure barely visible from behind bushy eyebrows and a chest-length beard opens the door and tosses up a hand in greeting. When his eyes land on me in the passenger seat, his hand drops. It's hard to say because of all the hair, but I'm pretty sure his leathery face tightens.

Mine feels kind of stiff as well. I don't know what I expected from Finn's uncle; maybe an older version of Finn with deeper creases at the corners of the eyes. But this guy's more *Duck Dynasty* than surfer dude. I've seen my fair share of salty, commercial fishermen, and a number of hardcore mountain men when we visited Mom's relatives in West Virginia, but I've never seen anyone like this guy on the Outer Banks. I try not to stare as Zeke approaches the Blazer.

Finn jumps down to the sand. They move to the back of the car and open the door.

I turn and smile. "Hi," I say.

Finn sort of smiles. But I think he's trying not to smile more than he's actually smiling, like he's in on a joke I missed. He hands Zeke several huge packs of batteries, gallons of water, and two cardboard boxes. Zeke stacks the supplies on the ground.

"Who's that?" Zeke asks in a gruff voice without acknowledging me.

"A friend from school. Her name's Sophie."

I don't know which shocks me more, Zeke's bad manners or Finn Sanders introducing me as a friend. Clearly, his definition of *friend* and mine vary.

"Too bad you won't be able to grab a quick set of waves. They've gone off the Richter in the last hour or two." Zeke turns to lift one of the boxes stacked on the sand.

Finn's voice drops. "Like how off the Richter?" He glances over his shoulder, like he's looking to see if I'm listening.

Not only am I listening, but alarm bells sound in my brain. I know enough about Finn to realize tempting him with waves *off the Richter* is like asking a stressed-out chocoholic if he wants a Hershey's bar.

I open my mouth to speak, but Finn beats me to it. "Sophie, you want to see something awesome?"

"Uh . . . *no*. I want to get off this island."

"Sorry, bro." Zeke slaps Finn on the back, then starts carting his goods inside. "I'm going out there before the waves get too serious."

Finn's the one who looks sick now, like someone set him

up on the world's most awkward blind date. He drags a hand through his shaggy hair when he speaks. "This is a once-in-a-lifetime opportunity, Bookworm. Can you give me like twenty minutes?"

"Twenty minutes to kill yourself? Sure. Have fun."

He ignores my sarcasm and snatches a wet suit from the tub in the backseat. Leaning over the top of the car, he unfastens hooks and latches on the board rack as he speaks. "You're the best. Make yourself comfortable."

"I was kidding!" I tell him.

I want to bang my head on the dashboard. I want to lecture him on the dangerous surf conditions. I want to close my eyes, wave a magic wand, and transport myself from this rattrap of a vehicle to the cab of Mom's truck. But there's no use arguing with him. I can tell he's going to do what he wants to do when he wants to do it.

I try to strike a bargain. "What if you're not back in twenty minutes?"

"I will be."

"If you're not, I'm leaving."

"Fine." He steps down from the running board, pulling a white surfboard off the roof and resting it on his shoulder.

I level my eyes on his face to make sure he knows I'm serious. "I'm leaving in your car."

He slings the wet suit over his other shoulder, hesitating for a second before responding. "We don't have to worry about that because I'll be back in twenty."

As I watch him jog off, I decide I'm fairly sure he's lying.

CHAPTER EIGHT

*When you meet triumph or disaster,
treat these imposters alike.*

ALFRED, LORD TENNYSON

Eighteen minutes later, I've flipped through two surfing
magazines and the book on natural eating and healing.
The sections pertaining to digestion are heavily highlighted
with notes scribbled in the margins. No wonder. The boy's a
walking gut bomb waiting to explode. I'm pretty sure he could
skip the research, eat real food, and eliminate whatever's upsetting his system.

After nineteen minutes, I glance over the dunes with mixed
emotions—half hoping Finn will come waltzing back with a goofy
smile, a wisecrack, and the desire to chauffeur me to Manteo
ASAP—half hoping he won't show so I can hit the road by myself.

At twenty minutes, I crawl into the driver's seat. I've never
driven a stick shift, but it can't be that difficult. Yesenia's mom
has a stick shift, and she explained how the clutch works. We
just never got around to practicing, since Yesenia hasn't bothered to get her driver's license. Between her siblings and me
being able to drive her around, she says there's no need.

My feet barely reach the pedals, so I scoot to the edge of the seat and turn the key in the ignition. The engine doesn't fire up or even sputter. Something near the keyhole *click, click, clicks*. That's about it. I try a second time. And a third. Nothing.

Finn's car looks like it's survived World War III, but it drove fine for him. I must be doing something wrong. I suck down a deep breath, trying to calm my racing heart and think clearly. This would be a great time to pull up a tutorial video online, but my service is still hovering at zero bars. I'm anxious enough without thinking about my phone and all the alerts and planner alarms I'm missing, so I try to focus on driving.

For the life of me, I don't know what I'm doing wrong. The car is in gear. I'm turning the key. It must have something to do with the clutch. I figure I can't hurt this beast of a vehicle, so I press the clutch to the floor and give it another try. The green ogre rumbles to life. With the clutch still mashed to the floor, I move the gearshift down to reverse and give it some gas. Ha! I'm not breaking any speed barriers, but I'm moving—that is until I attempt to stop, turn, and shift to first. The fickle monster sputters and dies.

I manage to restart the engine but stall out a second time before I close the gap between Zeke's shack and the dunes. It's no use. Driving this contraption solo is almost as dumb as surfing in the face of an oncoming hurricane, and I prefer not to do stupid. Defeated, I crawl back to the passenger seat to fume and curse the universe.

I don't want to give Finn the satisfaction of chasing after him, so I search the floorboard for something more interesting to read than surfing magazines or homeopathic textbooks. I accidentally knock the duct-taped book with the silly title off its spot on the donut box, and the reinforced cover falls open. The pages are dog-eared and highlighted all over the place. Annotations cover every speck of white space in the margins. Mr. Richards would be impressed. I'm pretty sure in middle school, Finn paid less-than-stellar attention to detail when reading and taking notes, but high school Finn is certainly invested in not sweating the small stuff.

Despite my curiosity, it seems like an invasion of privacy to mess with such a well-loved book, so I close it, returning it to its place of honor atop the Krispy Kreme shrine. Then I stare out the side window and draft a mental T-chart, weighing the pros and cons of going to get Finn versus waiting on him to return.

Pros: I want to get out of here. Now. For me, for Mom, for Mere, for Jim . . . for my general safety. For Finn's safety too, however little he seems to care about it.

The cons side of the T-chart remains empty. As I search for a reason to wait on Finn's return, besides my pride and the fact the sky has turned charcoal gray, I twist the key in the ignition to turn on the radio.

It crackles to life in the middle of another hurricane announcement. ". . . water is inches from Highway 12 in Hatteras. Dare County Emergency Management has started door-to-door inquiries to ensure residents have evacuated. Several factors have combined to create especially dangerous conditions. Repeat: please evacuate now."

Enough is enough. I flick the radio off in the middle of the man's dramatic pause, jump down to the sand, and storm toward the dunes. Movement in the tangled trees beside Zeke's shack catches my eye. I freeze, zeroing in on a chestnut horse hunkered down in the knotted stand of spindly trunks that camouflage him. The poor thing couldn't have picked a worse time to lose his herd. Wherever they are, they seem to have left him to fend for himself.

I turn away, unable to look at him once I realize just how much I feel like that lonely horse. Dull pressure squeezes my heart. As I tromp toward the ocean, I recite facts I learned from Dad about the horses he fought to protect. Humans generally do more harm than good when they interfere. A horse died a few years ago after tourists fed it apples and carrots and other treats its system couldn't handle. The fact I repeat again and again is how the horses have survived here for over five hundred years. They were left behind by Spanish explorers who couldn't scrape out a life. Humans wouldn't thrive here for several hundred years, but the horses did just fine under the harshest conditions.

The horse will be fine. And I will be too.

Breathless, I crest the mountain of sand and spot a pair of jeans, flip-flops, and a T-shirt piled on the ground. The beach is empty. But still, I would never just strip down to my underwear on the wide-open beach. Obviously, Finn has zero issues with that.

I glance out to sea and spy two white boards bobbing in the angry surf. Waving a hand above my head, I try to get Finn or Zeke's attention. Apparently, they're hyper-focused on staying afloat in the churning water and dimming light. As I watch, Finn angles his board toward the beach. His broad shoulders and strong strokes look determined. He rises with a forming wave. In one fluid movement, he pushes himself to standing. Turning parallel to the beach, he glides in front of the racing funnel of white until it consumes him and the back of the board. Air catches in my throat. There's no way he can escape the water surrounding him on all sides.

But he does.

Somehow, he shoots out a tiny opening in the funnel and races ahead of the collapsing wall of water. He shouts a cry of victory over the crashing waves. I watch, speechless. It's beautiful in a kind of terrifying way.

I shake off the trance. There is no way—*no way*—I'm going to be sucked in by his cool wetsuit or daring stunts. I wave both hands over my head, jumping up and down for added emphasis. By some miracle, he turns his head in my direction. When he does, the tail end of the wave he just outran charges in and capsizes him.

Holding my breath, I clamp my hand over my mouth. He's gone. I know what it's like to be knocked off a boogie board and dragged under on a typical summer day—to tumble and scrape against a carpet of crushed shells, to want to reach for the surface when you have no idea which direction is up or down. And today is anything but typical.

I run toward the water as Zeke paddles toward shore. Apparently he has eyes in the back of his head or something and saw the whole thing. "Finn!" he shouts.

A board rockets from the water fifty yards down the beach. There's no cocky surfer attached to it. I sprint toward it, but the loose sand makes speed difficult.

No. No. No. This can't be happening. I told him it was stupid. "Finn! Finn!" I scream as though he's going to hear me under the turbulent water.

The boy's arrogant and annoying and impulsive, and I told him this was idiotic. But I would never, never wish anything bad on him. And now it's my fault, my fault he's—I don't dare think the words.

"Dear God, please, please—" I'll pray, beg, whatever it takes to bring Finn to the surface. I couldn't live with myself or the guilt if he died. I should've been more emphatic about not surfing.

But I wasn't.

And now Finn is gone.

CHAPTER NINE

*Let the great world spin for ever down
the ringing grooves of change.*

ALFRED, LORD TENNYSON

There!" Zeke yells as he charges up the beach toward me.

I squint in the general direction of his pointed finger, but I don't see anything. Then the surf retreats, leaving behind a life-size lump of black. I take off. My calves scream in protest against the sand pulling at my feet. Zeke catches up to me seconds later. Without words, we each grab an arm and drag a limp Finn to safety.

Zeke rolls Finn onto his back for a better look.

He's not dead—not even unconscious. The idiot is laughing. *Laughing.*

"That was . . . awesome." He pushes himself up on an elbow.

My pulse pounds in my throat. I fight the urge to draw back and kick him in the ribs. Glaring down at him with my best death stare, I cross my arms over my chest. "You scared me, idiot."

One corner of his mouth turns up. "Aww, see, I knew you cared, Bookworm."

I almost growl. "You . . . you . . . jerk. You scared the crap out of me."

"*Jerk?* That's the best you've got . . ." His voice trails off as he wipes salt water from his face with the back of his hand.

Refusing to be baited into another ridiculous argument, I swipe at the tangled hair whipping around my face. "How can you even joke at a time like this? I thought you were dead."

The wind whips at the ocean frothing behind him. These are not your typical Outer Banks waves with their dependable and evenly timed crest-trough-crest rhythm. These waves are higher, harder breaking, and hungrier. They almost made a meal of Finn.

Dad once told me three things must work together to create waves like this—a hurricane force trifecta of speed, distance, and duration. Then I remember what one of the radio announcers said about the Category 2 storm and the timing of the high tide, and the sense of urgency I've been fighting to keep under wraps suddenly threatens to overflow.

Zeke offers Finn his hand. He takes it and lets himself be pulled to standing. "Not dead but close," Finn says. "I bet mouth-to-mouth would speed the recovery."

My jaw clicks when it falls open. "Not in this lifetime. By the way, Highway 12 is almost under water in Hatteras. We might want to get this show on the road unless we plan to ride it out here."

Zeke gives Finn a little shove toward the dunes. The man seems a thousand times more frightened by the thought of overnight, female company than he does by Finn's stupid stunt or the threat of an oncoming hurricane.

Ch-ching.

Score two for me.

In another lifetime, I might be curious about Zeke and his loner life out on the beach. In this lifetime, all I care about is getting to Mom. If she doesn't hear from me soon, she'll freak, and she can't afford to be distracted while pulling a heavy load and looking out for Mere.

"Hey, what about my board?" Finn asks.

"Dude, that thing's history," Zeke says as they follow me toward the dunes, and Finn looks sadder than I've ever seen him.

No one speaks till we reach the shack. Neither of them comments on the fact that the Blazer's parked in an entirely different spot or that the clouds are getting darker and we're losing sunlight.

"You sure you don't want to go with us?" Finn takes his sandy clothes from Zeke and steps around to the driver's side of the car. I study the ground, as there's absolutely no telling what the boy does or does not wear under his wetsuit. And I'm not taking any chances.

"Yes," Zeke says.

When I chance a quick look up, he's glancing toward the dark patch of trees behind the shack where I saw the horse.

"I have stuff to do here," he says. "I'll head to the lighthouse if things get bad. If the lighthouse goes, the island goes. If the island goes, I may as well go with her."

That's cheerful, I think. I chew on my bottom lip, glancing through the windows of the Blazer. As Finn wiggles into his shirt, I pull open the passenger-side door and slide in.

Finn tightens his belt as he walks toward Zeke and pulls him in for that shoulder-bump, back-slap thing guys call a hug. "Be safe," he says.

"Always, man." Zeke heads to the shack as if it's just another day in the life of an Outer Banks hermit.

Finn steps up onto the running board, then slides into the driver's seat and throws the Blazer in reverse. My head jerks backward, but I don't complain. I'm thrilled to finally be on the road, heading toward the mainland, heading toward safety, heading toward Mom.

We drive in silence. My practical backpack and duffel rest on the backseat right beside his water sports equipment and a Kit Kat wrapper. The wind blows harder now, and Finn has to drive much closer to the dunes on the ride south. I see no signs of the horses now—or any other wildlife. They've surely holed up somewhere away from the gale and the rising tide.

When we reach the paved road in Corolla, I almost start to relax, at least until Finn opens his big fat mouth.

"Since you're in a hurry, we can take a shortcut," he suggests, pointing toward a narrow street on our left.

The beach road here is paved and nothing like the four-wheel-drive beach road behind us, but it is the only main road this far north. During the summer, it's bumper to bumper almost every day. But this is October. There's nobody here and no reason to risk a downed power line or twists or turns or anything else on tight neighborhood streets, even if they shorten the distance some.

"No. Let's take the main road. It's safer."

"What's so great about *safety*? The best things in life aren't safe—surfing, hang gliding. Even driving a car isn't safe, is it?" He gives the steering wheel a quick turn, causing the front end to cross the yellow line as he whips us down a side street.

"You're . . . you're . . ." I grab the door handle. Words

that would traumatize Mom ricochet in my head, but I don't say them.

"Spit it out. Let it loose." He seems amused by my stuttering.

If this were a movie, I'd demand he stop the car, smack the smirk off his face, and then go storming off on my own into the hurricane. But I'm not in a movie, and I'm not that impulsive. I release my death grip on the door handle and ball my hands into fists in my lap. "You're a jerk, Finn Sanders." I spit the words in his general direction without meeting his eyes, realizing I've used the same insult twice now.

Laughing, he smacks the steering wheel. "You're funny, Sophie March."

Refusing to look at him, I study the road ahead, steadying myself when we feel another blast of wind. Honestly, I didn't know he remembered my last name. But clearly, he doesn't remember me that well, because I don't have a funny bone in my body—sarcastic, maybe. On a really good day, maybe even witty. Funny—not so much.

Before I can remind him that he doesn't know anything about me anymore, that we're not friends, that he stood me up for my first and only high school dance, something smashes into the windshield. He jerks the wheel, and the next thing I know we're lurching off the side of the road. He overcorrects, yanking us back onto the smooth asphalt. But the back of the Blazer fishtails, whipping back and forth. Somehow, we remain on the road. Time slows, magnifying the crash of glass and the squeal of brakes.

Some sort of self-defense mechanism must kick in, because I watch the action unfold in front of me like something happening to someone on TV. Bracing my hands on the dashboard, I calmly accept the inevitably of what's to come. Part of me wonders how Mom and Mere will make it without me. Part of me accepts the unavoidable. The ringing in my ears helps to mute the screech of metal on pavement.

A distant scream that might be Finn's hangs in the air. The last thing I see before a neck-jerking impact is the line of mailboxes and stand of dark pine trees barreling toward us.

CHAPTER TEN

To strive, to seek, to find,
and not to yield.

ALFRED, LORD TENNYSON

When something cold and wet smacks my cheek, I open my eyes. Blinking, I try to clear the fogginess clouding my thoughts. It's more dark than light outside. Icy drops of water prick my face through the missing glass in the windshield before me. I glance to my left at the shadowy figure slumped over his deflated airbag and steering wheel, and a wave of memories crashes over me. Oh, God. We are in deep, deep trouble.

I have no idea how much time has passed. It's probably only been a few minutes since the accident—otherwise it would be pitch dark by now. We're on the back end of twilight and speeding toward real-deal darkness, but there's still a bit of gray in the sky. However long it's been, it was long enough for the wind to increase from a whistle to a roar. The person hanging forward against his seat belt is Finn, and he's not cracking any jokes about mouth-to-mouth this time.

I push the airbag out of my lap and claw at my own seat

belt, desperate to escape. The picture of my family's crumpled car in the newspaper flashes behind my eyelids. I realize I could've died just now and left Mom with yet another tragedy.

A gust of wind rocks the car, distracting me from the panic gripping my heart and chest. When I squint into the murky shadows, the pine trees above us bend at precarious angles. Somewhere in the distance, a sharp crack of what sounds like splintering wood snaps above the droning wind.

I reach over to wiggle Finn's elbow. "Finn. Wake up. We've got to get out of here."

When I squeeze his shoulder, a groan escapes his pale lips. His head lolls to the side, eyelids fluttering a bit but not opening. I shiver as cold wind nibbles at the exposed skin on my face and neck. We need to hole up somewhere safe. Waiting for help is not an option, and anywhere would be better than a wrecked car beneath a stand of shallow-rooted pine trees.

Last I remember, we were racing down a residential side street. Then what must have been a massive tree branch hit us out of nowhere. The mailbox on the hood of the car means there must be at least one house beyond the trees and sandy hills to our left. I just have to find it in the dark. No, not *me*. *We* have to find it. Finn's not my favorite person, but I'm not leaving him out here to fend for himself. Plus, he doesn't look like he'll be able to fend for himself anytime soon.

I unbuckle my seat belt, prepared to do whatever I need to do to keep us both safe. He's in good shape. I didn't see an ounce of fat on him when he was dressing back at Zeke's—not that I was looking. Yet he's really tall and has to outweigh me by a lot. We're not going anywhere till he can walk.

"Finn, please. Wake up." I gently lift and tilt his head back against the headrest, thankful when his chest rises and falls. But he doesn't respond. My fingers graze a massive bump near his temple. It's too dark to tell how badly he's hit his head, but I start to worry about a concussion. When I unbuckle him, he slides to the left against the door. His head touches the glass. He winces, his eyes opening to slits. I wave my hand in front of his face. "Finn. Finn. It's Sophie."

His eyelids flutter again, threatening to close.

I lean in so close his shallow breath brushes my cheeks. "Finn, stay with me, please. Look at me. We've got to get out of here."

His lips part, but no sound comes out. The trees beside the car crackle and pop under the force of the wind. Finn's Adam's apple slides down his neck, and his eyes widen. He manages a wobbly nod, but even that seems to require tremendous effort.

"Look at me. Don't close your eyes. I'm coming around to your side." Without waiting for him to respond, I jump out of the Blazer. Obviously, I can't take all my stuff, not if I'm going to have to help Finn walk. I'll come back for the rest later, but I reach in the back, unzip my bag, and grab Mere's compass.

Yanking Finn's door open with one hand, I drag one of his long arms across my neck, then wiggle his legs out and pull him toward me. I wish he'd say something—anything—even something stupid. The cool wind and freezing rain bring him to his senses as I half drag, half lead him up a mound of sand that feels more like Mount Everest.

He finally speaks. "My head hurts like—" His voice breaks off as he doubles over, grabbing his ribs.

I clench my jaw, trying not to collapse under his weight.

"Shh. I've got you. Keep putting one foot in front of the other. We're almost there."

I'm totally lying, but he's not in a position to understand what's going on, much less argue about it. My thighs burn in agony under our combined weight. My wet hoodie sticks to my skin, weighing me down even further. My neck aches from the impact of the airbag and Finn's weight, and I contemplate sitting for a minute or two, but we're still overshadowed by a canopy of drunkenly swaying trees. Peering through the tunnel to the opening at the end of the drive, I spot the shadow of a lopsided bungalow on stilts. The dark outline of a possible shelter, no matter how poorly built, puffs my sails with a second wind.

"Finn. Come on. There's a house up ahead."

The weight across my shoulders lessens a bit when he lifts his head. "Yeah . . ."

He pauses for a second or two after every step to catch his breath. By the time we reach the deck at the top of the stairs, we're drenched through to our skin and shivering against each other. I unpeel his arm from my neck, lean him against the wall near the door, and bang on the window. When no one answers, I wiggle the knob.

Of course, it's locked.

I bang the glass again. Tears burn my eyes. There has to be a key somewhere. When I lean down to look under the mat and find nothing but wood, icy rainwater washes the tears away.

"You're . . . gonna have to break . . ." The howling wind cuts off bits and pieces of his weak speech, but I get the gist of it. Finn wants me to break into this house. I guess it would still be breaking and entering with a key, but it would seem a lot more civilized that way. I survey the windows. Maybe one's unlocked.

A terrifying bang overpowers the groaning of the wind. When I almost jump out of my skin, my foot hits a concrete frog near the door. Somehow, my heart restarts itself after a missed beat.

"Do it," Finn says.

Another bang, and another, cracks the night. I jump again and again. My imagination conjures images of drunk looters with guns shooting up the neighborhood and robbing homes.

"Sophie, it's just . . . the transformers blowing . . ."

Oh, right. Just those little transformers blowing. Nothing to worry about. We're stranded on a narrow strip of land, jutting out into the Atlantic in the middle of an oncoming Category 2 hurricane. Now our only source of power is apparently blowing up as we speak. Clearly, we're perfectly safe—nothing to stress about here, friends.

"Do it," he says a second time.

"Crap, crap, crap," I whisper under my breath.

Curse this boy.

Curse this hurricane.

Curse the transformers.

Curse it all—every last bit of this horrible nightmare.

Bending down, I grab the heavy frog. With a grunt, I heft it to my shoulder, then slam it through the glass.

CHAPTER ELEVEN

A sorrow's crown of sorrow is remembering happier times.

ALFRED, LORD TENNYSON

The house is cold and dark, but it's small, which makes finding the couch easy. I prop Finn in the corner cushions, then head back to the door and the light switch. Flicking the switch does nothing but confirm what Finn already said about the transformers: the power's out. I try a lamp and the TV remote out of desperation. Nothing.

I check my phone for the seventy-fifth time since I got in the car with Finn. Zero signal. Not much battery.

I step back to the couch. Finn's slumped over on his side in a fetal position, teeth chattering. I'm no expert, but I grew up on Dad's forest ranger stories. And it doesn't take a medical degree to realize Finn's headed down a one-way street to shock and maybe even hypothermia if I don't do something fast. Before the situation can spiral any further out of control, I wiggle his shoulder.

He groans and opens his eyes to slits.

"Don't blink. Don't blink," I order in my most authoritative voice as I slide my finger across my phone and switch on the flashlight. When I shine it in his eyes, he winces and blinks. As soon as his eyes obey my command, his pupils constrict to pinpoints under the glare of my flashlight. I know responsive pupils are a good sign that Finn didn't suffer a concussion, and I breathe a sigh of relief.

He rests his arm across his eyes. "Cut the light. It hurts."

"What day is it?"

"That's. A. Stupid. Question." His teeth chatter, chopping up his speech.

"Just tell me." If his pupils are responsive and he's alert to time and place, I can let him sleep for a few hours at a time.

"It's Wednesday. Leave me alone. I'm freezing." He shifts onto his side, clearly settling in for a while.

We really need to get out of our wet clothes.

"Finn!" I grip his shoulder, but he doesn't budge or make a sound. After a few seconds, I take a deep breath and tug his T-shirt down the arm nearest me. Once his elbow clears the armhole, I bend his arm, slipping it inside the body of his shirt. Using the tricks I learned from Mere's rehab nurses, I have him out of his shirt in just a minute. The jeans take longer because they have a button and a zipper. My insides turn all twisty when my fingers brush his stomach. Holding my breath, I stare at the fish mounted over the old fireplace instead of his body. I peel him from his wet jeans inch by inch. Avoiding an underwear malfunction slows me down even further.

When I finally have him stripped down to his SpongeBob boxers, I realize my mistake. He's freezing. Now his whole body moves in rhythm with his chattering teeth. I should have rounded up blankets first. I hate to leave him exposed and cold, but I have to find better supplies.

The kitchen, dining, and living areas are all one room. I push through the closed door opposite the couch. It's a bedroom. Without hesitating, I pull bedspread, blanket, and top sheet off an iron-frame bed with one aggressive yank and head back to Finn. I cover him from chin to toes and carefully tuck the covers in around him. The covers do nothing to lessen the shivering. I need to do something with his wet hair, so I hurry to the tiny L-shaped kitchen in search of dish towels.

I return with an armload of soft towels and hot pads, then drop to my knees beside the couch, thankful Finn appears to have dozed off. As I massage his head with a towel, a bit of color seeps back into his cheeks. When his teeth stop chattering, his face relaxes. He sinks into a deep sleep before my eyes, and something in my chest loosens. It's hard to be irritated with him when he looks so vulnerable—when he's not smirking, when he's not talking.

Maybe Finn's not the real problem. Maybe it's just his mouth. Maybe we'd be great friends if he didn't talk so much, and if we didn't have that little nightmare where he stood me up at the dance. But from what I've seen, the talking will never go away unless someone wires his jaw shut.

Pushing myself to my feet, I head back to the bedroom in search of dry clothes for me. If I'm going to take care of Finn, I need to take care of myself too. The person who owns the house either doesn't spend much time here or is some kind of super minimalist. There's one Crab Shack T-shirt, a pair of men's jeans, an East Carolina sweatshirt, and a pair of flannel drawstring pajama pants. I don't care how cold or wet I am or how incapacitated Finn is, I'd die before prancing around this house anything less than fully clothed.

I take off my wet clothes and tennis shoes, throw on the T-shirt, slip into the way-too-big pj pants that, to my happy surprise, have pockets, and head back to Finn with the jeans and sweatshirt for when he wakes up. He's breathing softly, face still relaxed, so I set to work. I remember this drill from childhood—back when we were still a four-person family with a dad. We rode out many a nor'easter and even a few Category 1 hurricanes. All Outer Banks residents know to be prepared 24/7 for unpredictable weather and power outages. There must be basic storm supplies here somewhere.

The logical place to start is in the kitchen. Trying to take advantage of the last bits of light before I can't see, I pick through the cabinets nearest the back door, methodically opening one, feeling around, and then moving to the next, finding a few cans of soup and other nonperishables as I go. I hit the jackpot when I open the drawer beside the sink—candles, matches, a flashlight, and a value pack of double-A batteries. I set them on the counter and run down my mental checklist.

Shelter—check. Light source—check. Canned goods in the cabinet—check. Water—*crap*.

I try the faucet. A few spurts of water and a bunch of air shoot out, then nothing. We won't make it long without water, so I grab every pot and pan I can find and charge out to the deck, arranging the makeshift buckets in a line near the railing. Securing them with the concrete frog and a couple of heavy flowerpots, I pray they'll withstand the predicted high winds. In an emergency, rainwater might be our only option. Shaking moisture from my hair, I step inside and bolt the door behind me.

There's nothing I can do now but wait for my clothes to dry, wait for Finn to wake, and listen to the rising wind. The house sways a little, and I remind myself that's what it's designed to do. The stilts do more than elevate the living space above water level; they also provide some give in strong winds. Staring into the blackness beyond the window, I tell myself I've got this. I'm pretty good at taking care of myself and everyone else. The boy sleeping soundly in the cocoon of warm blankets and sheets at my back is evidence of that.

But guilt nibbles at my insides. I should be taking care of Mom and Mere, not Finn. I should have told Mom about my tires. Maybe all of this could have been avoided if I had.

Sadly, there's nothing else I can do to improve our situation right now. I don't want to waste our light sources, so I sit in the dark, listening to Finn's steady breathing. I draft a mental to-do list of what needs to be done at daybreak and pray the storm will turn back out to the Atlantic. Or maybe some emergency personnel will find us on their door-to-door rounds.

A loud bang cracks the side of the house, and my head snaps. I realize I must have closed my eyes for a second and that debris is hitting the house, probably a trash can or lawn chair or something someone forgot to put away or tie down. My butt's numb from sitting on the hardwood floor, and my whole body aches. Common sense tells me to get some sleep, but my stubborn streak insists I stay alert—stay focused. When I yawn, I realize common sense is going to win.

I debate going to the bedroom, but I worry something could happen if Finn and I are separated, even by a wall. It's like that reality show where people have to survive naked in the wilderness for weeks at a time. They may fight like crazy, but anything is better than being alone. Finn's the last person I'd choose to be stranded with, but he's all I've got. And anybody is better than nobody.

I push myself to standing and arch my aching lower back. My spine pops. I survey the darkness again. We're surrounded by windows. If the winds bear down even harder, we'll have to move to a closet or the corner of the kitchen away from the threat of breaking glass. I gently sit on the edge of the couch in the bend behind Finn's knees and kind of recline on the arm of the couch. I don't have to touch anything but his calves and feet, which seems safe enough—no room for misinterpretation.

Trying to be very still, I rest my head against the back of the couch and concentrate on the wind. At some point I must have fallen into a deep sleep, or I'm still dreaming, because I'm nestled in blankets and . . . warm. And the world on the other side of my closed eyelids is no longer black. It's more charcoal gray.

I exhale, savoring one second of perfect quiet and warmth. Then soft laughter rips me to awareness. My eyes fly open.

Inches from my face is another face—a smiling face, framed by messy, towel-dried black hair.

"Morning, Sunshine." Finn winks at me. The goose egg on his forehead has already turned a greenish-gray.

My body stiffens. "Did the storm miss us?" I ask between mostly closed lips, praying he found the sweatshirt and jeans I laid out for him. If I weren't swaddled like a baby, I'd yank my hand to my mouth. I can only imagine the dragon breath I must have this morning. I wouldn't wish it on my worst enemy.

"No, I don't think we've seen the worst yet. But we'll be okay. The house is pretty well built." He moves slowly and carefully, like an old man, as he pushes himself up to a sitting position on the edge of the couch. He seems completely unfazed by the proximity of his body to mine.

I, on the other hand, can barely breathe.

"I want to say thanks," he says, changing the subject and saving me from the awkward silence.

"For what?" I haven't done anything. Maybe the bang to his head scrambled more than his face.

Turning sideways to face me, he playfully bumps my hip with his elbow, then lowers one eyebrow. His face is serious, but his eyes are speckled with mischief. "Uh, let's see. For the blankets, for the supplies I saw on the counter, for the pots on the deck, for the clothes . . ."

Thank you, God. Thank you. At least he's dressed.

"Thank you for saving me," he says.

"It was nothing." Anyone would have done the same thing in a similar situation.

Now even his eyes are serious. "It was *something*. I should have listened to you. It's my fault we're stranded. I'm sorry. Good thing you're like some kind of ninja-survivor girl."

Now I'm the one laughing—like a real, genuine laugh—which is completely absurd, considering the situation we're facing with the weather.

If the forecast hasn't changed, we could be in for a direct hit sometime in the next few hours, which means we have plans to prepare, decisions to make, and actions to take. And no time to lie around laughing like friends . . . or like anything else.

But for a second, laughing with Finn doesn't seem so bad.

CHAPTER TWELVE

*A life that is half-truth
is the darkest lie of all.*

ALFRED, LORD TENNYSON

Several hours pass as we wait to see what else the hurricane has in store. My phone hasn't had service since yesterday, and Finn's watch is no help. It must be at least midmorning. Maybe even noon. It's hard to say since the sky never advanced past slate-gray. Our cottage on stilts remains shrouded in gloom. We eat lukewarm chicken noodle soup I heat over a couple of candles.

"Won't your parents be worried about you?" I ask between bites.

He slurps a spoonful of squishy noodles and shrugs. "It's just me and my mom."

I could have sworn I remembered a mom *and* dad at school functions. Maybe his parents separated too. "Isn't that even more reason for her to worry?"

He leans forward to set his empty bowl on the driftwood table in front of the couch. The casual movement seems dreamlike with the sun camouflaged, the wind howling, and the house swaying beneath us. "She loves me. She worries, but we both learned one thing when my dad died—life is meant to be lived. *Really* lived. Like, suck every last drop of life out of life every day because today could be your last. That's why we moved back here—to be closer to Zeke and to the ocean."

A speck of chicken lodges in my throat. I had no idea he'd lost his dad. It must have been after he moved away. I just kind of figured from his happy-go-lucky attitude that he was like Yesenia, that he'd never come face-to-face with any of the big bad Ds—disability, divorce, death. The smile on his face doesn't match his death and dying comments, if you ask me. But he's not really asking me. I'm caught once again by the oxymoron that is Finn Sanders. His words are those of a wise old sage, but his face is more impish, stand-up comic.

"And she knew I might hang out with Zeke," he says.

When a Christmas-tree-size pine branch slaps the window, I jerk, sloshing soup out of the bowl. The wind is picking up.

I set my bowl beside his and begin grabbing the books and blankets I've piled up around us. "It's time," I say.

Without arguing, he stands. When he reaches for the flashlight and batteries on the table, he struggles to catch his breath. I stop to look at him, see his hand extended but frozen in place.

"You okay?" I ask.

"Yeah. Fine."

He's lying. The grimace on his face and the hand squeezing his ribs speak way louder than his hoarse voice.

"You're hurt."

"I'm fine." As if to prove it, he releases his side and grabs the flashlight and batteries.

I don't move until he nudges me toward the bedroom. It's a good thing the closet is on the interior wall and even better that it's pretty much empty. I fold the sheets and blankets to fit the floor. He grabs pillows from the bed. By the time we finish, we have a cozy hidey-hole I would have killed for back in elementary school. We have the books and a deck of cards I found with the emergency candles and other storm supplies.

"You take this thing everywhere you go?" He flicks Mere's compass, which I have hung around my neck.

I stand outside looking in, hoping he'll go first. For some reason, retreating to the closet seems like a big decision, like crossing some sort of invisible line, like an admission that our lives are at stake. "My sister's really attached to it," I say without explaining that Dad gave it to Mere, or that it was the only thing she hung on to after the accident, or that Mom and I packed our compasses away long ago. It's not like we'll have the money anytime soon to travel somewhere that requires orienteering equipment.

Finn leaves it at that, dramatically gesturing for me to enter. *"Mi casa es su casa."*

I try to smile, but I don't like it. I don't want to be trapped in a closet at the mercy of this stupid storm. But we have no choice, so I cross the threshold.

"Wait!" He grabs my shoulder.

"What?" I jump back, positive he's spotted a black widow or some mammoth rodent.

"We forgot the most important provision." He backs out of the room.

I examine the dim closet. We've got everything that was on my list to get us through tonight and into tomorrow. We agreed candles and matches would be too dangerous. We agreed canned goods would be too messy, which is why we ate before the retreat and stashed only a box of saltine crackers and a bag of gluten-free rice cakes in the closet.

I try to ignore the rain pelting the house harder than ever. These are not the plump drops of a summer storm. These raindrops are sharper, longer, more like miniature knives than precipitation. Hugging myself, I rub my upper arms and try not to think about wind, or rain, or knives.

As I wait for Finn to return, it hits me that this might be my last chance to pee for a really long time. When I scurry back from the bathroom, he's hiding something behind his back.

"Ta-da!" he announces, whipping out a box of Twinkies.

"How old are they?" I scrunch up my face.

"Who knows? Who cares? These things have enough preservatives to survive the apocalypse with the mutant cockroaches. And they're yummy." He places his fingers on my lower back, coaxing me forward.

I step inside again and plop down cross-legged at one end of the closet. He holds his side as he lowers himself to the floor at the opposite end. Sliding off his flip-flops, he stretches out his long legs. When he does, his toes brush my knee. The skin beneath my flannel pants tingles.

"Now what?" I ask, pulling the door shut on its creaky hinges and clicking the flashlight to its lowest setting.

"Truth or dare?"

I shake my head and try not to squirm under his gaze. "Maybe we could just rest for a little while." I lean my head back against the wall and close my eyes without waiting for him to respond.

The minutes creep into hours. The afternoon passes mostly in silence. My butt hurts. If we don't *do* something, I'm going to go stir crazy. "You want to play cards?" I ask.

He scans the closet dramatically. "I'd suggest spin the bottle, but there are only two of us and no bottle. How about high-stakes blackjack?"

I pull my knees toward my chest. "Um, I was thinking rummy."

"Boring." He picks up the deck of cards, then shuffles in the dim light without glancing down.

"I like rummy." I wrap my arms around my bent knees.

"Exactly."

"What's that supposed to mean?" I ask, my voice a little too loud in the cramped space.

"Nothing." He drums his fingers on the cards thoughtfully. "It just seems like you can't have fun if you never try anything new."

"I try new things." I unclasp my arms, sit up a bit, and lift my chin.

"Like what?" He shuffles the cards again, arches the deck, pushes them together, taps them on his leg, then repeats.

"I tried German last year."

"Oh! Wow! That was daring."

I don't need a lot of light to see the mischief in his eyes. Gritting my teeth, I decide not to rise to his bait.

"You weren't this uptight in ninth grade." He nudges my knee with his bare foot. "What happened?"

A muscle twitches in my jaw.

"Have I done something to offend you?" He finally gives the cards a rest.

Inhaling, I pause to check my words. Is he so inconsiderate that he's forgotten he stood me up? Or is he so insensitive that he has no idea how that would affect me—or any girl?

"Of course not," I lie, not wanting him to know how much I cared about the whole dance thing back in ninth grade and definitely not wanting to go into everything that's happened to my family in the last two years.

"Are you sure?"

"I'm sure. I'm just really stressed out, okay?" I force myself to meet his eyes.

"Okay," he says, interrupting my thoughts and handing me the deck of cards. "If you won't play blackjack, I guess rummy's better than nothing."

The cards are warm from his hands, and the deck's too thin. I start counting. "We're missing cards."

"It doesn't matter. Just deal." When he gestures for me to begin, his hand brushes mine.

I press my back against the wall and pull my feet toward me. "We're missing seven cards. We can't play rummy with that many missing cards."

"Dang." He snaps his fingers. "I guess that means no strip poker either."

"Darn." I drop my shoulders and smile in spite of myself.

"I guess we'll just have to play truth or dare, then." He grabs the box of Twinkies off the floor and rips open one end.

"I think we're a little old for truth or dare." I shake my head when he offers me one of the spongy torpedoes of sugar.

"Actually, it's a good icebreaker. Scientific evidence proves that people who know each other and feel comfortable together make better teams, especially in adverse situations. I think a hurricane qualifies as an adverse situation." He looks down his nose at me, like Mr. Richards does at a defiant student.

"Fine," I say, slightly taken aback by such technical reasoning to play a children's game. I'd rather sleep, or read, or have my wisdom teeth removed, but I don't want to hear another lecture on trying new things or answer any questions about my chilly behavior.

"You go first. Truth or dare?" He bites off half a Twinkie.

"Truth." I set my jaw, daring him to taunt me.

He smirks but doesn't comment on my choice. Seconds tick by as he scratches his chin. He's enjoying making me wait. "Got it. What's a secret talent nobody knows you have?"

"I can diagram sentences."

"Everyone knows you can diagram sentences."

"No, I can *really* diagram sentences."

When he lowers one eyebrow, his bottom lip shifts to the side, like he's thinking hard. "I don't know—"

"I can diagram the Pledge of Allegiance in fifty-seven seconds." I cross my arms.

"Impressive." He nods.

"Truth or dare?"

"Dare." More smirking.

Of. Course.

Ha! I smile as I reach behind the small stack of books against the wall. His confidence falters. Mine grows as I dangle the bag of gluten-free rice cakes back and forth in front of his face.

"The whole bag, buddy. The *whole* bag." For someone trapped in a closet, during an oncoming hurricane, I'm enjoying this a bit too much.

"Fine." He snatches the bag from my hands.

I lean back against the wall, cross my arms, and settle in to enjoy the show.

He untwists the tie, then lowers his nose to the partially open bag to take a whiff. His face screws up. "They smell like dirt."

"It's called real food."

He shoves an entire round in his mouth. A speck of puffed rice flies toward me as he shoves in a second and a third.

"Truth or dare?" he asks, holding the last cake near his mouth.

"Truth."

He swallows, then pauses dramatically before continuing. "Most embarrassing moment?"

That's easy. Waiting for a boy to show up for the ninth-grade dance with flowers in my hair and a dreamy smile on my face.

"Ummm . . ." I pluck the last rice cake from his hand to kill time.

His eyes remain locked on mine as he wipes a stray crumb from the corner of his mouth.

"Tracking horse manure onto the bus in fifth grade." I'm not being completely dishonest. The horse poop thing was really embarrassing. Kids called me Stinky Sophie for weeks.

"Truth or dare?" I ask.

"Dare." He smiles and does that cool-chin-jerk thing guys do.

"Lick the bottom of your flip-flop." I smile my super-sweet-little-church-girl smile.

Without hesitation, he reaches for his flip-flop.

"Stop." I smack his hand out of the way. "This is stupid. You'll do anything. I can lie, and you won't know the difference."

"Will I really do anything?" He peaks his fingers and squints one eye.

"You will."

"Okay, then give me a truth."

I don't want to play anymore, but I'm curious to know some of his secrets too. "What's *your* most embarrassing moment?" I ask.

"There are so many." He shrugs.

"Are you scared?" I contemplate feeling guilty, taunting him like that, but then I remind myself I'm not doing anything to him that he hasn't done to me.

This time he rubs his chin. "Probably that time I went to school with a hot dog in my pocket and the cops came with the drug dogs to search the building. The dogs went crazy, and everyone assumed I had drugs."

Oh my gosh! I had completely forgotten about the peculiar incident of Finn Sanders and the illicit hot dog. I meet his eyes and smile. When I do, I remember something else I had forgotten. He used to walk dogs at the Humane Society and foster them at his house. He had a beagle named Annie for months. The dog had thunder phobia, separation anxiety, and a bee allergy, but a passion for processed meat, especially bologna and hot dogs. He took her everywhere with him to socialize her. He would apologize to strangers in the pet store if she had a fear-incited accident and clean up after her without complaining. Our love of dogs was one of the things other than chess we had in common. And I'd completely forgotten about it.

I shake my head and try to change the subject again. "Let's read instead. Okay?" I hate the weak sound of my voice as I lift the stack of paperbacks to my lap.

"Whatever you say, Bookworm."

As I sift through the books, he sits up straighter. He looks all studious, but I know he's mocking me.

"*Deliverance?*" I hold up a yellowed paperback with a couple of commando-looking dudes on the cover.

"Way too dark for the circumstances." He snaps the rubber band securing the deck of cards.

"*The Last Song?*" I hold up a book with an almost-kissing couple on the cover, but I already know no self-respecting teenage boy would pick the Nicholas Sparks book.

"Don't those books always have sad endings?"

"Yeah. Somebody usually dies . . ." My voice trails off when I realize I've circled back to the subject I'd hoped to leave back in the living room.

His brow furrows. "There's a difference between sadness and dying, Sophie."

Straightening the blanket near the baseboard, I wait for him to go all mystical philosopher on me. Whether or not I meant to, I did bring this on myself.

"Sadness is being stuck. Not pursuing your dreams. Sacrificing. Compromising. Death can be really beautiful."

I try to look unconcerned, but I feel my face quivering, threatening to cave in on itself. My knuckles whiten against the blue book in my hand. Tears salt behind my eyes. I'm not sure whether I want to cry or hit something.

Losing someone you love is not beautiful.

Period.

"What else you got?" he asks, almost as if he can read my mind. Almost as if he knows I *need* him to change the subject.

"Stephen King." I hold up a book with a horrific clown on the front. "Somebody named Dean Koontz and a biography about some guy—Henry Van Dyke."

He reaches for the King novel. "Yes! *It*. My favorite."

"If guys being hunted in the woods is too dark, I'm pretty sure demonic clowns are too. The biography looks—"

"Safest."

"Well, it does." I shrug. The wind howls. Something scrapes across the roof, reinforcing my point. "I just don't think we need anything to put us further on edge."

"It's fine. You don't need to explain. Henry Van Dyke it is. I think we studied him in Lit." He rests his head on the wall behind him and rubs his side. "I'd kill for some beef jerky."

I ignore the jerky comment. "I didn't study him in my Lit class. I'd remember."

"I'm pretty sure I did." He closes his eyes. Clearly, the debate isn't worth his energy. "Just read. Okay?"

The first page reads like a history textbook, basically tracing Van Dyke's life from infancy through school. On the second page, I have to raise my voice a little. The rising wind is an unwelcome reminder of the serious situation outside the sanctuary of the closet. The author goes on to explain Van Dyke's work as an author and pastor. Chapter one ends with a long list of his songs, poems, and short stories.

I pause, listening for Finn's breathing over the racket outside. Nothing. But I see his sides rise and fall in a relaxed rhythm. He's asleep. I'm pretty sure it would take a gallon of allergy medicine or an elephant tranquilizer to put me to sleep right now. Yet he's totally unfazed by the threat of the hurricane.

I flip ahead a couple of chapters in hopes that Mr. Van Dyke's story picks up. Maybe he had scandalous affairs or addiction problems like so many famous writers. I need something to keep me distracted, especially if Finn isn't awake to do so, so I continue to read aloud.

My voice rises, battling the storm. By page twenty-seven, I'm pretty certain Van Dyke has no skeletons hiding in any of his closets. Chapter three closes with an inscription he wrote for a sundial to be placed in a friend's garden: "Time is Too Slow for those who Wait, Too Swift for those who Fear, Too Long for those who Grieve . . ."

I pause mid-poem to digest the words. They're familiar, but I have no idea where I've heard them. Maybe it's a text Lit teachers use. Maybe Finn's right. Much to my dismay, he frequently is. Maybe I did read Van Dyke for school.

Without opening his eyes, Finn finishes the last lines. "Too Short for those who Rejoice; But for those who Love, Time is not."

I close the book. "Is it from Lit?"

He shakes his head.

"Where?" I uncross my legs, straightening them alongside his down the center of the closet.

"My dad's funeral."

I don't respond. Thankfully, I don't have to.

"My dad picked it. Mom loved it. The preacher agreed it would be perfect. It's true if you think about it." When I still don't respond, he opens his eyes. "You don't believe me about the beautiful death thing, do you?"

I can't lie. Honestly, I can't speak, so I just lift my shoulders in a noncommittal shrug and pray he changes the subject.

"When we found out he wasn't going to beat the colon cancer, we made a pact to enjoy the time we had left." His eyes bore into mine.

I can't look away, so I open my big fat mouth. "I thought colon cancer was pretty treatable." Okay, that was stupid and insensitive.

"It usually is if you catch it early. His doctors didn't suspect it, though, because he was young, and healthy, and had a high tolerance to pain. By the time they did, it had spread. That's why we moved—for an experimental treatment in Charlottesville."

I refuse to open my mouth, refuse to spew some stupid medical thing I've read on the Internet, refuse to say anything about a stupid ninth-grade dance that suddenly seems trivial in the face of the loss he suffered. I bite the inside of my cheek instead.

"He had something called Lynch syndrome. Anyway, at the very end, he had to go to hospice for pain meds. They said he'd only make it a few days. He made it closer to a few weeks. Eventually, Mom and I had to take shifts. Life goes on outside even when someone you love is dying."

He isn't telling me anything I don't know. I mean, Mere isn't dead in the real sense of the word, but the big sister I knew and loved is gone forever. Granted, she's still physically alive, and I adore her, and I would do anything for her. But she's a different person now. She'll never dance again. She's not the big sister who ended the Stinky Sophie comments when I couldn't end them myself, or the sister who taught me how to apply eyeliner, and definitely not the daredevil who taught me to run barrels on old Jack. And I'm not the little sister urging Jack into tight turns at breakneck speed either.

In a weird way I can't even explain, her survival makes things more confusing. To people who didn't know Mere very well, there she is in her physical body, alive. They see an emotionally flat young woman who lacks physical coordination and seems to struggle with short-term memory issues. And there's nothing wrong with that, but that's not the sister I grew up with. She was a whirlwind of joy who left everyone she met floating in a wake of delight. She moved like a swan or a cheetah, depending on her mood.

Losing Mere as I knew her was the worst part of the accident for me. Part of me ended with her that day. My world got knocked out of orbit, but everybody else's lives, even Yesenia's, just kind of went along like nothing happened—like a gnat died, not my big sister. The doctors told us to be thankful she was alive, to create a new life for her and for ourselves. And we'd been trying, and I've been so thankful she's here.

But now I realize I'm still grieving.

Hard.

Sitting alone with Finn in a closet in the middle of a hurricane, I start to grasp what my school counselor has been trying to tell me for months. An idea swirls in my head like a cloud. It's there. I can see it, but if I reach for it, my hand goes right through. Are Finn and my evolving awareness of my feelings somehow connected?

After a long pause, Finn continues. "I was sitting in Algebra, near the end of ninth grade, at a new school. Dad had been at hospice for a while, but all of a sudden I just had to be there. I called Zeke to get me. As much as he hates leaving home, he drove all the way up to Virginia. We swung by the house and I grabbed a shoe box of pictures. When we got there, nothing had changed. Dad was unconscious like he had been for days. But instead of Mom leaving me with him while she went to return calls or shower or whatever she needed to do, she stayed." He stares at the wall above my head, reliving the memory. He smiles like he's talking about a wedding or a family reunion, not his father's death.

I sit frozen in place, hoping he won't notice my watery eyes or trembling lip. He covers my hand with his, and I realize he sees the eyes, the lip, and possibly a whole lot more. Oddly, I don't pull away. We sit for a second, hands touching. I try to remember the last time I intentionally touched anyone other than Mom, Mere, or Yesenia, but I honestly can't remember. Then something scrapes across the shingles, like fingernails on a chalkboard, and I slide my hand away.

Finn picks up where he left off. "The three of us scooted chairs up to the bed. I pulled some of my favorite pictures out of the shoe box. Dad fishing with Grandpa off the Nags Head pier. Mom shoving cake in Dad's mouth at their wedding. Me on his shoulders playing chicken at the pool. Zeke told a story about this psychotic dog that bit Dad in the butt. Mom told the story about how she threw up on their first date. We laughed a lot. The stories just kind of wound down. The sun was setting as I closed the shoe box."

He draws in a long, slow breath, then meets my eyes. "As soon as I closed the box and our laughter ended, Dad's breathing hitched. My mom told him it was okay to go. The three of us held hands around his bed. Zeke was singing 'Amazing Grace,' and then Dad just left us. I don't know how to explain it, but it was peaceful. I've never felt anything like it. All I can say is if that's what it's like to die, there's nothing to be afraid of."

He looks at my crossed arms and tilted jaw. "What?" he asks.

"You're not the only one who's experienced a loss, Finn." I pick a piece of lint off my pants. "And maybe it left you feeling all warm and fuzzy, but it ruined my family."

For once, he doesn't speak. He just sits there, waiting for me to continue—no smart-aleck comments, no Zen Buddhism. And once again, I open my mouth. I'm not sure if it's because of the dropping barometric pressure, the tug of the full moon, or just being locked in a closet with Finn Sanders during a hurricane.

"My sister was the center of our family. She was like a people magnet—old people, young people, you name it. They all loved her." Despite my racing pulse and fists, I continue. "I loved her—I still love her . . ." My voice cracks.

Finn sits like a hunter in a tree stand, hyper-focused on my face and perfectly still—like I'm a deer at the edge of a clearing, alert and ready to bolt at the first sign of danger.

But I don't bolt. I barrel ahead. "But my big sister never got her chance *to suck every drop of life out of life*." I pause to let him hear how ridiculous his words sound twisted and thrown back in his face.

"What happened?" he asks, his voice so quiet I can't be certain whether he said it or just mouthed the words.

Normally, this is where I would shut down, drop the steel door on my emotions, block out anyone and everyone—even Yesenia. But for some unexplainable reason, my mouth barrels ahead of my self-control.

"They were on their way home from the feed store on the mainland. Dad texted to say there was an accident on the bypass, and they were taking the beach road. Nobody knows for sure what happened next. All I know for sure is Dad hit a dump truck head-on. They had to cut him and my sister out of the car. They said it was a miracle they survived the impact. Dad walked away with a broken arm and some cuts and bruises, the other guy without a scratch. But we didn't know if Meredith would live. She did, but she had a TBI—" I skip the part about the truck driver accusing Dad of texting and driving. The police verified Dad's last text was sent several minutes *before* the crash. No charges were filed. Dad never talked about what he was doing with his phone at the time of the accident, and we never asked. The guilt was already eating at him. It seemed too cruel and too judgmental to push the subject despite the rumors that his forest ranger connections with local law enforcement might have encouraged the cops to look the other way.

Finn shakes his head, and I remember not everyone knows as much about the human brain as I do.

"She had a traumatic brain injury." I swallow, forcing myself to look at him. It's still hard for me to talk about it. "As if that wasn't bad enough, the day after the wreck she had a stroke. The doctors think it was a result of the trauma to the blood vessels in her brain. It messed her up—bad. She had to relearn how to walk, and swallow, and all sorts of horrible stuff. And it changed her. She was no longer the prima ballerina of our family, dancing her way through life. She was depressed and angry." My voice cracks again. "She'll never be the—"

Now I'm the one tilting my head back and closing my eyes.

It has nothing to do with my chill attitude and everything to do with trying not to cry.

He places a hand on my knee. This time I stiffen. I didn't tell him my story for sympathy. I told it to prove my point.

"Sophie, I'm sorry," he whispers.

I count to ten, then open my eyes. His face swims in my blurry vision. When I look at him, I believe him. He doesn't say *at least she's alive* or any of the other stupid things people tried to tell me after the accident.

There's no laughter in his eyes. He's not opening his mouth to argue his point. I don't know how to explain it. He just—*is*. He's in the moment, not fighting me, not fighting anything— just still and quiet . . . and serious.

Something else is weird. I don't feel exactly relaxed; it's definitely not peace. But it's like the fist gripping my chest unclenched a little when I shared my story out loud. It's like every muscle fiber in my body has been tight as a piano wire for so long, I forgot what it felt like to not be rigid.

Then glass shatters outside the closet, and whatever was happening to me—whatever was happening between us— is gone.

We sit frozen in place.

Listening.

What we hear is much, much worse than driving rain or gale-force winds.

CHAPTER THIRTEEN

The night comes on that knows not morn . . .

ALFRED, LORD TENNYSON

s that what I think it is?" I ask, shaking my head. We sit in the closet, paralyzed. I pray I'm wrong. Pray the water I hear is pounding rain or the sound of the ocean carried toward us on the wind. Pray it's not what I think it is.

But Finn nods and grabs my hand. I scoot toward him. I know what he's going to say before he opens his mouth. "It's the waves. Storm surge. We must be closer to shore than we realized."

Not good.

Not. Good. At. All.

I squeeze my eyes shut. This cannot be happening. I have no idea what time it is—maybe eight or nine. We've been in this closet for what feels like forever, or all day at the least. It's night again—maybe a little over twenty-four hours since Mom and Mere left for Williamston. Mom must be worried sick. And it's my fault. I thought I had everything under control. I should have found Jim sooner. I should have done something about my tires. I shouldn't have wasted time cleaning up trash.

"It's waves. We've got to move." He shoves on his flip-flops, and then pulls me to my feet, interrupting the thoughts spiraling in my head. We duck to avoid banging our heads on the hanging rod above us.

I lace on my still-damp shoes, thankful I thought to place them with the closet rations, then grab the compass hanging around my neck and tuck it inside my shirt. Seconds later, Finn pushes the closet door open. With the windows shattered on this side of the house and no door to muffle the sound, the ocean crashes, churns, and growls. I picture greedy waves devouring the dunes and our little sanctuary perched on the brink of disaster. If the house goes, we go. Finn and I both know the storm surge is a thousand times more powerful and deadly than the wind. If it gets a hold of us, we're toast—waterlogged toast.

Finn grabs the flashlight, pulling me through the living room. When he turns the knob on the door leading to the deck, the force of the wind slams it into his chest.

"Look out," he screams, then ducks his head and pulls me out into the storm.

We fight the wind to the deck rail and peer down into the dark. As my eyes adjust to the gloom, I realize the clumps of white creeping beneath the house aren't sand. They're sea foam, frothing ahead of the approaching surge of waves.

"We're going to have to run for it," he shouts over the wind.

"Where?" I ask, cupping my hand above my eyes to block out the shards of rain ripping at my face.

He pulls me toward the stairs leading down to the carport. "Farther inland. Anywhere."

He and I both know the dangers. We've heard the stories

of vehicles washed away by twelve inches of flood water moving a few miles per hour. We don't know the terrain, and it's pitch black. It wouldn't take much of an accident to cause a slip. We could be separated in an instant and one or both of us dragged out to sea, or whacked in the head with floating debris, or electrocuted by downed power lines in the water.

I shiver, and it's not from the freezing rain. Tightening my grip on his hand, I scurry after him down the stairs. Icy water rushes over my foot when I step down to the concrete pad under the house, and my flannel pajama pants twist around my ankles like gnarled hands. The ocean thunders around us from every direction. Hunched forward, hands clasped, we run headlong down the driveway. In a matter of minutes, we've gone from safe hidey-hole to out of control. What I thought was our sanctuary morphed into a deathtrap.

When Finn stops short, I slam into his back and remember to breathe.

My drenched shirt presses against his drenched shirt. The wind and rain drown out his next words, but he points at a fallen pine tree blocking our path. The thing could've killed us if it had fallen on our way to the house. He steps up onto the trunk and hops down on the far side. I press my hand against the lump under my shirt. I will not lose Mere's compass. It's my last link to her and Mom. Even if it's only a symbolic connection, I'm holding on to it for dear life.

Finn shouts something else I can't understand, but I get the gist of what he's trying to communicate from his hand gestures. He wants us to follow the yellow line in the middle of the road. I kind of want to follow him, but he's heading north—back the way we came. The houses spread out farther north, which means less chance for shelter. It seems illogical to head that way. We should head south toward civilization, where we're more likely to run into people riding out the storm or emergency personnel.

When he tugs on my hand a second time, I still don't budge. He turns to face me, eyes wide, rivers of water running down his face.

He leans in to my ear, shouting over the wind. "There's a volunteer fire department a few miles north, and Zeke's that way."

I want to argue, but his point about the volunteer fire department makes sense. They'll be first to get back power, phone service, and water after the storm. I compromise, telling myself this will go better than his *back-roads-will-save-time* reasoning, despite the painful twisting in my stomach.

We head north, bent at the waist like mountain climbers as we fight the wind. I have no idea how far we've gone. If I had to guess, not very far. Every step is a battle.

I study the ground immediately in front of my feet as we struggle forward. The second time Finn stops, I catch myself before barreling into him. He's pointing at a mailbox. Squinting, I try to read his lips.

"A house!" he shouts.

And he's right. A very large, very expensive, very sturdy house squats on a rise to our left, maybe a couple hundred yards farther inland than the last cottage. A glimmer of hope lights in my chest. Shaking a fist at the black sky, I tilt my head back and smile.

We're saved.

Our hope reignited, we move faster than before up a small rise to the large house sitting atop a four-car garage. As we approach, Finn grabs my hand and gestures up to the front windows. There appears to be a flickering light inside—a lantern maybe. I should be thrilled. But something about the quivering light and the horizontal sheets of rain in the dark night makes me shiver.

Cursing Dad and Mere for the horror movie marathons Mom never knew about, I shake off the worry. Where there is light without power, there must be humans. Where there are humans, there must be adults. There can't be any other teenagers trapped alone in this storm. That only happens in scary movies, and this is not a scary movie. This is as real as it gets. Plus, Finn doesn't seem worried as he drags me up the steps to the expansive deck that wraps around the entire house.

Where the roof extends over the front door, the wind isn't quite as piercing. I can hear Finn when he speaks.

"We made it, Bookworm!" He squeezes my shoulder, giving me a little shake.

As he lifts his heavy flashlight to bang on the door, I smile. "Yeah, we did."

After a few quick raps, the door swings open. A wide-eyed man older than my father stares at us. His eyes survey us one at a time and head to toe. Under other circumstances, he might frighten me. Under these circumstances, his sturdy house and massive lantern offer a promise of refuge from the weather. Besides, inviting two strangers into his home must be more of a risk for him than going in is for us.

When he gestures for us to enter, we scurry across the threshold. He shuts the door behind us, blocking out much of the noise from the storm.

"What are you two doing out in this?" he barks, then levels

his eyes on me. Something about his jittery eyes makes me nervous.

He wipes a sheen of sweat or rain—I can't be sure which—from his forehead.

"We wrecked," Finn says, seeming to sense my uneasiness.

I appreciate him answering and drawing the man's attention away from me. I glance around the high-ceilinged room as they talk and realize the house is made mostly of walls of glass. It's just as huge as it looked from the road but not nearly as sturdy, and the roof is already leaking in several places. To make matters worse, the man has lit candles all over the place, which everyone who knows anything about hurricanes knows is a major *no no*—it's the number one cause of fires during power outages.

The fear in my gut flares. Dad always said, "The key ingredients to handling any crisis are a clear plan and a calm head." This guy doesn't seem to have either.

Finn's eyes meet mine. He seems to be able to read my thoughts. "Maybe we should find a place with less glass farther inland," he says to the man.

"No!" the man growls, deep and low.

I take a step back.

Finn reaches a hand in front of his chest. It hits me that he looks way more adult than the adult in this situation. "You know the saying—run from water, hide from wind."

"What does it look like I'm doing?" The man gestures wildly around the room. "I'm inside, away from the wind."

"But all this glass is going to go eventually," Finn reasons.

"I'm not leaving. I sunk my life savings into this place, and I'm staying here to protect it."

Finn tries to speak. "Please—"

"Listen, kid. If you know everything, why don't you move on?"

Finn opens his mouth. When he does, a gust of wind whooshes under the crack in the door. A candle falls on the couch and smolders. The man rushes past me to snuff it out.

"It will be ruined!" he says as he beats the small flames into submission. "That couch cost five grand."

Finn looks at me, eyebrows raised in question. I know what he's thinking; this man is losing it. He doesn't realize the danger of his candles, and he's way more concerned about a couch than his own life.

"Let's go," I say.

Nodding, Finn grabs my hand and pulls me to the door.

"Hey, kids." The man raises a fist at us. "You and your friends better stay away after the storm. There won't be any looting around here."

My insides churn like the storm. I'm relieved to say goodbye to this irrational man with the wild eyes and the hazardous candles. At the same time, I'm terrified to face what an enraged Mother Nature has in store for us outside.

Finn shakes his head at the man. As he leads me toward the door, I bite my lip and pray for better luck at the next house.

CHAPTER FOURTEEN

*But the tender grace of a day that is
dead Will never come back to me.*

ALFRED, LORD TENNYSON

Now we're back where we started, trudging up the middle of the dark road and searching for shelter. The lack of sleep, stress overload, and storm effects must be making me delirious, because when the *doo-doo-DOO-doo* of the *Twilight Zone* theme song buzzes in my head, irrational laughter wells in my throat. I feel like we've been sucked through time and space into some low-quality black-and-white movie.

My calf muscles complain as we plod forward, reminding me this is no joke. I know Mom and Mere must be worried sick, and Mom's friend Carla too.

"Look out," Finn shouts as he jumps to the right.

But the wind is loud, and I'm so distracted that I don't move out of the way fast enough. Something whacks me in the shin. A beer bottle maybe. I scream through gritted teeth. I know I scream because the noise vibrates inside my head, but I can't hear it with my ears.

"Are you—" Before he finishes, something else grazes my shoulder.

It doesn't hurt like the bottle to the shin, so I press forward. As a warm rush of liquid pours down my arm, I realize I've got a problem. Finn turns back to me, his face hovering inches above mine. Concern registers in his eyes as he shines the flashlight he's been preserving on my cold face. He looks like something out of a scary movie with its light flickering on his wet face, eyes wide, mouth open, his black hair whipping in the wind like Medusa's snakes. When he lowers the flashlight to my shoulder, a pink stain spreads like spilled fruit punch across my shirt. And there's a lot of pink. I backpedal as he reaches toward my neck.

"Stop, Sophie. Let me see it," he shouts over the wind. The muscles in his cheek twitch as he pushes the flashlight into my hands. With both his hands free, he reaches toward my collarbone. I follow his movement with the light. When I spot the jagged shard protruding from the soft spot between my neck and shoulder, my knees go weak. It's hard to tell, but it looks like the twisted lid of a soup can. My God, the thing could have pierced my jugular. I could have . . . could have . . . died—bled out in the middle of an empty road in the center of the hurricane straight from Hades.

I blink, trying to keep my blurry world in focus. I will not pass out—will not pass out.

Finn grips my head in both his hands, then leans in to me. His lips brush the edge of my ear when he speaks. "That's got to come out."

Closing my eyes, I shake my head. Uh-uh. Not happening. I've seen this sort of thing in movies, and I'm pretty sure the person bleeds out when the arrow or knife or whatever is removed. The pink spreading down my arm and abdomen is bad enough. Spurts of blood would send me over the brink to hysteria. The wind changes directions suddenly, and I stagger. He tightens his grip on me.

"I know what you're thinking." The set of his jaw and the tone in his voice command my attention.

The boy gripping my face in his strong hands shares zero resemblance to the class clown I'm used to. Now he's all hardcore, one hundred percent rescuer doing everything he can to save me. I appreciate his help, but I need a second to think. I can't make any mistakes here. Mom and Mere's future hinges on me keeping myself safe as well.

He swats at a piece of newspaper swishing past our heads. The wind continues to strengthen. We won't be able to stay upright out here in the middle of the road much longer. We need shelter, and fast.

"Look at me," he says, waiting for me to meet his eyes. "Breathe. Listen. That's gotta come out."

I'm listening. I can agree with him on the heading north toward the fire department part of his plan. But the ripping the metal out of my already bloody shoulder part, I'm not so sure I can handle.

"We can't bandage it like that. It needs pressure to stop the bleeding. Plus . . . if it shifts, it could cause more damage." He grips my good shoulder with one hand. His other hand hovers near the ruined one.

I squeeze my eyes shut and lower my head, too exhausted to argue. Then a rip of pain tears through every fiber of my being. Muscles I didn't know I had around my stomach tighten. Some sort of primal snarl erupts from my guts and shreds the night. Curse him for yanking it out without warning me.

Obviously alarmed by my fury, he freezes. The pain constricts my lungs. I close my eyes again, trying to catch my breath. Then his strong hands clamp down on my injured shoulder. The deep pressure dulls the pain a bit.

He presses his forehead to mine. "Sophie, breathe." His words ebb and flow with the pressure he applies to my shoulder.

Closing my eyes, I exhale, then rock my upper body back and forth, back and forth, and try to block out the pain as he rips at his shirt with his free hand. Seconds later, he laces a piece of cloth under my armpit and over my shoulder.

"Breathe. Breathe. Breathe," he chants. As he fumbles around the wound, the cord I used to hang Mere's compass around my neck tangles in his fingers. He gently lifts it over my head.

"I think . . . I'm . . ." I whisper, my voice hoarse as he slides the compass into a pj pocket.

"Good job, Soph." He clamps down a little harder on my shoulder.

Despite the pain, despite the howling wind, despite the flying debris, something in my chest cracks or loosens. I can't be sure which. No one has called me *Soph* since before the accident.

No one has called me *Soph* since Dad left.

CHAPTER FIFTEEN

Half the night I waste in sighs.

ALFRED, LORD TENNYSON

When we finally reach the volunteer fire department, it's deserted, locked up tight. A metal pulley clangs a warning against the vacated flagpole. I should've gone with my gut—should've known the firefighters would have moved farther south to the more populated areas where they could be of more assistance. I don't have enough energy to be disappointed. I just want to sit down somewhere—anywhere. But there's nowhere to sit, and Finn just keeps walking.

He holds a massive trash can lid in front of us to deflect whatever the gale-force winds might throw at us next. If I weren't so exhausted, I might laugh. I mean, he's protecting me from flying debris with a trash can lid. It must be hard to play the chivalrous knight with such an awful shield. But he presses forward anyway.

All the houses up here are on the beach side of the road. They're bigger than the cottage we left behind. They're sturdier, but they're no safer from the encroaching storm surge. The middle of the road is looking like a pretty comfy spot to sit when Finn points to a driveway on the left.

Left is good. Left is inland. Left is farther from the rising tide.

A driveway disappears through a tangle of scrub brush
near the mailbox. The small trees and low bushes lining the
way bend at ninety-degree angles. The vengeful storm smashes
them against the sandy ground like grassy pancakes.

"Should we try it?" he screams at me over his shoulder.

I nod, too weak to answer. We trudge up the driveway.
When we break through the trees, we see not one but two
buildings perched on top of the dunes. Of course, I can't make
out any of the details, but two shadows are punctuating the
dark horizon, and I see no creepy flickering lights. Maybe this
is one of those expensive homes with its own guest cottage.

I should be happy the driveway's so steep. It means high
elevation and protection from the storm surge. It also means
more work, more climbing, and more energy. I'll never make it
if I don't sit down for a second.

"Finn!" I try to scream, but the strong wind squashes my
weak voice.

He tromps forward without acknowledging me. I should
follow, but I can't resist the temptation of the massive driftwood at the edge of the driveway. Easing myself down to the
log, I baby my bad shoulder, careful not to jostle it.

The compass slips from my pocket to the ground. I rest my
foot on its cord so it won't blow away. I'll grab it in a second.
I just need to sit still—to not move anything for a minute. I
clamp my teeth together and try to silence their chattering.

The one good thing about the icy rain is it numbs the pain
in my shoulder. It kind of numbs my thoughts too. Maybe
I'll just sit out the storm here. Careful to avoid any sudden

movements that might reignite the pain, I half slouch, half lean against a twisted arm of driftwood rising from the main trunk. I'm starting to think my plan is so basic, it might work.

Then my comical knight in shining armor with his improvised shield realizes I'm not with him and comes back determined to rescue me.

"Come on. We're almost there." He grabs my hand.

I shake my head, praying he'll leave me alone. "I just need to sit a minute. You go ahead."

"No." He tugs me to my feet. "I'm not going anywhere without you. We're in this together."

I want to argue. We're not in this together. I can take care of myself, but I don't have the energy to disagree.

He wraps an arm around my waist. "I'll carry you if I have to."

Based on the way he's been protecting his own injured ribs, I'm pretty sure he's bluffing. The thought of me slung over his shoulder with my butt in his face is an embarrassing enough mental image that I dig deep and fan the dying embers of my determination. "No. I can do it."

Somehow, we make it up the hill together, leaning into the wind and each other. Finn aims for the big house, but I steer us toward the smaller building on the left. It's kind of protected by the larger building in front of it, and we need all the protection we can get. Up here, we're totally safe from the storm surge, but the wind gusts are even stronger. The sound morphs from the roaring freight train I've grown accustomed to into a thunderous buzz, like something out of a science fiction movie. I clamp my hands over my ears to block out the disorienting sound. I want to sit down and curl up in the duck-and-cover position we practice at school during severe weather drills. But we're so close.

Finn rattles the door. Of course, it's locked. Unlike me back at the cottage, Finn doesn't hesitate to break the small, uncovered window on the door. Careful to avoid the jagged glass, he slips his hand through the opening, finds the knob, and opens the door. Once inside, I stagger toward a sectional sofa in the center of what appears to be an open kitchen and living area. Finn shines the light around the almost bare interior, and I decide some single guy must live here, because there are zero decorations and the TV is obnoxiously large. Luckily, the larger windows have been boarded up really well, and—thank God—there's a very masculine pile of firewood stacked beside what appears to be a working fireplace.

Finn leans against the closed door as I slump on the couch, trying to catch my breath. Hugging myself, I vow to get up in a minute. I just need to close my eyes and breathe. The throbbing in my shoulder should subside if I lie perfectly still. I hear Finn exploring the house, and once in a while a drawer opens and closes.

I try to calculate how many hours of this horror we have left. The few times I've ridden out storms at home, the worst never lasted more than twelve to twenty-four hours. The storm surge might be dangerous for a few days. We might be without power and water longer than that, but the winds should die down drastically by this time tomorrow.

We'll make it. People can survive anything for thirty-six hours, right? I mean, I've seen mares laboring to deliver their foals for two days.

I'm tough.

I can handle this.

I can.

I keep my eyes squeezed shut as Finn clanks around at the fireplace. A match strikes. The familiar sound of kindling crackling and popping punctuates the deafening buzz of the wind. Heat caresses my cheek, like Dad's hands when I was little.

I focus on breathing, and not moving, and not thinking about anything—just clearing my mind and breathing. When a warm hand wiggles mine, I jump. I was so focused on myself, I kind of lost track of Finn and his bumbling around the house.

"I'm so tired. What time is it?" I groan and blink, trying to clear the cobwebs from my aching head. Clearly, I need to stick to silence and stillness.

"It's late—the middle of the night, I think. You've been lying here awhile."

Reaching for the back of the couch, I wrestle myself to a half-seated position when the realization that I've lost Mere's compass hits me.

He places a firm hand on top of mine on the cushion. "Are you okay?"

I shake my head, unable to speak.

"Where does it hurt? What's wrong?" he asks.

I try to swing my legs off the side of the couch, but they barely move. "The compass. I lost the compass."

He shoulders relax. "I'll find the compass. We need to get you in some dry clothes first and clean your shoulder." Finn sits beside me on the couch, his hip pressing against mine, his face illuminated by the fire.

His *we* brings me to attention like a double shot of espresso.

We might be stranded together in this storm. *We* might even share a Twinkie and story time. But *we* are not changing my clothes or cleaning my shoulder. I'm learning to tolerate Finn Sanders, but I'm not ready to do anything more than that.

"I'm fine. I can—" Pain rips through my shoulder when I try to sit up. My throat burns. Hurricane winds are usually cold, but this place feels like the arctic.

"You took care of me earlier. It's my turn to take care of you."

No, sir. Not happening.

When his hand brushes my arm, his eyes widen. He lifts my hand a little, pressing it to his cheek, then rests his free hand on my forehead. His already wide eyes threaten to pop from his skull.

"Crap. You're freezing." He brushes matted hair off my cold cheek.

"It's the storm and this house," I say, praying his eyeballs don't fall into my lap.

"It's not the house or the storm. Were you feeling sick earlier?"

I shake my head, too tired to argue.

He rakes his fingers through his hair, then grabs a pillow and a cushion from the far end of the huge couch. "Maybe you've lost too much blood. We need to elevate your feet. And we need to make sure you stay hydrated and warm."

When he scurries away, I assume it's for blankets and something to drink.

Trying to stay warm like he said, I wedge my hands into my armpits. Fresh blood rushes down my chest. It's warm. That's for sure. Even in the dim light, the angry red fluid stains the Crab Shack T-shirt, making the old stains pale pink by comparison.

He reappears, blanket in hand, smiling encouragingly until his eyes drop from my face to the seeping stain on my shirt.

"Holy crap, Sophie! You're still bleeding."

"Yeah." The room spins, and I close my eyes. He shuffles around the couch. When he bumps into something, he curses under his breath. I'm too exhausted to care. A second later, he's kneeling on the floor beside me, reaching through the neck of my shirt and pressing a dark towel to my wound. I don't know if it's the blood loss or just the exhaustion from fighting the storm, but even with Finn so close, I can't seem to bring his face into focus. I squeeze my eyes shut to block out the fuzziness of the world around me.

He continues applying pressure to my shoulder as I continue breathing and squeezing my eyes shut. Finally, he gets up and bangs around the kitchen. The house moans and groans around us like it's fighting to stay upright. Every once in a while, a gunshot-like pierce of wood snapping punctuates the night.

We can't win. Up here, we're sitting ducks, waiting for the next gust of wind to blow us to smithereens. Gritting my teeth, I push myself a few inches higher on the couch pillows and try to survey the house for any noticeable damage.

As I peer around the shadowy room, Finn's bare feet shuffle across the wood floor. Our eyes meet when he steps in front of the fire. I try to smile but can't. The pain in my shoulder locks the muscles in my face. My stomach tightens at the sight of the bottles clutched against his chest. One of them looks like the Jack Daniels Dad grew so fond of before he jumped ship. I can't be certain, but it looks like he's also got honey and lemon juice and God only knows what else.

The last thing I want to do now is have some kind of pitiful hurricane party.

Scratch that. The last thing I want to do is become my father.

CHAPTER SIXTEEN

I found Him in the shining of the stars.

ALFRED, LORD TENNYSON

Finn peers down at me on the couch, his perceptive gaze on my face raising the temperature of my chilly cheeks several degrees. When I tell him I don't drink, he bursts out laughing.

"You seriously think I'm trying to get you drunk? In a hurricane? When you're sick?" He sets bottles and a pair of scissors on the coffee table, then settles beside me on the edge of the couch. His mouth is smiling, but the skin between his brows pinches together.

If I didn't know better, I'd think I hurt his feelings. "Maybe. Everybody says you'll do anything."

"Like what?"

"Like surf in a hurricane," I say pointedly. "And if you'll do that, you'll do . . ."

"Do what?" he asks as he plucks the whiskey bottle from the table and uncaps it.

"Just about anything . . . and . . ." Squirming, I hope he

doesn't ask why I've been listening to what people have been saying about him or why I would be interested. If the tips of my ears burn any hotter, they might warm my body and the entire room. I curl my toes into the couch cushions, wishing I could disappear, or at least create space between the two of us.

"We're not drinking this." He holds the whiskey up to my face. "It's for your shoulder. I think I got the bleeding stopped for good, but I couldn't find any first aid supplies or Tylenol."

"Oh," I say, sounding as awkward as I feel.

With his free hand, he plucks the scissors off the table and extends them to the collar of my shirt.

Wincing, I swat his hand away from my collarbone. "I can do it myself."

"You sure about that?" he asks, placing the scissors back on the table.

"I'm positive. Just help me up."

He sits frozen in place, mouth open a little, as if I've insulted him or surprised him. Tilting his head, he studies my face. "I can't believe it. You don't trust me, do you?"

Uhhh, maybe. Maybe not.

"I didn't say that."

"You don't have to. Your face did."

"Just help me to the bathroom. I'll do what you say." I gesture at the supplies on the table.

He holds my elbow as I hoist myself to my feet, then guides me to a cramped bathroom at the back of the dark house. The room spins as I lower myself to the icy toilet seat. If the living room was arctic, the bathroom is a freaking tundra. I try to keep from shivering as he heads back to the living room. When he returns a minute later, he lines the bottles on the counter beside me, then waits for me to meet his eyes.

"This is what I want you to do. Rinse your shoulder with the whiskey—gently. We don't want any more bleeding. The whiskey's not as good as rubbing alcohol or peroxide, but it's better than dirty water or nothing. Then squeeze lemon juice on the wound. It will burn, but the acid in the lemon will kill some of the tougher germs."

"We're not marinating a steak," I argue, careful not to move too suddenly.

"No. It's more like dressing a turkey." He pauses, smirking, clearly impressed with his little play on words. If my shoulder didn't hurt so badly, I might have a comeback, but I'm too exhausted to argue.

"What's the honey for?" I ask, concentrating on one spot on the floor so the room won't tilt or spin.

"Honey has natural antibiotic properties."

"How do you know all this stuff?" I stall, waiting for him to leave the room. I'm not taking off my shirt until he's on the other side of a closed door.

"Mom and I spent as much time searching for homeopathic remedies and miracle cures as we did sitting in doctors' office waiting rooms. I told you we accepted Dad's death, and it was peaceful. But that doesn't mean we just gave up as soon as he was diagnosed. We would have done anything to keep him alive. But when the suffering set in, we loved him too much . . ."

"I see," I say, pushing myself to my feet and clutching the edge of the counter with my cold fingers. I'm not so sure I do see. But I don't want to be rude, and if I don't do what he says fast, I might pass out. "Okay. Jack Daniels, lemon, honey. Got it."

He leaves his flashlight on the counter, then backs out of the room, pulling the door closed behind him. I exhale slowly then look in the medicine cabinet, but it's empty. No pain reliever. When I swing its door closed, my reflection in the mirror looks like something out of a horror film. The beam of the flashlight illuminates the bottom half of my pale face. The top half is camouflaged by shadows. My normally light brown hair hangs like dark curtains down either side of my pale face. My eyes sink into my skull zombie style.

Holding my breath, I attempt to wiggle free of my shirt. A wave of pain washes over me as the tight space closes in even further. Despite the discomfort, I refuse to cut this shirt before I know there's a replacement somewhere in this house. I wait for the room to stop spinning before I grit my teeth and yank the sleeve away from my injured shoulder. My fingers snag in the armhole, stopping the momentum of my arm, causing my shoulder to jam. I wince and watch as the floor rises to swallow my face. There's nothing I can do but wait for the impact and pray I don't further injure myself.

Snagging the edge of the counter on my descent, I lessen the severity of my collision with the floor, but probably not enough to completely hide the sound from Finn. Sure enough, seconds later, he's lifting me and cradling me against his chest. I unsuccessfully will myself to shake off the wooziness, but the thumping of his heart hypnotizes me.

At some point, the mental fog lifts, and I peer at my surroundings through one slitted eye. The fire to my right flickers and cracks, the wavering light casting ghostly fingers on the stone hearth. I'm back on the couch. It takes all my strength to glance around the room in search of Finn. He's nowhere to be found, but a smile tugs at the corners of my mouth when I spy Mere's compass propped up on the mantel.

How in the world? He found it, which means he's been outside.

Then I notice something else. I'm not wearing a T-shirt. I'm wearing a man's flannel shirt. Squeezing my eyes shut, I shiver. Sweet Jesus, he . . . he . . . changed my shirt. Maybe I should just close my eyes and die right now.

I try.

It doesn't work.

"Finn?" I call for him, but the house is eerily silent. I have no idea how long I was asleep, but I'm pretty certain not long enough to have skirted the hurricane. We must be in the eye of the storm. But where's Finn? Why would he leave me now?

If he's outside, he could get hurt. If he gets hurt, I'm alone. So much for his whole *we're in this together* motto. I steel myself for an inevitable stab of pain as I push, pull, and wiggle my way to a seated position in the corner of the couch. There is pain, but instead of the ripping and stabbing I expect, it's more pressure and bruising.

His home remedy might not be a modern-day miracle or prescription pain meds, but it's something. I definitely feel less achy, and the pain in my shoulder has lessened a bit.

Finn is taking good care of me. I could almost do more than tolerate him. I could almost . . . like him again. But that's ridiculous. I mean, maybe we could be friends here, in the isolated world of this storm, where it's just the two of us. But in the outside world, we have nothing in common, and my life is too complicated now for anything resembling romance.

This storm has thrown us together, that's all. And that's how I want it to stay. I certainly don't want to be stranded on my own. "Finn," I call, louder this time.

There's still no answer, so I drag myself to the front door. The shutters have protected us, but they also keep me blind to the rest of the world. As I pull open the door, a gust of air whips my hair. The wind may have weakened in the eye of the storm, but it's still blowing. Thankfully, it seems to have given up on the whistling and screaming. I squint into the night, pleased my eyes work better than I would have expected in the murky darkness. If nothing else, this stupid storm is teaching me to appreciate the wonders of the human body—of my human body. I had no idea I could see this well at night.

The full moon helps a bit. It's not shining like it normally would on a clear fall night, but it seems to be trying to break through a layer of clouds stretched like thin cotton balls. Movement in front of the other, larger building catches my eye. I blink, positive my eyes are playing tricks on me.

First, a pointed spire tops what I thought was the main house to our guest cottage. I blink again, and my fuzzy brain clears. It's not a spire. It's a steeple, a white church steeple rising toward the outline of a golden moon.

I thought I knew this part of the beach so well, but I had no idea this little church was tucked behind the tangled trees near the road. Something flaps in front of the church, distracting me from my surprise. No bird with an ounce of avian intelligence would be out in this hurricane, unless it were sick or injured. Plus, it's way too large for a bird. It's some sort of black material flapping in the wind—a flag maybe. No. I zero in on the movement at the front of the church.

Beyond the wide double doors of the main building is a weathered deck. The building and deck perch on a rise of sand. What appears to be some sort of railing made from twisted pickets of driftwood and maritime forest separate the deck from what must be a steep drop-off in front. From there, you would probably have a bird's-eye view of the Atlantic.

It's an eerily beautiful scene, like something out of one of the gothic romances Mom used to read before she quit romance—before Dad bolted. The black flapping draws my attention again, distracting me from the ironic loveliness of the white church outlined against the backdrop of the storm-swept barrier islands.

The wind spreads the material. My chest tightens. It's not a flag. It has arms. Strong, straight, graceful surfer's arms. It's Finn in a black windbreaker, arms stretched wide, head thrown back. He's standing atop a rickety railing in the eye of a hurricane doing his thing. What was it he said back at the first cottage? Something about sucking every last drop of life out of life.

A corner of the moon peeks through a slit in the clouds, like some prophetic spotlight shining on his face—his smiling face. He doesn't just smile. He beams, basking in the moment. I can't even remember what that kind of joy, or freedom, feels like. The closest thing I can think of is riding bareback on the beach at sunrise by myself with nothing but the pounding of hooves and waves for company, and I haven't done that in a long time.

My stomach twists when I realize Finn has something I

want. Something I don't have, or at least haven't had since I was much younger—contentment. He accepts whatever life throws at him. No, he doesn't just accept it. He embraces it. And he looks a heck of a lot happier than me or anyone else I know.

I quietly close the door and retreat to the couch, my ego as bruised as my shoulder.

Is it possible Finn knows more about life than I do? More about living than I do? Have I been doing this all wrong? Wind gusts in the chimney. A dying ember crackles to life as I ease back against the couch cushions, careful not to reopen the wound on my shoulder. I glance at the fire, avoiding the compass staring down at me from the mantel.

Finn won't be as easy to avoid when he returns.

CHAPTER SEVENTEEN

And our spirits rushed together
at the touching of the lips.

ALFRED, LORD TENNYSON

A little while later, footsteps sound on the deck outside the door. I hunch down on the couch fake sleeping, not yet prepared to talk to Finn, much less look into his face— the beautiful face I witnessed outside in the storm.

The door creaks open. After it clicks shut, it sounds like Finn's taking off his jacket and flip-flops. A second later, footsteps pad toward the couch. I concentrate on the rhythmic breath of my pretend sleep. I wish he'd just go away. I need time to think.

But. No.

Of course not.

What does he do?

He moseys right over to my couch, lifts my feet, and plops down with my feet in his lap.

And I can't do a thing about it because I'm supposed to be *sound asleep*. Ugh.

So I just lie there, trying not to wiggle the feet in his lap.

His lap. His lap. Augh. My feet don't know what to do. I don't know what to do. I have no experience with boys. I mean, I don't think the slobbery, braces-clicking kisses with Pete Jones in eighth grade count. That experience didn't exactly inspire a wave of hormonal boy craziness. Then Dad and Mere wrecked. Dad disintegrated, and boys weren't a very high priority.

Now I realize how completely inexperienced and clumsy I am with the opposite sex.

Dear God, I'm going to die. Die.

Not from an injured shoulder.

Not from a horrific hurricane.

From . . . awkwardness.

The fire pops, and I jump.

"Soph?" Finn wiggles my feet—the feet resting awkwardly in his lap.

I almost laugh out loud. God must have a sense of humor, or he wouldn't have dropped me in this storm with this boy. Put me in AP Spanish, I'm your girl. AP English, I can write an analysis essay to knock your socks off. Biology, horses, you name it. I've got it covered. Heck, toss me a Rubik's Cube or challenge me in a game of speed chess. I'll take your challenge. Put me on a couch in the dark—with one Y chromosome—and I wilt like a Christmas poinsettia in July.

"Soph?" he asks again.

He can see my open eyes. I have to say something. "Yeah." Wow, Mr. Richards would be impressed by the complexity of my diction.

"How you feeling?" He squeezes my foot.

"Um—a little better, actually."

"Jack Daniels is an amazing thing." He laughs, gently lifting my feet out of his lap. He steps toward the hearth and throws another log on the fire. My jaw unclenches. My toes uncurl. I think I might survive.

"We're in the eye of the storm," he says.

"Yeah." *I kind of, sort of know this, because I've been spying on you and fake sleeping for a while now.*

"The sun will be up soon. There's something I want you to see."

"Okay."

"It's outside."

Without asking, I know beyond a shadow of a doubt what he's up to. He wants me to stand on that rickety railing.

Some deceitful, backstabbing voice that doesn't belong to me whispers something to the effect of *what's so wrong with that?*

Dang it. "Okay." I must have lost my mind.

"You mean it?" When he turns to face me, one eye narrows—like he's waiting for a *but.*

"I said okay."

He smiles. "You're going to love this. I promise."

I kind of doubt it. But I'm stuck now.

He leans down, cupping my elbow in his hand. "Oh, wait. I found something else you're going to like." He scurries off to the kitchen. When he returns, he holds something behind his back.

"More Twinkies?" I ask, expecting some disgusting excuse for food.

"Better."

Better than Twinkies.

"You're a very lucky girl." He holds out two pill bottles. "Advil *and* Tylenol."

"Where did you find them?" When I was in the bathroom, the medicine cabinet was completely empty.

"I might have borrowed them from a neighbor." He pops the cap off the Tylenol. "Now, don't get me wrong. I prefer homeopathic remedies, but when something hurts, it hurts."

"You broke into another house?" I watch as he counts out a few pills, then offers them to me. I accept, our fingers brushing as he reaches for a glass of water on the coffee table.

"I didn't take anything else. Trust me."

The boy is wearing me down. Trust him? I'm not as sure about that. But I am getting tired of arguing with him.

"Now, come on," he says. "We're going outside."

He brings me my tennis shoes and a yellow raincoat. I swallow the nausea rising in my throat along with the pills. I shouldn't have said yes. But I did. I really have lost my mind.

I slide into my shoes and push myself to standing.

Finn keeps a tight grip on the door when he opens it so it doesn't smack us in the face. Wind lifts my hair as we step outside and into the eye of the storm. He must be right about the time. The sky is dark, but it's more charcoal than black. We survived the storm's approach in the first cottage. We've almost survived its impact and another night together here in this house. This storm can't last much longer.

With the overcast skies, we might not witness the sun cresting the horizon this morning, but it will rise nevertheless. In the fading darkness, I can make out the gnarled trees at the bottom of the hill.

Sure enough, Finn leads me to the front of the church and the spindly railing. He pats the rail. "You can see forever from up here."

"You want—" My voice cracks. "You want me to stand on top of that?"

"Yes. I know you prefer to play it safe." He's challenging me. "But this is worth it. Trust me." He keeps saying that—*trust me.* "Have I ever given you a reason not to trust me?"

"Well . . ." He did blow me off for homecoming without so much as a *sorry* and doesn't seem to remember or care about it.

"Have I?" He does things I would never do—breaks into houses without a care in the world, explores the world around him in the eye of a storm, surfs in the face of oncoming hurricanes. But he also delivered supplies to a relative in need, saved Mere's compass, and cared for me when I needed him. This situation is morphing into a whole lot of confusing.

But here I am lifting my leg to the top of the railing, very ungracefully I might add, and standing on the shaky contraption. But I can't be certain whether it's the railing that's shaking or my legs. Something is trembling enough to rattle my teeth, though. Finn grips my legs around my knees. His fingers feel terrifying and tender all at the same time. I want to tell him to let go, that I've got this, but I don't. I can't stand up here alone.

I open one eye a sliver, biting down on my lower lip and bracing for the plummet to my death. Instead, I exhale. He's right. The scenery is beautiful, like an Ansel Adams photograph. Strokes of ash paint the sky. Ebony ink colors the sea. Pearly waves crash on aged-ivory sand. I never knew something so devoid of color could be so beautiful.

I drink in the pre-dawn beauty with Finn. The wind brushes my cheeks like stiff feathers. The sea oats flap, the ocean churns, the world rushes around us. Nature scuttles in a million different directions but in perfect harmony, like a well-trained orchestra. The wind, the water, the oats bend and roll and sway in rhythm.

Then a frantic, out-of-sync movement catches my eye. Careful not to move my lower body, I tilt my head, peering into the darkness down near the beach. The angry ocean has already devoured the first row of dunes. But farther back, tangled in what appears to be one of those silt fences used to protect the receding dunes, is a struggling animal—a large, struggling animal.

"Finn?"

He doesn't hear me. "Finn?" I reach behind me for his hand. When I glance over my shoulder, he looks up at me, eyebrows raised.

"There's something out there on the dunes."

"Huh?" he asks as he helps me down to the deck. "What is it?"

I open my mouth to speak, but my voice hangs in my throat. He grips both my shoulders. "What is it, Sophie?"

I wave a hand near my face as if that will somehow help me swallow or jump-start my voice or both. He steadies his eyes on my face and waits.

"It's . . . it's a horse. One of the wild ponies is trapped out there on the dunes." I grab his hand, then pull him toward the stairs leading down to the boardwalk that intersects with the main road below. "We have to do something."

"I don't see how—"

"I don't either. But it's there. Maybe it swam around the fence or maybe there's a break somewhere. I don't know. Maybe it jumped a fence."

He stares at me skeptically.

I yank him toward the boardwalk. "We have to do something," I say again.

He leans back, digging his flip-flops in and not moving. "I'm not sure. That surf is dangerous even for me," he shouts over the wind.

"Really?" My heart races. "This is the *one* time you're going to play it safe? I can't believe it. When there's an actual reason to take a risk, you're going to pass?"

He winces as though I slapped him.

I charge down the boardwalk without a backward glance. Halfway to the road, my toe catches on a loose board. I skid across several slick boards and then across gritty sand, crashing and burning in epic style. I lie facedown for a second—afraid to move, afraid I broke something important, like an ankle. When I work up the nerve to test my limbs and joints, everything seems to be in working order. The shoulder doesn't seem any worse than it already was. As I roll to my back, Finn drops to his knees beside me.

"Are you okay?" he asks.

I nod, thankful he doesn't crack a joke about my clumsiness.

He reaches for my hand. "Back there." He gestures toward the church up the hill. "I wasn't thinking about me when I said we should wait. I was thinking about you being hurt."

I glance down at my shoulder. The home remedies mixed with the two Tylenol are doing their job, but there's still some tenderness there. I won't be ready for an intense upper-body workout anytime soon. Sudden movement still makes the world tilt a bit. But the horse's dire situation did briefly distract me from my own pain and unsteadiness.

I accept his hand, allowing him to help me to my feet. "My

shoulder is fine." I twist my face into a smile. It's kind of hard with sand gritting my teeth and lips, but I'm determined.

He brushes a lock of tangled hair off my cheek. "If we're going to save the horse, we might need to keep ourselves alive for the time being." His mouth is set in a firm line, but I'm pretty sure he's trying not to laugh at me.

He clutches my hand as we cross the deserted road and cut a trail between two widely spaced oceanfront mansions. Crashing waves overpower the wind and our senses as we near the beach. We pause at the top of a sandy hill to scan the dunes. Bits and pieces of the silt fence wind back and forth through sea oats, brush, and sand, but we see no sign of the pony.

"Which way?" I ask.

"That way." He points left, shouting over the roaring surf.

I don't move. "Are you sure?"

"No." He descends the hill.

"I think it was closer." Without hard evidence or a valid argument, I find myself hesitating. I remember how Finn's gut led us to Zeke's shack, and how his gut told him to remove the metal from my shoulder. Suddenly, I want to follow my gut. I don't know how it will work out, but Finn's gut seems to work for him. I tell myself mine can work for me as I trudge down the hill in front of him. When another, steeper hill rises in front of us, I ascend it diagonally. He tags along. We pause at the crest to survey our surroundings.

Sure enough, right where I predicted, the silt fence twists and jerks. A chestnut-brown horse lies on its side, back legs tangled in the fence, thrashing for its life. It looks like the horse I saw hunkered down in the brush back at Zeke's—the one separated from his herd.

Mom and Dad's warnings about the horses swirl in my head, bringing a bit of doubt. When I was a child, my family spent thousands of hours researching, observing, and fighting to protect these animals. When other families went to the movies or bowling, we visited Eastern North Carolina libraries to find tidbits of information on these horses, which could be traced back five hundred years to the Spanish explorers who brought them here.

If my parents told me once, they told me a thousand times, *Sophie, these are not pets like our horses. These are wild animals. They need to be respected and treated as such—for their safety and for ours.* Even domesticated horses can be dangerous. A kick to the head or chest can cause permanent damage, even death. The widow of the guy who used to shoe our horses can vouch for that. An eight- to twelve-hundred-pound horse can wield a powerful kick.

As we approach, the horse's nostrils flare. He smells us. Even from this distance, the red flesh lining the insides of his nose and the whites of his wild eyes are visible. His ears flick back and forth, trying to get a read on us.

"Sophie. Wait." Finn grabs my arm, pulling me to a stop several yards from the fence. "Let's think about this a minute."

I point over his shoulder. "We don't have a minute."

In the gray pre-dawn light, angry clouds swirl to the south. Our window of calm will slam shut soon. The backside of this storm is preparing to drop on us like a sledgehammer. We can't be caught out in the open. That didn't work so well for me or my shoulder last time. Now we don't even have Finn's puny trash can lid for armor.

"We need to cut him loose," I say, raising my voice over the pounding surf and rising wind.

"Cut?" His face screws up like I'm speaking a different language. "We don't have a knife. We're going to have to get close and yank."

Clearly, he knows nothing about horses. Dealing with a panicked, wild horse's back legs is a death wish.

"I have an idea," I tell him.

"It better be good," he says, stepping aside.

The horse lifts his head from the sand, snorting and wild-eyed. I can't explain it, but as we lock eyes, I can read his mind, or at least his terror—that threatened, out-of-control, under-attack terror that constricts the chest and squeezes the air from your lungs. My palms sweat for him. I'm pretty sure I'm panting. This whole situation is beyond awful.

But it's not just the horse or the storm. It's the way everything seems to go in my life. Sisters shouldn't suffer brain injuries. Dads shouldn't choose Jim Beam over flesh-and-blood daughters. Okay, maybe human beings are a train wreck. As much as I hate to admit it, maybe we do deserve a bit of the suffering we create. But not animals—not innocent animals. This beautiful horse never did anything to anyone. And if he dies, there won't be any of Finn's peaceful beauty here. We don't even have drugs to put him out of his misery. If he dies, it's going to be slow and painful and terrifying, cut off from his herd and confused, chewed up and swallowed by the ravenous surf.

As if to prove my point, the horse shrieks. His sides heave as he tries to drag himself to his feet. With his front legs curled under his chest, he manages to heft his heavy front end a few inches above the sand. When he tries to pull his hind legs under his belly, for leverage, the silt fence cuts into his skin. Blood oozes from the leg where the fence pinches his flesh.

A rush of adrenaline shoots through my arms and legs, and instinct kicks in. I know what we have to do. I've seen Doc Wiggins do it with sick and panicked horses. One of us has to get control of the big guy's head. If we control the head, we control the rest of him. The other needs to do the untangling.

"It's now or never." Finn takes a step forward.

"Wait." I reach for his arm, but he slips away. "I know what I'm doing, Finn." I can't let him rush in headlong. I have to take the lead here. But I'd rather not risk my life. Mom needs me. Another accident would kill her—if not physically, then emotionally. And Mere needs her. If Mom loses it, there's no one to care for Mere. I vowed to take care of them both, and I will.

But this horse is a lot like Mere. He needs someone who can problem solve for him. I have to do something.

Before I can stop Finn, he steps within reach of the horse's back hooves. With the strength that comes only from adrenaline and panic, the horse manages to kick despite the fence tangling his legs. A sharp hoof grazes Finn's side. His mouth opens in a silent scream as he doubles at the waist and retreats to where I stand.

I grip his upper arm with one hand and run the other down his side, feeling for protruding ribs.

"I . . . I'm . . . fine. It just scared me." He shakes his shaggy hair out of his eyes and presses his lips together. "I'm just not sure how we're going to do this."

He looks defeated, which is such a foreign look on him, it kind of scares me.

"I told you I've got this," I say. "I've seen my vet deal with horses like this."

His face hardens a bit. "Sophie, I told you—"

"Just give me your windbreaker."

He looks doubtful, but he does what I ask. As he's slipping out of his jacket, I bend down and remove a lace from one of my tennis shoes. His eyebrows lift.

I step close to him, tilting my face up to his so I don't have to shout and further frighten the horse. "Horses are stimulated by their vision. I'm going to cover his eyes and ears with this." I hold up the jacket.

"What about that?" He points at the shoelace.

"Trust me." I toss his words back at him. After a short pause, he laughs, deep and true from his belly, then steps back to watch as I inch toward the horse's head.

"It's okay, buddy. It's okay, buddy. I got you. I got you," I chant rhythmically. He lifts his head to struggle, but the fight's gone from him. Holding my breath, I crouch behind his head for half a second. Then in one swift movement, I drape the jacket over his ears and eyes, just like I've seen Doc do. My reflexes kick in, like they always do when I'm confronted with an animal in crisis. Without pausing to think, I gently swing one thigh over the horse's neck, straddling him. Breathing deeply, I tighten the jacket around the top half of his head.

Glancing over my shoulder at Finn, I flash a thumbs-up. With my free hand, I wrap the shoelace around the horse's top lip. But I need more leverage to create the makeshift twitch Dad showed me how to use. The calming distraction works on our horses when they're spooked. I hope it will work on the wild pony too.

"Help. Please," I hiss, lifting my jaw toward Finn and handing him the shoelace. The horse's neck tenses between my thighs. One wrong move and one or both of us could be bitten, kicked, or crushed. "Loop it. Twirl it tight and hand it back to me."

Our eyes lock for a fraction of a second. He passes me the twisted lace without question. When I tilt my head toward the horse's muscular hind end, Finn nods and steps toward the horse's back legs. Sheets of muscle ripple beneath my thighs, but the horse's shrouded head remains flat on the sand. I loop the lace around his top lip, tight enough to make him think about it, but not tight enough to hurt. His jaw spasms, and the lace slips through my slick palm. We're pressing our luck here. This situation has the potential to get really ugly, really quickly.

I don't have to tell Finn to approach from a different angle this time. He's a quick learner. There's no way to completely avoid the horse's back legs, but he gets a somewhat safer angle by approaching the horse from above instead of from directly behind. I focus on immobilizing the horse's head and neck as Finn reaches toward the silt fence and the thrashing legs. Gritting my teeth, I squeeze my eyes shut, refusing to be dislodged as the horse squirms beneath me.

I count to one hundred to maintain my calm focus. When a hand clamps my good shoulder, I startle. Of course, it's Finn. He's grinning ear to ear. He nods at the horse's back legs. Blinking, I exhale. We did it. The horse is untangled—free.

"Stand back," I say, releasing the twisted shoelace and dismounting the horse's neck. Sliding the windbreaker from its head, I retreat. Finn follows close behind. From the safety of the next dune, I turn to check on our horse. He's standing, but his head hangs below his withers, and he sways tiredly.

The wind picks up as I turn back to Finn. "We did it," I murmur.

Holding my gaze, he pulls me into a hug. "*You* did it," he says against my hair.

As I look up at his face, a ripple of heat passes from my cheeks, to my chest, to my belly, where it settles and spreads to the rest of me. The world buzzes around me in a blur of white noise. This time it's not from the storm around me. It's from something inside me. My vision narrows until all I see is his face, his eyes, his . . . lips.

My breath catches, but I don't pull away. My lips part, and I don't try to stop them. He leans closer. When his lower lip brushes mine, I can taste the salt on him. My head tilts. It's kind of like riding a galloping horse. Your body just kind of knows if you want to stay on, you have to lean into it. And all of me is leaning in.

Finn's hand slides around the back of my neck. My chest rises and falls, like I'm running. My pulse pounds in my ears. I've never wanted anything so desperately in my life. It's instinctual. I couldn't stop this train if I wanted to.

A crack of lightning rips the sky.

But Mother Nature sure can.

My eyes fly open. Finn's hand drops from my neck. Without speaking, we bolt hand in hand for the safety of the church and its little parish house. We've lived through enough hurricanes to know lightning and hurricanes don't mix. At best, this is a strange development in the weather. At worst, it's the precursor to weather the likes of which the Outer Banks hasn't seen in the last century.

CHAPTER EIGHTEEN

Theirs not to reason why,
Theirs but to do and die.

ALFRED, LORD TENNYSON

There isn't time to discuss the significance of the thunder and lightning, but by how fast Finn's running, it's pretty obvious he's thinking what I'm thinking. Hurricanes don't generally spawn lightning. It has something to do with lightning being formed by vertical winds, and the hurricanes being made up of mostly horizontal winds. When a storm like this discharges the kind of lightning we just witnessed, it signals something bizarre at work. If I were a betting girl, I'd put money on some kind of super weather event in the making.

In the two or three minutes it takes us to reach the road and the boardwalk leading up to the church, the wind increases dramatically. The hair on my arms and the back of my neck tingles from the electricity in the air. I glance over my shoulder near the top of the hill to check on our wild pony friend. My heart sinks at the sight of him swaying on three legs, his fourth tucked up like he doesn't want to put weight on it. In that condition, he won't reach the next dune. He won't escape the storm surge. He won't make it.

"This sucks," I grumble. With hands balled into fists at my sides, I rack my brain for a last-ditch rescue attempt—something brave and heroic. Maybe I could craft a halter and lead rope out of belts and clothing and coax the horse to safety with my super Spidey horse sense.

But neither of us is wearing a belt or any extra clothes. And this isn't a domesticated horse. This is a wild animal.

"It sucks big time," Finn agrees.

Despite my clenched-jaw determination, I know in my heart Mom, Dad, and Doc Wiggins would all tell me to let go and trust the animal and its instincts. I could concoct some epic rescue—like the well-meaning tourists who tried to herd an escaped horse to safety but ended up herding the panicked animal into oncoming traffic—and cause more harm than good.

Finn tugs on my hand, his face as grim as mine feels. With tears welling in my eyes, we race the last fifty yards to shelter. As we enter the house, Finn slams the door behind us. Leaning back against the door, he pants. I stumble to the couch. Resting my elbows on my knees, I grip my head in my hands. Our little sanctuary on higher ground doesn't feel so safe anymore—not with the backside of the storm bearing down on us and that poor horse out there on his own.

"Sophie, I think we might want to hole up in the closet till this passes."

I nod. The rising wind speaks for itself as I race around the living area grabbing pillows and blankets. Trying to remain calm, I remind myself we're out of reach of the storm surge. In most cases, water is more dangerous than wind. But this hurricane, with its freakish lightning, suddenly makes me doubt what I know to be true—that and the tension of the air. I swear I can feel some sort of magnetic force pushing and pulling on the frame of the house. I don't know whether to be afraid it will splinter and scatter or afraid it will implode on us.

"This way." Finn motions to the back room I haven't explored.

I clutch the linens against my chest and follow. "Do you think—"

"We're going to be fine. I know," he says. But the crease between his eyebrows is deep. He grunts as he chucks clothes and shoes out of the closet to make room inside for the two of us. We work in silence, lining the floor with pillows and blankets. When a gust of wind rattles the bedroom windows, Finn pulls me inside the cramped space and closes the door. Our ragged breathing and the muffled wind camouflage the silence.

We sit side by side this time, with our backs pressed against the rear wall and our knees drawn to our chests. When I shiver, Finn drapes an arm across my neck, careful to avoid my injured shoulder. I lean into his side, careful to avoid his bad ribs. We're wrecks.

"We've got to quit meeting in dark closets. People will talk," he says, joking as he bumps his knee against mine.

I glance around our hiding spot. I can't see Finn's face, but I can smell him—all sticky salt and rainwater. "What time do you think it is?" I ask.

He shrugs. "Before noon. It doesn't really matter. Does it?"

"Do you think it will last much longer?"

He shrugs again. "No idea."

I turn my face toward where his should be, inches from mine in the darkness. "You don't care about anything, do you?"

"I care about a lot of things." His breath brushes my cheek, and I know he's turned to face me as well. "I just try not to worry about stuff I can't control."

Here we go again. "I prefer to think of it as using resources wisely. I can get more done in eight hours than most people can in twelve."

"You know about *chronos* and *kairos*, right?" he asks.

"Yes, Finn. I know my Greek mythology." Seriously? Where is he going with this? He called us *friends* back at Zeke's. Anyone who knows anything about me knows I've got some mean mythology chops.

"Yeah, but I'm not talking about the gods. I'm talking about the words."

"They both mean *time*." I interrupt, trying to ward off another one of his lectures.

"Yes and no," he says. "Yes, they both mean *time*. But chronos is clock time—schedules, calendars, and alarms. Kairos is more like *moment* than *time*. It's like nirvana. It's riding the perfect wave. It's the blush of sunrise on a deserted beach. It's not keeping track of time. It's losing sight of it—being lost in the moment—in the zone."

Despite his poetic little monologue and the warmth of his body beside mine, I feel my defenses going up.

"You're saying I'm too uptight about time?" I scoot a little toward my end of the closet.

"I didn't say that."

"You didn't have to."

"But think about it. It is kind of a trade-off. If you focus on one, you lose the other. You can't have both."

I can't take it any longer. I need him to shut up, to stop all this talk of being lost in the moment. Before I can control it, my body commits the ultimate act of treachery. The upper half of me tilts forward, close enough to brush the corner of his mouth with my lips.

When he nibbles my lower lip, my insides melt. I'm pretty sure my brain melts. I lace my hands behind his neck just as he pulls back an inch.

Drawing my hands from behind his neck, he grasps them against his pounding heart. "Are you *sure* you want to do this?"

My heart snaps in my chest like a rubber band. Maybe I read his signs all wrong. "Do you?"

He lets out a breathy laugh. "Are donuts a delicacy?"

Shaking my head, I try to make sense of his confusing answer. The awkward pause lasts just long enough to clear my head.

"I'm . . . not sure what I want," I say, being totally honest.

"That's what I thought."

"You're wrong about one thing, though."

"What's that?"

"I'm not all chronos."

The laugh I'm growing dangerously fond of erupts from his belly. He squeezes my hand. "When this storm ends and we're not trapped in a closet, I want to see more of *that* Sophie."

I squeeze his hand in return, trying to picture the two of us together back in the real world—me with my schedules and responsibilities and calendars, him a free spirit going wherever the next wind or wave takes him.

"Finn?"

"Yeah?"

I want to ask him what he was thinking back in ninth grade when he didn't show up for the dance, moved away, and didn't call. But I don't want to make a big deal out of something that was obviously not a big deal to him.

"Ummm . . ." If I had a free foot, I'd kick myself in hopes of restarting my voice.

"I'm all ears here." He rests his head on the wall close to mine as though he's got all day, and I guess he does.

I say in a small voice, "I just—I've always wondered why you never got in touch or explained about standing me up. I mean, now I know about your dad . . . but still . . ."

"Standing you up?" The air between us shifts when he lifts his head away from the wall.

Surely I wasn't so unimportant that he can't even remember we were supposed to meet at the dance. I try to slide my hand out of his, but he squeezes a little tighter. "Yeah. You know. We were going to meet at the ninth-grade homecoming dance. I mean, it was our first high school dance. I was pretty excited . . ." I hate the way my voice keeps trailing off, betraying me with its weakness.

"All the teachers knew about my dad. I thought one of them would have said something to everyone."

My posture's so stiff, I'm brittle—a puff of air and I might disintegrate. I don't answer.

"They didn't tell you, did they? About my dad?" he asks, like he recognizes the hurt in my voice despite my best attempt to hide it. "It happened so fast—him being selected for the trial. But I should've told you in person. I'm so sorry, Sophie. I—"

He swallows. "That's why you've been so distant with me, isn't it? Because I didn't show up for the dance?" He sounds relieved, like he just remembered where he left his phone or keys.

My chest untightens a notch, and it hits me. I've been so worried about my hurt feelings, I've barely considered how awful it must have been to leave so suddenly under such horrible circumstances. My broken heart abruptly seems a little immature and a little overly dramatic.

When he pulls me to his side, my frayed nerves untangle a bit. "I was stupid—" I lean into the warmth of his side.

"You could never be stupid, Bookworm." He rests the side of his face on the top of my head.

I can't be certain in the pitch dark if he's smiling, but something in his voice makes it sound like he is.

If we survive this storm together, I think I may be able to find a way to give him a second chance.

CHAPTER NINETEEN

A beam in the darkness: let it grow.

ALFRED, LORD TENNYSON

We sit for what seems like a lifetime in the dark without saying a word. Finn's arm never leaves my shoulders. Despite the blackness, I occasionally feel his gaze on my face.

"Can we lie down?" he asks. "My back's killing me."

"Yeah." I try to sound cool, but I'm not sure how that's going to work. Are we going to lie face-to-face? I lick my gums and teeth in a lame attempt to freshen my breath.

"Here," he says, patting the flannel blanket on the floor as he squishes against the back wall of the closet. I lie parallel to his body like a two-by-four. When I shiver, he pulls me back against his chest, and it doesn't feel weird or awkward. It feels safe.

It's suddenly hard to believe I thought I needed to protect myself from this—from Finn. Hard to believe I thought closing my heart, keeping it safe, was more important than the warm embrace of a boy I care about—really care about.

Yesenia would be so happy. She loves being right. The swishy feeling in my stomach kind of affirms that Tennyson quotation she's always repeating. Plus, she'd finally get to add a few checks to the bucket list she's been keeping for me all these years.

When something crashes in the distance, I flinch and remind myself I have to survive this storm if I hope to check anything off Yesenia's silly list.

"I wish we had music or a book or something," I say over the racket of my pulse and racing heart.

"We could talk." His breath brushes the edge of my ear and sends tickly shivers along my throat and neck.

"About what?" I ask.

"Anything."

"How much longer do you think this will last?"

"Anything but the weather. Okay?"

"Okay." I browse my mental file cabinet but come up blank, suddenly realizing how small my world is. My life is pretty much school, school, school, the barn, and worrying about Mere and Mom and . . . school. "Um, I love to read."

"Everybody knows that. Tell me something I don't know. Greatest fear?"

Everything. I can't tell him there are too many choices to pick just one.

He squeezes my hip. "Come on, give me something here. What's your greatest fear?"

I remain frozen in place, not wanting to sever the line from his arm to his hand to my hip but not wanting to answer his question either. No. It's more than that. I don't know *how* to answer his question. "I don't know."

"Yes, you do." He jostles my hip again.

"What are you afraid of?" I whisper.

"I'm afraid of spiders and snakes and opossums."

"Opossums? No, you're not." I nudge him in the stomach with my elbow. There's no way a guy who surfs in hurricane waters can be afraid of a furry, pointy-nosed critter. He must be kidding.

"Wait. Wait." The wind howls while he thinks. "Got it—climate change."

"Really? You're afraid of climate change?"

"Yep. It's serious. If we don't do something to reverse the arctic ice melt, we'll be under water—Outer Banks, bye-bye."

"Hmm."

"What?"

"I just thought you'd be afraid of something . . . scarier."

"What's scarier than melting polar icecaps and rising sea levels?"

"For me—losing something I love." My words drape over us like a heavy quilt.

"Losing things we love is a part of life, Sophie. We can't avoid it."

"Yes, but . . ." I tell myself to stop, abort, shut up.

"But what?"

"It's not just my sister I lost in the accident. I mean . . . You know what I mean. I lost my dad too."

"Oh, Soph. I'm sorry. I didn't know he died—"

"He didn't." I force air through tight lips. "It was worse than that."

"Worse?"

I blink back the tears in my eyes. "Yes." I take a deep breath and swallow before continuing. "He didn't die. He . . . he walked out on us." I've never said this out loud to anyone. Of course,

Yesenia knows, but she respects my silence. We haven't talked about it since the week after Dad left, when she asked about his absence. I said he needed space, but Yesenia's smart. She didn't miss the increasing number of beer cans on the coffee table or the way Dad's complexion turned from golden brown to sickly yellow.

Finn squeezes me even tighter, resting his chin on top of my head. We lie in silence for several long minutes.

"It's bad to lose someone you love because of an accident or sickness. It's worse when the person makes a conscious decision to walk away and not look back." Pinching my eyes closed, I will myself not to cry.

"When did it happen?"

"It was a few months after the accident. He couldn't handle Mere's disability, the mounting medical bills, or his own guilt. He was the one driving. He started drinking and taking too many pills to deal with the pain and just never stopped."

"Would it have been better if he died?"

"No. Yes. I don't know." I bite the inside of my cheek. "It's why . . . I just can't . . . It just seems like I always lose people. I can't lose anyone else."

"I don't know—you're pretty tough." He rubs his fisted knuckles playfully in my hair, the same way Dad did when I was a kid.

I don't laugh. "No, Finn. I'm serious. I'm not like you."

The closet is quiet. For once, he doesn't have anything to say. He lets the stillness settle around us. After what seems like forever, he finally speaks. "Then I guess you better get some cats or something."

"That's a pretty good idea, actually." I laugh, trying to

sound unconcerned and trying not to think about how much I miss Jim's little whiskered face.

"You might change your mind," he mumbles a minute later, unable to disguise the exhaustion in his voice. We've been going like this for too long.

"Doubtful," I whisper, lying perfectly still, and then listening to his rhythmic breathing. I don't begrudge him the sleep. We're both drained. If we're going to think clearly, we both need rest.

But I can't sleep. I lie awake rehashing our conversation. I can say I won't open my heart to that kind of risk ever again. But the truth is I think I already have. Finn seems to have weakened my defenses and snuck inside when I wasn't looking.

like glimpses of forgotten dreams.

ALFRED, LORD TENNYSON

When I open my eyes, I feel like I've aged seventy years. My bones hurt. My muscles ache. My shoulder throbs, reminding me I should probably take some more Tylenol. But when I hear Finn's soft breathing beside me, I smile despite the discomfort.

I lift my head a couple of inches off the floor. Nothing tilts or spins. I must be improving. Cocking my ear to the door, I listen for the storm. But the house is silent. The world is silent. Sitting up, I reach around in the dark for the doorknob on the inside of the closet. The room outside the door is slightly less black than the closet around us.

Part of me wants to rest, but an image of that poor horse invades my thoughts. He probably didn't make it in his condition. My heartstrings stretch until they threaten to snap when I think about the wild horse out there alone. If he managed to survive but didn't get far, he'll need fresh water.

I hate to wake Finn, but I have to check on that horse. We also need a plan. We need a phone and probably medical attention for both of us.

"Finn, wake up." I wiggle his shoulder, ready to do something—anything. I have to let Mom know I'm okay. I'm sure she and Mere are fine. They left with time to spare. But I need to *know* they're okay, and despite my text, Mom must be going crazy by now. "I think the storm has passed."

"Umm hmm," he answers, but makes no effort to move.

"We have to get out of here and get help." I clap my hands in the general vicinity of his face when he still doesn't budge. The sharp noise brings him to attention, accomplishing what my voice couldn't.

He sits up, banging his head on the wall and grunting. "Huh? What? Oh. Right. The storm." Standing, he grips his lower leg and shakes it like it fell asleep or something.

"I think it's passed. It's quiet out there." Rubbing my sore back, I push myself to standing. "And we need to go look for that horse."

Finn hobbles around behind me, oddly quiet. We move toward the living room like wounded warriors. His shoulder pops when he stretches. Soft light filters in through the boarded-up windows, shining on the gray embers in the fireplace. As I hold my breath, we approach the front door together. Without speaking, we step across the threshold and onto the deck.

Wind blows the hair off my face, but it's more like a really brisk breeze than a gale-force wind. Tree limbs crisscross the driveway like pickup sticks. The railing at the front of the church that supported my weight yesterday leans forward precariously. One strong gust will send it tumbling down the sand. Shards of stained glass reach up from the bottom of a large round window, pointing at the disgruntled clouds churning northward.

Standing tall and straight, the church steeple remains in stark contrast to all the destruction surrounding us. The trees around the buildings have been leveled like one of Aunt Mae's pastures in the wake of her Bush Hog. Blown in from who knows where, an overturned lawn chair lies on its side. Broken glass, torn shingles, and a tattered flag litter the parking lot beside the church.

"Let's see if we have a better view from the church," Finn says without looking at me.

"Do you think it's safe?" I drag my feet, wondering if we're pushing our luck up here.

"It looks solid. Just don't get too close to the edge."

"Don't worry, I won't," I say, stepping over a stick blocking our path. Soon we're standing on the church deck, scanning the horizon, the dunes, the shoreline. There's nothing, no one—no emergency personnel cruising the road below, no Coast Guard helicopter patrolling the beach. We're on our own. That's something only coastal natives and hurricane survivors fully understand. Just because you survive the high winds and actual storm doesn't mean you're safe. Very often lives are lost *after* a storm because of flooding or injury or plain old stupidity.

We can't let our guard down. We need to be careful. But I can't stop thinking about the injured horse.

Finn seems to read my mind. "He's fine, Sophie. Those horses are like dinosaurs. They'll survive everything short of a nuclear event or a great asteroid."

"But he was alone and injured." I squint down at the dunes, but it's useless. Without the advantage of standing on the railing, I can make out only a thin sliver of sand at the ridge of the dune line.

"He didn't have to go far. Just beyond the storm surge." Finn's voice is optimistic, but his sentences are oddly short and to the point.

I chew on my lip, wondering if I've done something to offend Finn. Or said something to annoy him. Or maybe he just woke up on the wrong side of the closet; the boy hasn't cracked a joke since he woke up. It doesn't matter. We don't have time to stand around chatting anyway.

"He'll be hungry." My stomach growls in sympathy.

"You're hungry," Finn says, obviously trying to distract me from my concern and change the subject. "Under the right conditions, animals can go without food for days—maybe weeks."

I'm not going to be dissuaded so easily. "These aren't the *right* conditions. And he can't go days or weeks without water. Please—let's just look around."

He runs a hand through his hair. The *please* seems to crack his resolve. "Okay. But we need to eat and clean your shoulder before we go traipsing down to the beach. And if we can't find him quickly, he's on his own. He'll be fine."

Back in the kitchen, we scrounge around in the cabinets for something to eat. I find a box of unopened crackers and a jar of peanut butter. He finds a bottle of apple juice in the fridge and a gallon of milk. Finn was smart to leave the refrigerator door closed last night. The juice isn't cold, but it's not warm either. We agree it's fine to drink. We can't drink the milk, but I have an idea for the container.

Sitting at the small round table, we share a knife but don't talk. We should be giddy with excitement. We survived. It may take a few hours or most of the day, but we'll find help. Someone will be out looking for survivors now that the storm has passed.

Standing, I brush cracker crumbs from my lap, pour the milk down the drain, then head toward the bathroom with the empty jug.

"What're you doing?" he asks.

"Going to get water from the toilet tank in case we find the horse."

His forehead wrinkles with doubt.

"It's not ideal, but it'll work," I say, stopping to down the Advil he left on the table with the last of my juice.

I know one gallon of water isn't going to do much for a horse that size, but a little bit of something is better than a whole lot of nothing. On the way back from the bathroom, I grab Mere's compass from the mantel. There's no way I'm losing it again.

Finn sits at the kitchen table, gripping his head in his hands. He doesn't speak when I set the water and compass near him on the table or when I start digging around in the kitchen drawers.

Lifting his head, he tracks me with his eyes. "What are you looking for?"

"This." I turn around after pulling pen and paper from the drawer beside the phone.

"Are we taking notes or something?"

"No. We're *leaving* notes." I turn back to the counter and lean down to start writing. *Dear Homeowner* . . .

Finn moves up behind me. "We didn't leave a note at the other place."

"We didn't have time—" I stop when he reaches into the drawer at my hip and starts rummaging around.

"What the—" He pulls out a small cardboard box with a picture of a radio on the front. "This would have come in handy yesterday."

"It probably needs batteries," I say without looking up from my thank-you note to the person whose house we invaded.

"No. Look. It's genius." He taps the box. *"Uses rechargeable lithium-ion battery, hand crank, or solar power."* He drops the unopened box into a plastic grocery bag. "We're taking this with us."

Capping the pen, I cross my arms. "We can't take anything. The storm's passed. It was different when we didn't know if we'd survive."

"Sophie, we still don't know if we'll survive. We take the radio."

His terseness throws me off. "Okay. Whatever." I uncap the pen and write a P.S.—*hope you don't mind we borrowed the weather radio as well.*

Finn drops a handful of granola bars in the plastic bag, then shoves each arm through one of the handles, like he's wearing a makeshift backpack. He and I both reach for the milk jug on the table and bump hands.

"I can carry something." I pull the water from his grasp.

He doesn't even argue. Now I *know* something is wrong.

"Finn, are you okay?"

"Sure." His lips curve into what would be a genuine smile on anyone else. But without a sparkle in his eyes to match, he's not fooling me. When he smiles, his eyes always light up—always.

"You're never this serious—or this quiet."

"I'm good. I think this storm just knocked the wind out of me or something." He pauses before nudging my good shoulder with his free hand. "Pun intended. Get it? Knocked the *wind* out of me?"

He's trying a little too hard, but at least he seems more like himself with the goofy word play.

"Let's hit it," he says, moving toward the door and holding it open for me.

We comb the dunes without speaking. The roiling storm surge makes it too noisy to hear each other without shouting. The water rose at least five feet overnight and ripped away huge mounds of sand. The sea oats and dune where we rescued the wild horse are completely submerged.

My insides twist like a rip current. The only signs of our four-legged friend are a few smudged hoof prints.

Finn turns to face me and leans close so I can hear him. "He must've headed inland."

"Or been dragged out to sea." I peer out over the angry Atlantic.

"Why do you always have to be that way?" he barks over the waves, his jaw firm.

"What do you mean?" I ask, taking a step back.

"You always expect the worst." The words are harmless enough, but his voice sounds accusatory.

I wasn't expecting that from him, and I wasn't expecting how those five simple words could hurt like a fist to my mid-section. "I don't know." I brush the tangled hair from my face so I can see him better.

There's pain in his eyes, as though I hurt him.

"Finn, you're right. I'm sorry. I shouldn't be so nega-tive. We have a lot to be thankful for. We're alive. We made it—together. I just . . . I just can't bear the thought of that poor animal, all alone . . ." My gut tells me to accept it—there's a good chance the horse didn't make it. But my heart reminds me that Finn has been right more than once. Maybe he'll be right again.

A shadow swoops over us. We glance toward the racing clouds in unison. What looks like a black-and-white cross punctuates the sky above our heads. When the black cross-pieces flap, I realize it's not a levitating religious symbol. It's a bird—a massive bird, like Pteranodon size. He glides on the brisk wind, inches above our heads. Peering at us from a beady black eye, he squawks, then rises on a current of air.

"Was that an—" Finn's mouth hangs open on his unfinished sentence.

"Ha!" I shake my fist in the air, beaming. My face stretches when I smile, really smile. "An albatross!"

"No way. They don't travel this far south." Puzzled, he squints at the gargantuan bird as it tips one wing, rocking to one side and then the other.

If I didn't know better, I'd think the bird was teasing us. "They don't *normally* travel this far south. But that's an albatross. The storm must've blown it off course or something." I track it as it glides farther and farther away.

"How do you know it's an albatross?"

"I just do. Trust me." I don't go into how Doc Wiggins is like a part of my family or how he's an avid bird-watcher. I remember the pictures of the Hawaiian nesting grounds Doc Wiggins visited two years ago. He lectured me on the birds when he returned.

"That was definitely an albatross," I say again.

"It doesn't make sense, though. The only thing less sensible would be a penguin sighting."

He's right. It doesn't make sense, and I'm really tired of things that don't make sense. I'm starting to realize life might be easier if I quit trying to make sense of everything. It's hard to believe so much has changed in two short days. It's hard to believe how much I've changed in two short days.

Not knowing how to deal with the dead-serious Finn in front of me, I place a playful hand on my hip, hoping for a reaction from the boy I've grown close to during this storm. "Thank you, Captain Obvious."

He cups his hand over his eyes, squinting for one last glance at the massive bird, and ignores my attempt at humor. "You know they're a good omen, right? Like good luck on steroids."

I let my hand fall to my side. "Um, have you ever read *The Rime of the Ancient Mariner*?"

"Exactly."

My jaw drops, and I prepare my argument about how wrong Finn is about this. The stupid mariner shoots the bird that leads them out of the ice jam in Antarctic waters. The guy's doomed with a capital *D* when the rest of the ship's crew turns on him for killing the bird. They force him to wear the massive, dead bird as some sort of symbol of regret or something. That's where the saying *an albatross around your neck* comes from. That's quite a burden to have on a ghost ship lost at sea.

But before mariner-dude killed the bird—I never could figure out why he killed it—the bird was the lucky charm that brought the wind they needed to escape the Arctic Sea. To this day, sailors believe albatross are a good omen—a symbol of land. Which is totally wrong. The birds can live at sea for years without access to land.

But suddenly, I don't want to argue. I want to hope. I want Finn to be right. I want this to be a sign from the universe—a sign that everything is going to be okay.

CHAPTER TWENTY-ONE

I slip, I slide, I gloom, I glance.

ALFRED, LORD TENNYSON

Finn finally turns away from the speck of black and white receding on the horizon. "Let's get out of here. When they allow residents back on the island, the Wild Horse Fund volunteers will be tracking the horses and checking the fence line."

He's correct, of course. One way or the other, the horse is gone. I have to focus on Mom and Mere now.

"Okay, let's go," I say, scanning the dunes again and praying for an equestrian miracle. When no natural or supernatural horses materialize, I lift my shoulders and prepare for the final chapter in my and Finn's hurricane survival story.

He stops beside a clump of sea oats and pauses for a second. His shoulders lift, like he's preparing to deliver a speech. "I kind of thought we might . . ."

"Kind of thought we might what?" I ask, glancing over my shoulder at him.

"I kind of thought we might go check for Zeke at the lighthouse before we head south. I mean, the storm was worse than any of us expected. I think we should offer to take him to the mainland with us."

Head north. Again? Away from safety. Away from Mom and Mere.

Um.

No.

"Finn, I can't. I have to get to Manteo. Now. My mom is going to be freaking out if I don't get in touch with her."

He shoves his hands in his pockets. "Fine."

He trudges up the dune in front of us, his back stiff and straight. I remind myself that Zeke is his family. Finn is probably just as worried as my mom is.

"How long do you think it will take to get to Manteo?" I ask.

"Not long."

"Really?" It must be at least fifteen miles, maybe more. On foot, with the possibility of flooding and downed power lines, it seems it would take quite some time. "How?"

"Yeah. We're going to borrow a car."

Borrow? He says it so casually, like he's going to borrow a friend's pencil in class. As we crest the last mound of sand before the level road, I look both ways for traffic. Of course, the road is desolate—not a car in sight, but there are plenty of downed branches.

"Where will we find a car to borrow?" I ask. "What about keys?"

"In a garage. If we can't find keys, I've got this." He taps his pointer finger against his temple.

"You're going to fire the engine with your brain power?" I slow down, assuming he'll stop to explain. But he presses forward.

I don't like this. Our crimes are escalating. First, it was breaking and entering for self-preservation. Then petty theft for convenience and safety. But grand theft auto sounds like something that could haunt us on our college applications and resumes.

I tell myself I would want someone to borrow my truck if it would save a life or reunite a family. Plus, we'll be careful, and it will get me to Mom and Mere faster. I have no better solution of my own, so I tag along behind him.

We backtrack to the houses we passed on our way to our church parsonage sanctuary. But Finn's optimism is misplaced. There's nothing but drifts of sand and seaweed and broken timbers in the first garage. The next three are pretty much the same except for the overturned fishing boat wedged sideways in the second. I guess these people were smart enough to evacuate all their vehicles. That's what Mom and I were trying to do.

The devastation around and between the houses is beyond depressing. The wreckage everywhere I look makes me wonder what Mom and I have to look forward to when we're finally allowed to go home. Outer Banks residents, like their horses and their ancestors, are tough and resilient, but it's going to take more than a strong will to put this mess back together. It's going to take lots and lots of money and time—months, if not years, to piece back together what a vengeful Mother Nature ripped apart.

The sky darkens, and a light mist tickles my cheeks as we head away from what appears to be the last house as far as we can see.

"Now what?" I ask, glancing at the ominous sky. The outer bands of wind and rain that follow behind a hurricane may not be as dangerous as what we've experienced, but I'm not exactly keen on enduring more severe weather.

Finn seems to read my mind. "Don't worry about the weather, Sophie."

"Me, worry?" I deadpan. Then I sigh. "It can't get any worse, I guess. You're right."

He chuckles for the first time today, and the weight in my heart eases a bit.

"My two favorite words," he says, smiling and surveying the road to the north and south. "Now I need to be right about finding us some transportation."

It doesn't look promising. "What about your car?"

"It's wrecked, Bookworm. Remember?"

"The windshield's busted, that's for sure. And it's off the side of the road. But if we could get it back on the road and not drive too fast, it might get us to Manteo?" I shrug, wanting to get this show on the road and not caring much about what kind of ride we take. Plus, it would be kind of nice to avoid felony charges and a prison stay.

"I like how you think. Let's try it," he says, grabbing my hand and leading me down the center of the road.

"How's your side?" I ask as we head south.

"Not bad. How's the shoulder?"

"Not too bad. The Tylenol helps." The medicine eases the pain in my shoulder, and something about holding his hand eases some of the pain in my heart. It feels good, normal, healthy to be physically connected to another person—a boy I like, not a family member I'm holding on to for dear life.

We walk without talking. The wind and surf drown out the need for conversation. The Blazer comes into view several minutes later. Less than forty-eight hours ago, we'd fought the wind and were delayed by my shoulder injury. When we evacuated the first cottage, it seemed like we'd hiked miles in the dark.

Now, in daylight with the wind at our backs, I realize our great retreat was maybe a mile, two miles at best. Finn breaks into a jog as we near the vehicle. I scurry to catch up.

He smacks the Blazer like an old mule. "You're one tough girl," he says. His enthusiasm dies when he gets a better angle of the front of the car. The hood's dented, the windshield smashed out.

I give him space as he peeks inside the front seat. "It's pretty nasty in there." He glances over his shoulder at me, like he expects me to complain.

"I can handle nasty if you can get it back on the road." I try not to look at the spear-like tree limb protruding from the crack in the glass. A couple of feet in either direction could have ended with one of us as a human shish kebab.

Finn yanks the driver's side door, reaches around the steering wheel, and wiggles the key in the ignition. Something clicks under the hood, and that's it. His tough old girl just sits there. Cursing under his breath, he pulls a lever under the dashboard, and the hood pops up. As he steps to the front of the car to inspect the engine, I step to the back of the Blazer to check out the cargo area. Lying on top of several boxes are a couple of beach towels. I yank the rear swinging door with the intent of grabbing the towels, but it doesn't budge.

"You need help?" Finn peeks around the raised hood.

"I've got it." I force a smile and give the handle a fierce pull.

"Bang down with your fist," he says, then ducks back under the hood.

I follow his instructions, and *the old girl* opens on the third try—just like he said she would.

Reaching for the towels, I glance up at the sky. The clouds are dark. More rain is on the way. It's going to be difficult navigating the roads with all the downed trees. I don't want to think about driving in the rain with reduced visibility and no windshield to protect us from the elements. Trying to keep my mind off Mom and Mere and the weather, I keep busy drying off the front seats with the towels.

Finn steps around the hood and toward me. "I think I've got it," he says.

"Well, start it, and let's go." I can't take another minute of standing around.

"No. You start her. I push," he says, heading to the back of the car.

I scrunch up my face, studying the precarious angle of the Blazer's back tires. I'm not an engineer, but it looks risky. It looks like if the car shifts back or to the right, anyone behind it could be trapped, maybe even crushed by the back tires.

"I don't know . . ."

"Sophie, I've done this a million times. She gets good traction. You drive. I'll push, and we'll be out of here in no time."

I want to believe him. He's done this *a million times*, and we need to get going. I take the keys when he hands them to me.

Ignoring the pain in my shoulder, I place the last dry towel on the seat and slide in behind the steering wheel. My feet swish in water pooling on the floor mat, and I notice the homeopathic book is waterlogged. An empty Doritos bag bobs in the mess. But Finn's *Don't Sweat the Small Stuff* somehow survived the crash, pressed in between the donut box and the underside of the dashboard.

"Fire her up," he calls.

When I turn the key in the ignition this time, I remember to press down on the clutch as well. But Finn's *tough old girl* seems a bit under the weather—literally. She wheezes, then sputters out a wet cough. There is no roar of an engine. No spark. No nothing. I glance back through the rear window at Finn. He gestures for me to try again. I twist the key and hold this time. An unhappy metal-scraping-metal sound complains from under the dented hood. I turn the key back to its starting position, afraid I'm going to blow up the beloved Blazer.

"Third times a charm," Finn calls, and then slaps the rear window.

Squeezing my eyes shut, I turn the key and pray hard. The metal-scraping-metal drowns out the light sounds of the mist and breeze.

"Give her gas," Finn shouts. "Come on. Come on," he chants.

The beast of a vehicle rumbles to life as if she understands Finn.

He flashes a thumbs-up. "You know how to drive a stick, right?"

I shake my head. "Not really," I say, trying not to think about my jerking and stopping and starting back at Zeke's. We should have discussed this before I fired up the beast.

"It's easy. Just let off the clutch and press the gas—gently and at the same time." His head drops from sight in the rearview mirror as he prepares to push.

I let off the clutch a bit, but nothing happens. Biting the inside of my cheek, I apply pressure to the gas—gently like he said. But I'm so focused on my gentle pressing, I lose track of the clutch and release it completely. The car lurches forward.

My chest smashes against the steering wheel. Cursing from behind the Blazer interrupts my wincing.

Glancing in the rearview mirror, I check for Finn. "You okay?" I call.

He coughs and sputters as I put the car in gear and turn off the engine. When I step out, I see him face first in the sand near the rear bumper.

"Finn, I'm so sorry." I rush to help him as he struggles to a seated position.

I offer my hand. He accepts, and I pull him forward.

"Do you want me to try it again?" I ask.

"No." He signals me to halt with one hand and massages his ribs with the other. "Let me try."

I cross my fingers as he slides in behind the steering wheel. He turns the key and *his girl* fires right up. My breath catches, and my chest expands. Sucking down air, I realize it's become almost second nature to hold my breath. Please, please, let him get the Blazer on the road.

The engine revs higher and higher as Finn presses the gas pedal, but the Blazer doesn't budge. He gives her more gas. An angry stream of sand shoots from beneath the back tires. They dig in deeper and deeper. Clamping my mouth shut, I'm right back to holding my breath. I want to scream. Why can't we catch a break?

"Maybe we should just keep moving." I hug myself and rub my upper arms. I'm not exactly drenched, but the mist has picked up. The clouds hang so low I can almost touch them. My clothes and hair act like sponges, absorbing thick moisture from the air.

"No. I have an idea." Determination etches his face. "I've got this."

I follow as he moves toward the back of the vehicle. Opening the rear door a second time, he removes boogie boards, a lacrosse stick, and other sporting equipment I can't identify. He piles everything on the ground beside the car.

I help without speaking, not wanting to interrupt his thinking. Eventually, he uncovers a long wooden board and gives it a tug. But it's stuck, wedged in place beneath a stack of books. Pulling them toward me, I can't help but notice the first title—*To Test or Not to Test: The Pros and Cons of Genetic Counseling.*

I glance over at Finn. In some ways, this ordeal has brought us much closer. I feel like I know him. There's more to him than the class clown he portrays at school. But in other ways, he's as much an enigma as always. I mean, who eats the way he does, lives the way he does, and studies homeopathic medicine *and* genetic counseling?

The top book slips to the sand, unveiling the next title— *Illness in the Family.* Finn looks up. Our eyes lock. His lips part like he wants to say something. His face tightens, as though he's in pain.

"I'm sorry, Finn," I whisper, suddenly understanding what he was trying to tell me back at the cottage about his father's death. There was a lot of pain. I see that clearly now, but he chooses to remember and relive the beauty. In his mind, the beauty and the pain are all woven together like some intricate tapestry. I was listening to only half of what he was saying.

"Sorry about what?" Tilting his head, he releases the board and focuses on me.

I form my words carefully. I can't put a finger on it, but I feel like we're talking two different languages, like if I'm not careful I'm going to say something terribly wrong. "I'm sorry about . . . your dad."

"Yeah. Me too." His shoulders relax as he leans on the bumper.

I point at the stack of books cradled in my arms. "Your dad's illness—it must have been tough. My comments were rude about the way you handled his death. I'm a stubborn, opinionated jerk." My emotions tangle in my stomach. I feel my mouth smiling at the same time my eyes fight back tears. "And I hope you can forgive me, because I've been thinking, and I really want us to be—" I choke on the sob welling in my throat before I can say *together.*

He gently removes the books from my arms and sets them back in the car. Without breaking eye contact, he pulls me to the bumper beside him.

I can't explain what's happening, but something big is coming. I just know it. I've experienced enough tragedy to recognize the sizzle of electricity in the air that precedes bad news. He lifts one of my hands, squeezing it between both of his, and waits for me to meet his eyes. My mind jumps from image to image—waking up facing him on the couch at the first cottage, my feet in his lap at the second house. It keeps returning to our kiss on the beach and in the closet. My lips tingle. Have I done something wrong? Is he mad I said I wasn't sure what I wanted last night?

I've watched enough romantic comedies to know that look on a boy's face. He's about to let me down easy, which is pretty ironic considering I'm the one who's been running away from him. "Sophie, you're smart, pretty . . ."

Okay, now I'm definitely not breathing. I'm certain my

digestive, circulatory, and nervous systems have shut down as well. I'm literally frozen in place.

"I've always liked you—even when you insult my intelligence and think I'm just a big, dumb surfer guy." He bumps his shoulder against mine. "You're the only person who ever really challenged me."

But?

"There's something I need to tell you."

"Okay." I try to sound nonchalant, but my voice cracks. What was I thinking, opening my heart to Finn Sanders? I never should have allowed him to distract me from my primary goal—getting to Manteo and taking care of Mom and Mere. When I blew a tire, I should have set out on foot.

"What you said last night about your dad—and what you told me before about your sister . . . about how you couldn't handle losing anyone else you cared about . . ."

"Finn, spit it out. What are you trying to say?" My pulse churns in my ears, louder than the distant ocean.

"I need to tell you something." Mist glistens like spiders' webs on his eyelashes.

"You said that already."

"Yeah. Right." He's utterly tongue-tied. The boy who never shuts up is speechless. His Adam's apple catches halfway down his neck when he tries to swallow. "It's just that I wasn't completely honest with you about my dad."

"He didn't die of colon cancer?"

"He did, but it wasn't your typical colon cancer. The Lynch syndrome thing I mentioned? It's complicated. I don't think I explained it very well. Or at all."

"Okay." I exhale a little. I remember him saying something

about that when he first told me about his father. Maybe this really isn't about me—about us. It's all about his dad's death. And he just needs to get something off his chest.

"It's a genetic thing. There's a fifty-fifty chance I inherited the gene." He holds my stare, neither of us blinking.

I stay perfectly still, trying to understand what he's saying.

"My dad had an unusually early onset, which means if I inherited the gene, my onset will probably be early—possibly even earlier than his." His stops talking, like he's waiting for me to connect the dots. "It's a really ugly disease, Sophie. After what you said in the closet . . ."

My cheeks warm when he mentions the closet.

"I just thought maybe we shouldn't . . . What I mean is . . . I know you're not the kind of girl to kiss just anyone. And I don't think you'd want to get close to someone who might be checking in at the Horizontal Hilton when you don't have a reservation." One side of his mouth turns up. Obviously, he thinks his joke is clever. When he finally blinks, a tiny drop of mist falls from his lashes to his cheek.

Before I can stop myself, my heart and mind race from visions of his slow death, to me at his funeral, to me curled in a fetal position in my room unable to drag myself out of bed and clean stalls.

"Sophie, say something."

"What is there to say? I don't even know what to think."

"Say you agree or disagree. Say it's a deal breaker, or you don't care—just say something." He shrugs.

Shaking my head, I lick the salty mist from my lips and concentrate on not letting my teeth chatter. Thoughts ricochet in my head, banging against my skull. I like him. I really do. And as much as I hate to admit it, he's right. Everyone dies. I should be big enough and brave enough to face the facts. I can't grieve for Dad and Mere forever. I have to move forward eventually.

But there's a big difference between eventually and right now. And I *can* grieve until Mom and Mere are taken care of. I can stick to my original goals. I can stick to my well-laid plans. I can put off vet school until Mom is more financially stable, until she can afford to pay someone to help with the barn and Mere. And I can certainly put off girlish crushes, no matter how tempting and fun they might be. I can go back to the self-control I was so good at before this stupid storm. I can totally put a stop to the silly idea of learning to open up and take risks. That may work for some people, but I'm not *some people*. I'm the girl with an overworked mom, a disabled sister, and an absentee dad.

Finn wiggles his eyebrows. "Or say I'm irresistible and sexy and you have to be with me no matter what. Just say something."

I don't have the energy to speak, much less laugh. He looks so hopeful. I wish I could at least fake a smile, but I'm completely drained. I thought maybe I was strong enough to do this. I was wrong. I can't. And I need to bring this emotional train to a grinding halt before it runs away and jumps the rails.

"I'm sorry."

With my free hand, I pull at a loose thread on my shirt. It snaps. He shrugs, like my non-answer is no big deal, but the look on his face totally disagrees with his set jaw and dropped shoulders.

His hand grazes mine as he pushes off the bumper. He pulls it away quickly, turning back to the wooden board. We're separated by only a few inches of salty air, but it may as well be the entire Atlantic Ocean.

CHAPTER TWENTY-TWO

Shape your heart to front the hour,
but dream not that the hours will last.

ALFRED, LORD TENNYSON

After a minute of pushing, pulling, and grunting, Finn successfully frees the wooden board from the back of the Blazer. Unable to concentrate on what he's doing with the genetic counseling books staring up at me, I scoot them back where I found them. Now I'm trying to listen to Finn's explanation about the board.

"It's sort of like a reverse lever," he says. Without glancing back at me, he shovels handfuls of sand from under the rear tire.

"Right." I agree, but my heart isn't into his science lesson. Our previous conversation occupies every crevice of my heart and my mind.

"We should get enough traction from this wheel to be out of here in no time."

No. Time.

Chronos.

Kairos.

The mist stops, and the angry sky lightens to a meditative

gray as I contemplate the symbols of growing light and passing time. I feel the day getting away from us as I fidget at the side of the road.

"We're ready," Finn says, gesturing for me to slide into the front seat.

I follow orders, thankful he accepted my lame apology without pressing me for an explanation of exactly what I was sorry about. The Blazer starts on the first try, like it really wants to please him. He deals with the clutch and gas in one smooth motion, the way I mount a horse. The engine revs.

Then bing, bang, boom. She exhales, and we're off. The temporary world and lives we experienced during our crisis slip farther away with each rotation of the tires, like minutes ticked off on a clock.

Finn twists the knob on the radio. Static greets us on every station, and he clicks it off. The tires bump and crack over twigs, patches of sand, and broken glass littering the road. My brain drafts a mental to-do list that could rival Santa's naughty-or-nice scroll. I need to check things at the house, at the barn, at school.

The distance between Finn and me grows as we head south. I stare out the passenger-side window—my body numb, my emotions numb. Everything numb. I squint for signs of our four-legged friend or other survivors. When Finn slams on the brakes, I snap to attention, turning to the road ahead. My seat belt tightens and holds against my chest as I digest the obstacle in our way.

A downed tree blocks the road. Finn puts the car in park, then bangs his fist on the steering wheel. So much for his staying calm during a crisis. His nerves are finally fraying too.

"Now what are we going to do?" I wave my hand toward the tangled mass of limbs and leaves and trunk blocking our path. "There's no way we're moving that."

His fist tightens on the steering wheel as he turns to face me. "Typical."

"What are you talking about?" Now my fists clench beside my thighs.

"Why do you want to give up every time things get hard?"

I realize this isn't just about the tree in the road. I open my mouth, but my tongue seizes. How dare he? Heat rises from my neck to my ears.

I. Am. Not. A. Quitter.

And I resent him saying it. I've never quit on my family. I've never quit on school. I cross my arms with a huff. "I do *not* quit."

"Humph." He places his hand on the door handle, dismissing me.

"You wait just a minute, Finn Sanders." I reach for his arm, but he pulls away, leaving my hand hanging awkwardly in midair. "I am not a quitter," I say.

He turns back to me, eyes narrow. "You're not?"

"No—I'm not. What have I ever quit on?"

The breeze picks up, blowing in through the smashed windshield and ruffling my tangled hair. "You're quitting on us—on friendship or anything else because you're afraid of getting hurt."

"I never said I—"

"You don't have to say anything." He opens his door and steps down to the road. "You quit on your dad."

I shake my head, certain I misunderstood him. I quit on

my dad? *I* quit on my dad? Of all the nerve. "You don't know what you're talking about, Finn."

"You wrote him off when he hurt you. Will you give *him* another chance?"

"He wrote me off. He doesn't deserve another chance." I can't believe I'm arguing with him. He doesn't know what he's talking about. It's like trying to reason with a child or a crazy person. "And he doesn't want another chance."

"If he did, would you give him one?" There's a challenge in his tone.

I glare at him. I can't answer his stupid question. And I don't appreciate the way he acts like he knows me better than I know myself. And we don't have time for this crap right now.

He doesn't know me that well. Period. End of story.

He steps out of the car and leaves me seething inside. My feet squish in junk food wrappers and rainwater when I shift in my seat. He examines the tree from every angle, then approaches the heavier trunk end and pushes till his face turns red. The tree doesn't budge. He tries the other end. Nothing. He finally resorts to kicking it, which accomplishes nothing. But I bet his toes will be sore for a few days. Worse if they're broken.

He sulks back to the Blazer, seemingly none the worse. "It's not moving."

Seventeen sarcastic comments pepper my tongue, but I bite them back.

"We've got two options—leave the car and find transportation on the other side . . ." He slides into the driver's seat.

"Or?"

"Or find a chainsaw."

When he slicks his wet hair back and away from his eyes, I see the full weight of his stress. He looks way more man than boy. This storm has aged him as well.

I speak slowly and carefully. "Or we could walk the entire way—not steal anything or vandalize anything else."

He rakes his already raked hair, pausing to grip his head for a minute before continuing. "Or . . ."

He releases his head and pumps the gas. The engine revs. My heart tightens. He grins, like the psycho dad in that Stephen King movie. He extends his arm in front of my chest. A second later, we're crashing into the tree, our necks snapping from the impact. Fortunately, we didn't have enough space to build up much speed, so he didn't kill us. Unfortunately, we didn't have enough space to build up much speed, and the tree didn't budge.

"Have you completely lost your freaking mind?" He is out of control.

Ignoring my question, he turns the key in the ignition. The Blazer sputters and dies.

"We know your mom and sister evacuated safely. We should have gone to get Zeke *first*. He has a chainsaw and supplies and better transportation. Though this storm was also worse than we thought it would be . . ."

I tried to tell him the storm was going to be bad, but I keep my mouth shut.

"I have to make sure he's okay," he says.

"I know you do." I'm tired of arguing. That doesn't make me a quitter. It makes me . . . tired. I blink back tears, determined not to cry now. "I just . . . I need to find my mom."

"And I need to find Zeke. But I guess I'll do that after I

deal with this tree and get you to Manteo." He steps out of the vehicle, striding toward the tree still without so much as a limp. So much for the broken toe hypothesis. He vaults the tree like it's nothing and heads up the center line of the road on the other side.

As he walks away, I realize I need to let him find his uncle. All we've managed to do today is argue, and I can't take it anymore. I need to find Mom and Mere on my own.

I survey the mess that is his car, the mess that is my current reality. I contemplate just getting out. Heading my own way. The storm has passed. Finn and I don't truly owe each other anything now. He can take care of himself and go find Zeke. I can take care of myself and my people. We can pretend none of this ever happened. I mean what happened, really?

Two frightened people trapped alone in a storm kissed. Not much of a big deal in that. So maybe we exposed a few emotions as well. That's not anything that wouldn't happen in a game of truth or dare or around a bonfire or whatever.

He's fire. I'm ice. We're night and day, water and oil, and every other cliché ever written about opposites. Leaving now is logical—like ripping off a Band-Aid. Leaving now is practical and cautious. And I don't care what Finn says. Being cautious is not the same as quitting.

Being cautious is wise.

But . . .

No buts, Sophie.

I wait for him to turn down a side road before reaching for the door handle. Then, holding my breath, I pull the handle and the heavy door creaks a warning. I freeze, but Finn doesn't come running back to me.

I step down to the asphalt. As I carefully close the door, a worm of guilt wiggles in my gut. I can't just walk out on him. We've been in this together. Plus, I don't want him to be right. I don't want to be a quitter. Ugh.

I find a dry scrap of paper and a colored pencil in his console and leave a quick note telling him to go find Zeke and assuring him I'll be fine.

Pushing the door open, I step down to the road again. This time I slam the door without peering back inside. As I tromp away from the Blazer, I ignore the rear windows and the books piled there.

Determination sets in. My head and feet make a decision before my heart has time to sway them.

With Mere's compass tucked in my pocket, I widen the chasm between Finn and me. Even the wind seems to be against me as I head south. It impedes my progress, literally pushing against my forward momentum and scraping my ankles with bits of sand. I clench and unclench my fists. I'm cold. I'm tired. Honestly, I'm not even sure I can make it the rest of the way.

I tell myself my normal world and predictable routine are just across the bridge at the southern tip of this island. All I have to do now is figure out how to get there on my own.

CHAPTER TWENTY-THREE

*My life has crept so long
on a broken wing . . .*

ALFRED, LORD TENNYSON

I trudge south, contemplating the last few days, contemplating the grumbling of the ocean and the swooshing of the seagrass and the weight of the heavy air. It's hard to believe the amount of sand that's been displaced and redeposited by the storm. Just moving sand—not to mention clearing downed trees and power lines, repairing roofs, and rebuilding homes— will take residents ages to complete.

As I walk, I listen carefully, telling myself I'm listening for the sound of rescue personnel or the horse. If I'm honest, though, I have to admit I'm listening for the Blazer and Finn chasing after me, begging me for another chance. In reality that would only make things more difficult, and yet I can't help my traitorous heart.

But I don't have to worry about what to say to him because the wind and waves make the only sounds in my world.

Rubbing my thumb back and forth against the compass in my pocket, I count the broken yellow stripes in the middle of the road. My stomach grumbles. Too bad I didn't snag a granola bar before heading out on my great, solitary adventure. I lose count of the yellow lines somewhere around two hundred and twenty and start again at one.

A foreign thump breaks the monotony of the ocean's somber melody, and I jump a foot in the air. If it's Finn, I don't know what I'll say—how I'll explain setting out on my own. I hear it again, and it's not his beloved Blazer. It's something even better. It's the unmistakable thump of a helicopter. My heart rises above the fog and mist as I bolt toward higher ground on my left. Clawing and scrabbling for the top of the dunes, I cup my hands over my eyebrows, straining for better visibility.

Brushing sand from my hands and arms, I squint out to sea and spy what looks like an intoxicated housefly zigging and zagging over the open ocean. It must be the Coast Guard, but they're totally not searching for stranded islanders. Someone or something must be lost at sea. I shiver, trying to imagine surviving the brutal tumult of the Atlantic in anything smaller than the aircraft carrier Dad and I toured in Virginia Beach two summers ago.

I watch until the helicopter disappears completely from view and swipe hot tears from my face. Up here, perched on a high dune, I have a clear view of the ravenous storm surge. I have no idea what time it is. I don't even remember where I last saw my phone. Was it that first night at the cottage?

A shadow of movement catches my eyes near the frothy bubbles at the high tide mark. Shaking my head, I blink to clear my vision, sure my eyes are playing tricks on me. It's the chestnut horse Finn and I saved from the silt fence. He's favoring his back leg and not moving very fast. But he survived. He really, truly survived.

The horse spots me dancing and swinging my arms over my head and stops to stare, ears flicking back and forth as he assesses the situation. My celebration is short-lived when I realize the poor guy can't have found fresh water. Years ago, the horses pawed through the sand for freshwater drinking holes. But I don't think horses can balance on only two legs. Plus, these animals have become a bit acclimated to human support. I can't remember if the Wild Horse Fund volunteers provide freshwater sources, but I can't risk it. It could be days before rescue workers find him—if they find him. Their first priority will be human survivors.

The weight of the situation presses down on my shoulders and on the rest of me as I track the horse's slow progress in the sand. He turns his heavy head and takes a faltering step, obviously deciding the crazy girl on the dunes is too far away to present much of a threat. I glance south toward Manteo. The magnetic force of Mom and Mere tugs on my heart.

Lifting my shoulders, I turn toward the most important people in my life. When I do, I almost step on a perfectly formed sand dollar. It's still gray. We haven't had enough sun or heat in recent days to bleach and harden the brittle shell. But it's miraculous that such a delicate creature could survive the crashing surf and still wash up intact.

Then a kaleidoscope of memories punches me in the gut, taking me back to the day Dad left. There was a sand dollar that day too. I'd found several conch shells and a sand dollar while walking alone on the beach. I was bringing them home to Mere and found Dad leaving. We argued. Pointing at the sand dollar in my hand, he said things weren't always as they appeared.

"Some people are just really good at seeing what they want to see," I'd shouted.

He plucked the delicate treasure from my grasp, cracked it into two halves, and tapped one half on his palm. Then he reminded me about the five doves at the center of the starfish and explained how everyone tries so hard to find and preserve the shell that they forget about the beauty at its heart.

I told him if there was beauty in his heart, he wouldn't abandon his wife and children.

He said, "Your mother's tough, Soph. She can take care of herself and what's left of our family."

"Is that your excuse for leaving us?" I screamed at the top of my lungs, effectively silencing him.

When he leaned forward to hug me, I whispered, "I hate you."

And we haven't spoken since.

As much as I hate to admit he's right, he is. Mom is way tougher than the sand dollar at my feet. It dawns on me that my mother may not need me as much as I need her to need me. All this time alone with nothing but my thoughts is making me crazy. Either that, or Finn and all his meditative psychobabble are messing with my head. It doesn't really matter whether Dad's right or Finn's right. The truth is I can't do anything to help Mom or Mere right now. I couldn't do anything to save Mere in the accident. I couldn't stop Dad from walking out on us.

But I can help that horse.

I remember something else—something my favorite teacher

said in middle school. We were collecting money for a homeless shelter up north. She and the other kids were so excited we had collected almost a thousand dollars. She asked me why I wasn't joining the celebration. I told her it wouldn't be enough to take care of the huge homeless problem in the city. I expected her to disagree—to feed me a motivational quote or something. But she told me she understood exactly what I was saying, then proceeded to share her philosophy—that God doesn't expect us to take care of *all* the problems in the world. He expects us to help the specific people placed in our lives and on our hearts. The Richmond homeless shelter was placed on our hearts when one of the girls in our class lost her father there. He overdosed and died sad and alone in that shelter.

I totally get what she was saying now. I can't help *all* the wild horses. I can't do a lot of things right now. But I can help *that* horse—the one that's been placed in my life a second time in as many days. I can steer him toward the safety of his herd north of the fence. I can find freshwater for him. And that's exactly what I'm going to do. I'm not quite sure how, but I'll figure something out. At home with buckets and oats, this would be much simpler. But if I want to be a vet someday, I have to learn how to help all the animals in need, not just the easy ones.

And I am not—repeat, *am not*—a quitter.

CHAPTER TWENTY-FOUR

If you don't concentrate on what you are doing then the thing that you are doing is not what you are thinking.

ALFRED, LORD TENNYSON

I follow the hobbling horse as the mist picks up and the wind shifts. My feet drag the sand. Because of high tide and the angry storm surge, I have to hug the dunes, which means loose sand, which means more effort. We finally near what appears to be a weathered house in the distance. My shoulder shrieks in protest, but I refuse to listen.

The horse hasn't wavered from his northward march, following the pencil-line path between surf and dunes. I know what I must do—employ the ole toilet tank water recovery mission a second time. I hunch forward and drag myself step-by-step up and over the dunes, onto the boardwalk, and to the leaning tower of cedar-sided gray wood posing as a summer home.

The storm already shattered several windows, so reaching through the door and letting myself in hardly even feels like breaking and entering. Either that or my moral compass has completely failed. I slosh through standing water in the living room, soggy books and magazines swishing in my wake. I spot a half bath off the side of the living room and splash in that direction. An overturned plastic trash can rests beside the toilet. I grab it, make sure it's empty, then fill it with water from the toilet tank. Carrying the water down the uneven boardwalk to the beach without spilling it requires balance and upper-body strength, both of which I'm short on today. But somehow I suck it up and press forward, trying not to think about my shoulder injury or slipping and breaking my neck. If the horse weren't injured worse than me, I would never catch him.

But I do. My superhuman determination to save him and prove to myself and maybe Finn that I'm not a quitter fuels my charge up the beach. It does nothing to ease my huffing and puffing or grunting and groaning. As I close in, the horse seems to dig into a reserve of his own and picks up his pace. I'm close enough now to make out the oozing flesh on his back leg. But once I'm within about thirty feet, I can't seem to shrink the gap any farther.

This isn't going to work.

The average horse is used to following, not leading. That's why a wild horse can't survive without a herd. Their herding instinct, which shares a lot of similarities with a game of follow-the-leader, is as strong as their fight-or-flight instinct. As long as I approach from behind, he's going to keep moving away from me faster and faster until he can't take another step. I need to be ahead of him so I can place the water in his direct path, then pray his survival instinct is enough to make him drink.

I decide to try something that works with my own horses.

Normally a human must have a bond with a horse to activate his desire to follow, but I don't have any other genius ideas here. The humming wind and the mist hanging in the air are going to make it difficult for the horse to hear my movements. But it can't hurt to try.

I stop and pause to the count of ten. As I turn around, I pray for the best. After several steps in the opposite direction, I peek over my shoulder. And miracle of miracles, my horse-whisperer plan kind of worked. The horse didn't turn to follow me. I didn't expect him to. But he did at least stop. He has to need a break himself. Even from thirty-plus feet, I can see his ribs rising and falling with each labored breath. His head hangs low. He makes no effort to avoid the frothy waves lapping at his hooves.

Hot beads of sweat form at my hairline, mixing with the chilly drizzle. Carrying several gallons of water is taking its toll. Acting quickly to take advantage of his stillness, I scurry back up and over the dunes. He's blocked from my sight as I head north, parallel to the dunes.

"Don't move, big guy. Don't move," I plead as I hurry forward.

The short trek constricts my lungs and cramps my muscles. I force myself to go an extra five to ten yards to be safe before hefting my heavy feet and legs back up and over the dunes.

"Thank you. Thank you," I whisper to the wind when I realize I have in fact gotten in front of the pony. He lifts his head a bit as I approach, his ears flicking in my direction.

"Easy, big guy. Easy." I keep my voice low and my speech slow as I take another half step in his direction. "Easy."

His head turns to the right on his long neck as though he's

contemplating a retreat, but his legs remain locked firmly in place. The wild look is gone from his eyes. No white is visible now. Actually, his eyes are oddly sunken back in his head, a sure sign of severe dehydration. I notice he's either drifted closer to shore or the tide's coming in again, because the water is splashing higher and higher on his legs. I need to hurry.

I inch forward as far as I dare and deposit the trash can as close to him as possible. Before withdrawing, I splash my hand around in the water, hoping to interest him. His ears flick, and he lowers his head an inch or two. I climb halfway up the dune at my back and plop butt-first in the sand—partially to give him space, partially because if I don't sit down I'm going to die.

The horse doesn't move, and I feel sick to my stomach. All this time, all this effort, and it hasn't done any good. Dropping my face in my hands, I let the hot tears overflow my eyes and seep between my fingers. I really just want to lie down and sleep. When the breeze shifts, I lift my head and see the horse has moved within inches of the trash can.

I hold my breath. Digging my hands in the sand near my legs, I will him to close the gap. He half hops, half steps to the trash can, and a fresh wave of tears spills down my cheeks.

The splitting pain in my shoulder and calves from climbing up and down the dunes is worth it. When he drops his head and slurps water from the plastic trash can, my heart glides out to sea like the albatross Finn and I spotted yesterday. If I can get a wild horse to drink from a trash can in close proximity to me, surely I can get him to safety north of the sound-to-sea fence. Then it's due south for me. Do not pass go. Do not collect two hundred dollars. Get to Mom and Mere and our own horses and put our lives back into order.

The horse drains the trash can, then flicks it to the side with his nose. Neither of us moves for several long minutes. After giving us both a chance to rest, I move in a few steps from behind the exhausted horse. I hate to push him in his condition, but I need to get him to safety. Thankfully, he plows ahead when I approach from behind. The water seems to have refreshed him a bit, and the salty wash of surf on his lower legs seems to have cleaned his wounds and possibly even lessened the pain.

He's not setting any records, but he hobbles forward at a steady rate. I struggle to keep up. When I swipe the water from my cheeks and forehead, my forehead feels hot—steamy. I shake it off, quickly dismissing the alarm bells that start ringing in my head. My senses are probably still a bit off from the loss of blood and shock. Besides, I seriously doubt an infection could set in this quickly. I probably need rest and lots of water myself. If I do get an infection, which is pretty common in post-hurricane nastiness, that's what antibiotics are for. I'll be fine for a few more hours, and this guy needs me.

I dig deep into my last reserves and press forward. Each step is like trying to swim through chocolate pudding. We struggle along in silence, our roles reversed in this backward game of follow-the-leader. With single-minded focus, I advance from one hoof print to the next, counting as I go. At three hundred and eight, my right calf cramps. There's no way I'm going to make it all the way to the fence. Lifting my eyes from the charcoal sand littered with shell fragments, twisted cans, broken bottles, and God knows what else, I look for somewhere to sit. A nice hunk of driftwood would be dreamy. Something brown up ahead catches my eye. I shake my head.

It can't be what I think it is.

But it is.

It's the freaking fence. The fence. The fence. I find my seventieth wind and press forward despite the knotted muscle in my leg.

We did it. We did it.

I did it.

If I had the energy, I'd dance, or flip, or even just fist bump the turbulent air. Instead I rest my hands on my thighs and breathe a sigh of relief. My joy deflates as I scan the fence.

Yes, we made it.

But there's no break in sight, no wild horses in sight, which means I have no safe place to deposit my new friend.

We've traveled all this way for nothing.

CHAPTER TWENTY-FIVE

*The shell must break
before the bird can fly.*

ALFRED, LORD TENNYSON

When cold water brushes my feet, my eyes fly open, and I lift the side of my face from the sand where I collapsed. My shoulder throbs. The ocean roars. I just want to go home. But that's not an option, and neither is lying here and drowning. So I brace my hands in the sand and push up to my knees. Sand cakes every crack and crevice of my body. I need a hot shower or ten.

Rising unsteadily from the sand, I spy my wild pal. His head swivels in my direction. If I didn't know better, I'd swear he was shaking his head at me.

"I know. I know. I'm pathetic," I say to him, a little concerned about my mental stability. I can't remember the last time I ate or drank anything. It seems like it was ages ago. My world has been reduced to jagged, chopped-off ridges of sand, roiling waves, and flattened and sideways houses. And this horse.

"Let's do this." I wave my arms in his direction. He plods forward as though he knows the drill, and he looks much better than I feel. With the fence guiding him on one side and me on the other, slightly behind, it's much easier to steer him in the direction I want him to go. He got out somehow, and I'm going to find the break he escaped through if it kills me.

It might.

The farther we travel, the more I begin to wonder if this is a lost cause. If he swam around the fence, which is highly unlikely, or jumped it, which is technically impossible, I've got a big problem. My epic rescue will be an epic fail without some way of crossing the fence.

Lost in thought and trying to calculate how much fence I have left to inspect, I don't realize my buddy has stopped till I'm almost within arm's reach of his hindquarters. He lifts his head, trying to get a read on something in the distance. His ears twitch back and forth between me and a new development up ahead.

I squint but don't see anything but an endless landscape of sand and clouds and a straight, unbroken line of fence. Horses have better hearing and smell than humans, so maybe he's zeroing in on something he can't even see. My heart lifts at the possibility that maybe the Coast Guard helicopter has turned inland.

Determined we must be nearing the end of this trek, I swish my hands toward his rump, encouraging him to proceed. My hamstrings protest as we ascend what must be the spine of the island. Then we're descending on the other side, and the protest transfers to the fronts of my thighs as I brace myself against gravity. Honestly, it would be easier to roll or stumble down the dune, but I don't want to frighten my charge. As I contemplate sitting for a second, a new sound interrupts the rush of wind and waves, rumbling in the background despite our distance from the sea.

It's a mechanical whining—not a helicopter, not a boat, more like a car. But there's no way anyone's up here in a car. It would take some powerful all-wheel drive to reach this part of the island. I'm not even sure Dad's truck or Finn's Blazer would make it up here.

But someone or something has to be operating that engine—hopefully a fireman or an EMT. At the bottom of the ridge, the noise grows louder. As we round a clump of scrub brush, an absurd monster truck materializes in the distance. The tires stand taller than I do, above my head. Some sort of thick canvas webbing fills the side windows in place of glass. Based on the various colors of the rusty cab and bed, I'm pretty sure the thing was pieced together from the corpses of trucks that haven't seen anything but the back lot of a junkyard for the last few years, possibly the last few decades.

If there's a live person to go with the Franken-truck, I have no choice. I must proceed. I could use some help here, and that scary excuse for a vehicle might be my ticket to the mainland.

"Hello," I call, but the trifecta of wind, sea, and monster truck completely drown out my voice.

I inhale deeply, cup my hands around my mouth, and call again. "Hello!"

Nothing.

As I suck in a lungful of air and prepare to scream at the top of my lungs, the engine stops, and a *Duck Dynasty* beard with a wiry body attached to it steps out of the truck. Holy crap! If I weren't so mentally and physically exhausted, I might laugh or cry. Instead, I simply stare. The irony of the universe is not wasted on me when I realize the man scurrying toward us is Finn's uncle, Zeke—the same Zeke I said could fend for himself, the same Zeke I chose to head away from in favor of the mainland and my mother and sister. I roll my eyes at the heavens.

"Over here!" He waves his hands over his head as if I could miss his beard. Or his truck. His enthusiasm throws me off balance. I'm not sure whether it's some strange side effect of the storm, or surprise, or what, but this Zeke is way happier to see me than the Zeke of two days ago. He jogs across the sand to meet us, and the wild horse whinnies softly, almost as if he recognizes Zeke, which is impossible. There is no way these two know each other.

"Guillermo! Guillermo!" Zeke's happier than I've seen him, like he's reconnecting with a lost loved one instead of a strange girl and a bedraggled horse. "Guillermo, you made it, buddy. I was looking for you."

He has eyes only for the horse. My fatigued brain struggles to keep up as he approaches and pats my *wild* horse on the shoulder. I begin to doubt everything I've always believed about these horses. And now I'm really skeptical of Zeke as well. I'm pretty sure he can get in big trouble with Fish and Game and the cops for interfering with these protected animals.

When he finally makes eye contact, I realize he has a mouth, and lips, and teeth, because there's something resembling a smile behind all that hair. But it fades quickly.

"I thought you guys evacuated." His eyes dart to the stand of scrubby trees behind me. "Where's Finn?"

That's a really good question with no really good answer. "We wrecked. We stayed in a house south of here during the storm . . ."

216

His eyes narrow on my face as he runs a leathery hand through his beard. "So where's Finn?"

"We . . . uh . . . separated . . ."

"Why in the—" He stops himself before the profanity flies and glances at the horse like he's afraid he'll spook him. "Why would you do that?"

Because I wanted to. Because I can take care of myself.

Because maybe I'm afraid of getting close to Finn, which makes him kind of right and me all wrong, and kind of a liar, and maybe even a quitter.

I shrug. That's all I can do with my heart deflating inside my chest.

"So where is he?" Clearly, he's not going to let it go, and I can't blame him.

"Looking for a chainsaw to clear a road." I shake my head, unable to hide my irritation.

"And you?" He gestures from me to the horse.

"And I what?"

"And you just happened to pair up with Guillermo here and head away from civilization." His eyebrows drop so low, they may meet the beard, swallow his face, and blind him for all eternity.

"It's kind of a long story." I shift my weight from one tired leg to the other.

"We've got nothing but time." He studies Guillermo's back leg, frowning, and waits for me to answer.

Actually, *he* may have nothing but time. I really need to get to the mainland.

He crosses his arms in front of his chest, like he can wait all day, and I cave.

217

"I was headed to the mainland, but I saw him." I gesture to my wild horse friend, who Zeke keeps calling Guillermo. "Finn and I saw the horse before—caught in a silt fence."

Massaging his chest with his fist, Zeke waits for me to continue. Concern etches his face.

"He was tangled badly and making his leg worse struggling to free himself. Then I was heading south today and saw him again. He was dehydrated, and I knew he wouldn't survive without his herd."

"That's pretty impressive you decided to help him." His forehead rises, revealing his eyes again. My chest expands a little.

"Well, my parents invested a lot of their lives into protecting those horses and building that fence." I nod toward the power cable barrier to my right.

"What's your name again?" he asks, rubbing Guillermo between the ears.

"Sophie. Sophie March."

His eyes widen. "You Doug March's girl?"

"Yes." I wait for him to explain how he knows my dad.

"Your dad and I went to school together. We made rescue calls together before the fence went up. He's cool—haven't seen him in a while, though."

Me neither.

"I heard he hit on hard times." He shakes his head. "Your daddy was the only person other than family to visit me in rehab. He was always the first person to lend a hand when one of our buddies needed help. He's done a lot of good, that man. Hope you and your pretty mama are giving him lots of support when he needs it."

I don't answer. I can't. A butterfly of guilt flaps its wings in my chest, initiating a tiny waft of air. Zeke is right. My dad was always there for everyone until the wreck. He was always there for me, Mom, and Mere. He never missed a single Daddy and Donuts in elementary school. Never missed a father-daughter dance. Never ignored us to play golf or watch football. Mom said he was her knight in shining armor—until he wasn't.

"And I haven't seen you since you were knee-high to a grasshopper. Never would've recognized you. You were a little show-off, always trying to impress your daddy. Kept him on his toes too—running after you about as much as the horses, if I remember correctly."

With no means of escape from my tight chest, the puff of butterfly wind in my lungs begins to swirl in a circular motion.

"Yeah." I force out the single syllable.

I haven't thought about my childhood relationship with Dad in a long time—how he and I were the two amigos. Back then, Mere was more likely to stay home with Mom, where she could dance when she finished working around the house or barn. They were joined at the hip. I wanted to be in the truck with Dad, windows rolled down, racing head-on to a new adventure.

It's funny what a difference a decade makes—how the years work on us like an ocean current shaping, moving, and reshaping a sandbar. It's mind-boggling to think how quickly your entire life can change. If there hadn't been an accident on the bypass that day, Dad wouldn't have been on the beach road. If he hadn't been distracted by the change of plans, or his phone, or whatever, maybe he and Mere wouldn't have wrecked. Even if they had still wrecked, maybe he wouldn't have let the guilt eat him alive if he hadn't been messing with his phone around the time of the accident. I doubt anyone except Dad will ever know for sure exactly what happened that day. Maybe he was telling the truth when he said it all happened too fast to remember the details. I'm too physically and emotionally exhausted to think about it right now.

Whatever happened, he let it eat at him, and his solution was prescription pain meds and alcohol. I could forgive him for anything—the addiction, the depression, anything—but I could not forgive him for walking out.

"I don't recognize you either," I say, trying to sound casual and ignore the cyclone of emotions churning inside of me.

"Back then, I had more hair up here." He smiles and pats the top of his head. "And less here." He tugs on his beard.

I have no response for that. "So about Guillermo—what do you propose we do?"

"He's a young male, so that makes it tough," Zeke says, then runs his hand along Guillermo's rump. "The stallion in the band runs off the young males when they near maturity. Generally, these guys take up with a band of other bachelors until they can recruit a harem of their own. But this guy's been hanging around the shack. I've tried to ignore him, but he's still too comfortable with humans and will probably have to be rehomed."

"How are we going to get him back to his herd?" I nod toward the fence, ready to get this show on the road and for a minute to gather my thoughts. It's hard to think properly with this strange hermit staring me down—a strange hermit who's not acting hermit-y at all because he likes my dad and because I earned some respect for risking my safety to protect a wild horse.

"One thing at a time. We need to find Finn, and I need to

know where you found Guillermo," he says, not answering my question.

"I'm pretty sure Finn can take care of himself." Unless some gnarly waves distract him, or he amputates his leg with a chainsaw, or he runs off the road in a *borrowed* vehicle. For a second, I really miss him. I mean, we were kind of a good team. He brought out some of the adventurous little girl tucked so deep inside of me, I'd completely forgotten she was there.

"I know we were south of Duck but not sure how far south." I shrug. It doesn't seem that important now that we're back here at the fence. Zeke rests his hand on Guillermo's rump as he leans in for a closer inspection of the wound. "Let me clean that wound and give him some water. Then we find Finn. Then we take it from there."

"I really need to get the horse to safety so I can find my mom." I glance at his monster truck, hoping he'll offer me a ride to Manteo.

"*Safety* is an interesting term under the circumstances."

"Yeah." He's not getting the I-need-a-ride facial clues, so I cut to the point. "Look, my mom and sister need me. Can you get me to Manteo?"

"Sure—after we get Guillermo squared away." He twists the tip of his long beard around his index finger as he stares off into the distance. "And find Finn."

I try to be patient. I do. But I can't stand it any longer. "Do you at least have a phone I can use?"

"No signal up here even without a hurricane." He shrugs.

Without responding, I blink and step toward the truck. I don't have the energy to respond. I barely have the energy to drag myself across the sand to lean on one of the giant tires.

I've given one hundred percent and then some, and it still wasn't enough. My blood, sweat, and tears weren't enough. I'm not enough—never was, never will be.

I'm done.

What's the point in fighting Mother Nature? Zeke? Finn? There is no point. I'm completely at their mercy.

Closing my eyes, I slide toward the sand until my butt rests on the lower half of the tire.

I'm defeated.

I quit.

CHAPTER TWENTY-SIX

Knowledge comes, but wisdom lingers.

ALFRED, LORD TENNYSON

As I cross my arms and settle in to wait for the next wave of emotional turmoil, the sound of a gunshot breaks the air. My heart skips a beat. "Wh-what was that?" I ask. With my heart lodged firmly in my throat, I jump from Zeke's unsteady chair. It's like I'm stuck in some survival reality TV show. Every time I overcome some great obstacle or press through some physical or emotional challenge, the producers throw in another insane trial.

Zeke hums and pours liniment on Guillermo's leg. He doesn't even look up from his work. He's completely unfazed, as if the sound of a gunshot on an isolated northern beach in the wake of a hurricane is nothing to be concerned about. Even Guillermo seems untroubled by the noise.

Finally, Zeke smiles at me, seeming to have sensed my fear. "It's just Finn's car backfiring. That kid's amazing. He found us."

Is amazing really a suitable adjective for Finn? Maybe frustrating or shocking or . . . sort of amazing.

Sure enough, a few seconds later, the vomit-green Blazer

rumbles into sight, barreling around the scrub brush in the distance. She looks more horrendous than usual with broken glass for a windshield, and she kind of lists to one side like two of her tires are flat.

To my utter surprise, I feel my face break into a goofy smile. And Yesenia's all-time favorite Tennyson quote repeats in my head. I can hear her as though she's standing beside me. "'Tis better to have loved and lost than never to have loved at all."

I always thought that particular tidbit was a pile of romantic mumbo jumbo. Now I'm not so sure. Right this second, with Guillermo, who I feel at least partially responsible for saving, close by and Finn approaching, I totally get it. It's about taking risks as much as it's about love. It's better to take a risk and fail than to live in fear.

I hope Finn and I can make amends and at least be friends. Yesenia and Tennyson are right. I've learned from him, from our time together, from this stupid storm. I never would have wished for this hurricane. I never would have wished for a flat tire or a horse to be caught in a fence and injured. But I can learn from these experiences. I've learned a lot about taking risks for myself and for others. Now it's time to take the risk to end all risks.

After what seems like ages but is probably just a minute or two, the Blazer stops a few yards from us, sputters, and then dies. The door opens with a painful groan as Finn steps down to the sand.

He jogs toward me, his face quickly transforming from surprise to skepticism. "You're here."

"I'm here." I hold his eyes, willing him to keep an open mind. To understand that I'm not going anywhere anymore.

He nods, then steps toward Zeke. "I've been looking for you everywhere." He slaps Zeke on the back. Then his head jerks back in my direction. "Isn't this the horse that was tangled in the fence?"

"Yes."

"And you two tamed him, or what?"

"It's a long story," Zeke and I answer in unison. I shrug. He chuckles a bit.

Finn glances back and forth between me and Zeke, like he's contemplating what happened between the two of us while he was gone.

"So what now?" Finn asks.

As much as I want to race to Manteo, I know I couldn't live with myself if we left Guillermo alone up here. "We find the break in the fence and get the horse back where he belongs."

Zeke caps the bottle of liniment and turns toward me. "There's no break in the fence."

"There has to be. How else would a horse get over here?" I ask, circling back to the real discussion.

"I don't know."

I try not to roll my eyes, but this conversation feels like it's about to derail.

"It doesn't really matter, does it—how he got over here. What's done is done." Zeke puts down the liniment bottle, hitches up his Hawaiian shorts, and turns back to Guillermo, who stands dozing near the fence. "What matters is how we deal with the present situation and how we get him north of that fence."

"How're we going to do that without a break in the fence?" I glance at Finn, willing him to jump in and help.

"We break it ourselves, herd him through. Then you two head to Manteo, and I'll stay here until rescuers arrive."

My brain says his plan is ridiculous. My gut says it might just work.

"That fence is solid. How do you plan to take it down?" I turn to Zeke, praying he has a good answer.

"We could dig up two posts and push them down with both vehicles, but that could take several hours." He rubs his beard.

I don't have several hours. I need to let Mom and Mere know I'm okay. I'm glad I got the horse to Zeke. I'm glad Finn found us. I would make the same choices if I had to do it all over again. But there has to be a faster way.

"What if we skip the digging part and just use the trucks to knock down a couple of posts?" I say. I thought Finn was being an idiot when he crashed into the fallen tree in an attempt to move it, and now that's exactly what I'm suggesting—using not one but two vehicles as battering rams. But I don't see any other way.

No one speaks for several seconds. A steady wind ruffles Guillermo's tail and Zeke's beard, but it's no longer the god-awful gale of the hurricane. I roll my head from side to side, trying to loosen the knots in my lower neck and shoulders.

"It could work," Finn says. "But if we wreck the trucks beyond repair, it could be another day before we get to Manteo."

Ugh. Good point.

He pushes black hair away from his face, revealing the knot on his forehead. The thing is still massive, but it's even more yellow-green now, not purple-black. I find myself feeling relieved.

Finn points at the gray sky like he has a genius idea. "What if we use the Blazer to push and save Zeke's truck for pulling?" He points at the rusty but huge winch on the back of Zeke's Franken-truck.

"Let's do it," Zeke says, then claps his hands. "Finn, you push. I'll pull. Sophie, you keep an eye on Guillermo."

Shaking my head, I meet his eyes. "No. Guillermo is more comfortable with you. You keep an eye on him. I'll help Finn with the fence," I say, placing my hands on my hips Wonder-Woman style, ready to stand my ground if he argues.

Zeke glances at Finn with raised eyebrows.

Finn nods. "If she says she can do it, I trust her."

And just like that, we're ready to save Guillermo for good—that is, of course, if I can drive Franken-truck and kick this fence's butt.

I haven't felt like kicking much butt lately, but suddenly I'm ready to give it a whirl.

A few minutes later, I'm banging my fist on the steering wheel, gritting my teeth, and screaming, "Come on. Come on."

This has to work. It has to.

I believed. I trusted. I took a risk. But the fence post is *not* budging. I peek in the rearview mirror to see if Finn's making more progress than me in his Blazer. Then I take a deep breath and prepare to drive Franken-truck forward one more time. Between the dirt on my rear window, the jagged glass in his windshield, and the shaggy black hair falling in his face, I can't read his facial expression. But I can read my own. It looks like it's about to crumple in on itself—much like the crumpled front end of Finn's Blazer.

"Ugggh! Come on!" The screaming originates from somewhere deeper than my throat. It's more of a fierce growl than individual words. My upper body jerks back and forth, slamming the seat behind me despite my still-tender shoulder.

As I will the behemoth forward, I press the gas pedal halfway to the floor. The engine screams louder than I do, threatening to rip out from under the hood if I give it more gas. If I blow up this truck, we're in deep trouble. We have no back-up plan. The Blazer might have one more semi-solid push on the post in her before she's immobile and wrecked beyond repair.

My pulse throbs in my neck. Zeke stands in the distance, too far away to yell advice over the earsplitting engine, too far away for me to make out his facial expression either. I look to Finn in the rearview mirror a second time. I think he nods.

And I go for it.

I just do it.

I stomp on the gas.

The truck rocks and bucks. The engine shrieks. But nothing happens. The post doesn't budge.

"Grrrrrr." Hanging on to the steering wheel for dear life, I lift my butt off the seat for better leverage and manage to press the gas pedal the last half-centimeter to the floor. In the time it takes me to blink, the truck lurches forward, rocketing across the sand. My heart races. The truck races. But my brain remains frozen, suspended for a millisecond before it fires the signal to my foot to brake.

Lifting my foot off the gas, I stomp the brake, desperate to stop before I hit the stand of saplings and scrub brush head-on. The truck halts suddenly, and the massive fence post whiplashes, smacking the back of the truck with enough force to slam me chest first into the steering wheel.

CHAPTER TWENTY-SEVEN

Words, like nature, half reveal and half conceal the soul within.

ALFRED, LORD TENNYSON

I grip my side, gasping for air, but nothing's happening. I can't breathe. I can't speak.

I collapse against the seat. When I do, my lungs open enough to suck in half a breath. Something's squeezing my chest. I struggle to breathe. "Oh, God!" I moan, certain I've injured myself. But each plea for help carries a bit more oxygen to my lungs, and I realize I haven't broken ribs or punctured a lung. I knocked the wind out of myself.

I close my eyes and concentrate on inhaling and exhaling.

"Sophie? Sophie! Are you okay?"

I open one eye. Finn stands on the running board, peering in at me. If his eyes open any wider, they might pop out of his face.

I strain to form something resembling a smile, but don't have the energy. "I knew you cared, Wild Man," I croak.

"Not funny. You scared the crap out of me. I thought you hurt yourself or—" His jaw clenches, like he's imagining the worst.

"I'm surprised you didn't try mouth-to-mouth," I say, my voice a tiny bit less bull-froggy.

He jerks as if I slapped him, then squints at me carefully. "Wait. Was that a joke?"

A genuine smile tugs at the corners of my mouth. "Yeah. Yeah, it was."

When he drops from the running board to the sand, we're eye level. "And you took down that beast of a fence."

He lifts the door handle, pulling the door open.

I shake my head. "*We* took down the fence."

He lifts my arm from the steering wheel and drapes it over his shoulders. Then he's half guiding, half carrying me to Zeke and Guillermo. "My tough old girl died just before you gunned it. You did that all by yourself." He waves his free hand in the direction of the overturned fence post and the long section of cable stretched across the sand.

"It doesn't matter when the Blazer died." I stop and wait for him to meet my eyes. "I couldn't have . . . I mean . . . I wouldn't have ever done that without you."

He nods and maintains eye contact. We stand like that for several seconds. Then I wrap my arms around his neck and hug him, thankful that he doesn't ask questions or push me away. He seems to understand my desire for silence. I release his neck in favor of his hand.

Zeke beams as we approach. "Good work, kids." He pulls both of us in for a hug, apparently not caring how long it's been since any of us had a shower. Guillermo stands watching from a safe distance.

"Now what?" I ask.

"Guillermo goes back where he belongs. I toss out a bunch

of hay in hopes of drawing the bachelor band this way." He points to the ridge in the distance. "Then we let nature take her course."

"And we head to Manteo?" I ask.

"You and Finn head to Manteo in my truck. I'll stay here and keep an eye on things and go check out the shack if I feel up to it."

Finn and I help Zeke transfer water, hay, and first aid necessities from Franken-truck to the Blazer. The Blazer is pretty much a hollowed-out shell now, but all Zeke needs is a place to rest and store supplies, so it works perfectly for him.

"Catch you on the flip," he says, patting Finn on the back before turning to me. "Thanks, Sophie. You did a good thing."

"You're welcome. I was glad to help." And I was. Rescuing Guillermo gave me a real taste of what it would feel like to be a veterinarian, and it boosted my confidence too. I resolve to talk to Doc Wiggins about creative paths to vet school when things settle down.

After we say our good-byes, Finn and I head for the monster truck. We haven't technically spoken since we were reunited, and I have to say something before I chicken out.

"Uh . . . Finn?"

"Yeah?" He slows down a bit.

"You remember our conversation when we were trying to get your Blazer back on the road?" Of course he remembers. He thinks I shot him down.

"Yes."

"It's not a deal breaker."

He cocks his head, the familiar crease forming between his eyebrows.

"The genetic thing—it's not a deal breaker. I want to be friends . . . or whatever . . ." Heat rises on my neck. I sound like I've reverted to third grade and am communicating through those check-box messages. *Do you like me? Check yes or no or maybe.* "What I'm trying to say is I'm not quitting you."

He squeezes my hand, pulling me to a stop. "Even without guarantees?"

"Even without guarantees . . . and . . ." My palm sweats, but he doesn't seem to notice. Or if he does, it doesn't bother him.

"And?"

"You're *semi*-irresistible." I repeat almost exactly what he suggested I say earlier on the side of the road.

He bursts out laughing. When he pulls me under his arm for a side hug, his whole face lights up, including his dark green eyes. "And sexy?"

"Let's not get too crazy."

"Okay—not *too* crazy." He playfully pokes me in the side. "You ready to hit the road?"

"Beyond ready."

He gestures toward Zeke's truck. "Your carriage awaits."

It's not a glass carriage, and I don't feel like Cinderella. But who needs a carriage when you have an indestructible Franken-truck?

CHAPTER TWENTY-EIGHT

Ring out the false, ring in the true.

ALFRED, LORD TENNYSON

Squinting into the wind blowing through Franken-truck's mesh windows, I study the buildings and landscape as we head south. My mind reels at the stark contrasts. In some places, homes are leveled, stoplights are smashed on the road like Legos, and vehicles are overturned. Then a quarter mile down the road, some random house stands perfectly unscathed, looking out over the surrounding destruction, and asking *what happened?*

Finn's not speeding, or teasing me, or jerking the steering wheel today. He drives well below the speed limit, scanning the road for downed power lines and other dangers. We stick to the main bypass, only detouring if a portion is blocked. The rain has finally stopped, but standing water covers large sections of the road. When we stop at an intersection, there's no wind. It's like Zeke said—things are always changing.

One minute the wind blows, knocking down buildings. The next minute it's drying puddles after the storm. One minute it's blowing families apart. The next it's blowing a handful of random people together, teaching them to work together and opening their eyes to new ways of thinking.

Finn slows almost to a crawl, creeping around a bicycle lying on its side in the middle of the road. We've yet to encounter survivors or emergency personnel. Amid the chaos and destruction in the heart of Kitty Hawk, a flock of seagulls gathers in an empty parking lot—specks of white on a sheet of black asphalt.

"I guess it's a good sign the gulls are back," I say, pointing at the birds.

Finn nods but keeps his eyes glued to the road.

We pass the turn to school, and I wonder how Yesenia weathered the evacuation. She probably made a game out of it, or a party, or used it as an opportunity to check items off her bucket list.

Her bucket list.

Priority number one on her bucket list: Ask someone to the dance.

It would be fun to rock Yesenia's world—to go straight to the top of the list. She may never believe me, but it's worth a shot.

"When do you think we'll go back to school?" I ask, easing myself toward the epic question.

He shrugs. "Maybe next week—you know how islanders are about getting back to business."

The bridge to Manteo comes into view, completely unharmed by the storm of the century, like a tribute to modern-day engineering.

"You're ready to go back to school?" he asks, gripping the steering wheel with two hands. He hugs the side of the road to avoid a downed sign.

"I don't know yet. I guess it depends on Mom and Mere and how much we have to do at the house." I swallow reflexively.

I know Finn likes me. So why is this so terrifying? "Well . . . uh . . . if we have the dance next week, do you want to go?" I just spit it out.

"Huh?"

Franken-truck mounts the bridge and begins her ascent. Whitecaps froth the Albemarle Sound beneath us. If I didn't know better, I'd think we were crossing the ocean, not a shallow coastal inlet.

"Do you . . ." *Spit out the rest, Sophie.* "If we have a dance, do you want to go? With me, I mean?"

Finn stops the truck on the empty bridge. "Really?"

"Really."

He takes one hand off the steering wheel to squeeze my hand. I lace my fingers through his as we start moving again, and just like that we're cresting the bridge and descending. Sandbags and police cruisers block the road into Manteo. The grumpy old guy who was willing to go down with his house would be happy to know the cops are being super conscientious about who gets on the island to ward off looting before it starts. It looks like they're not letting anyone from the mainland onto the islands. Eventually, they'll allow people with proof of residence in areas deemed safe and then go from there. Thankfully, they wave us toward the mainland.

Even though I told Mom I was safe, albeit days ago, and even though she knows cell towers have been out, she must have been worried sick. So seeing her and Mere pressed up against the temporary barriers just past the police cruisers comes as no surprise. I wouldn't put it past her to be the first person to request access across the bridge. My heart soars when I see her messy ponytail and baggy *Horse hair, don't care* sweatshirt.

The small crowd gathered at the blockade watches our approach.

When I step out of Franken-truck, Mom's hands fly to her mouth. I break into a run. Finn follows close behind.

"Sophie! Sophie!" Mere waves. She clutches a sweater to her chest.

Without slowing down, I wave back.

The air whooshes from my lungs when I spot the clean-shaven, bright-eyed man standing behind her. And although his face is pinched with worry, his clothes are clean and his posture straight. I haven't seen this version of Dad in over a year.

My jaw tightens. I'm not prepared for this. I don't know what to say to him or how to act. I slow to a walk. Finn catches up.

"You okay?" he asks, seeming to sense something's not right.

"My dad's here," I say, my voice barely a whisper.

His eyes dart to the onlookers. "Are you good with that?"

"I'm not sure. I think." My eyes lock on Dad's frozen expression. He looks like he might crack down the middle.

Mom barrels toward me, tears streaming down her face. When she grabs me and pulls me against her chest, I lose sight of him.

"I was so worried." She tightens her hold on me.

"I'm fine, Mom." And I am.

Dad hangs several steps behind her, but Mere jumps into the group embrace with more enthusiasm than I've seen from her in a long time. Dad and Finn wait, seeming to understand we need a minute together. When I smile over Mere's shoulder at Finn, he flashes a thumbs-up.

Dad steps forward. His hand lifts as if he's going to touch my shoulder, but he catches himself. "Hi, Soph," he says.

I blink. I've practiced a million cold, spiteful comebacks in hopes that one day I'd have the opportunity to use one of them on him. My lips part, but most of the resentment's gone.

I swallow. "Hi . . . Dad."

I'm not welcoming him home with open arms, but I'm not shutting him out either. Reconciling with an absentee father wasn't exactly on Yesenia's bucket list, but she'd be proud of me anyway for taking the emotional risk.

I pull back from Mom and Mere, motioning Finn forward. "Do y'all remember Finn?"

"Yes! Yes, of course," Mom says.

Mere smiles and nods. Dad stands there, apparently uncertain whether he's part of the *y'all*.

"Finn, this is my family." I gesture toward all three of them.

When I glance over at Finn, a hint of sun breaks through the clouds above his head. It's the first time I've seen the sun in two days. Or is it three?

I've totally lost track of time.

And I'm good with that. In fact, I'm better than good.

I'm perfectly content to lose myself in this moment, surrounded by people I care about. There will be plenty of time tomorrow, and the next day, and the next for clocks, schedules, calendars, and alarms.

Right now, I choose to ride this perfect wave and to enjoy the blush of sun on my cheeks.

I choose my family.

And Finn.

And *kairos*.

CHAPTER TWENTY-NINE

'Tis not too late to seek a newer world.

ALFRED, LORD TENNYSON

It's amazing how the storm of the century shook up our lives. We still have tarps on the barn roof and fences that need to be patched. We lost a good saddle and some other tack. But two weeks after the super storm, the barn, house, and school are mostly back to normal. My physical world suffered damage but nothing that power tools and hard work won't eventually fix. My emotional world, on the other hand, evolved into something completely new and different.

I glance at myself in the full-length mirror, checking to make sure my lip gloss goes with my sleeveless peach dress, completely unembarrassed by the angry bruises and the long scab on my shoulder. In fact, I'm kind of proud of my injury. It's a reminder that no matter how horrible things look in the middle of a storm, chances are the sun will eventually peek out again.

"You look pretty," Mere says from her spot on my bed.

Jim completes a couple of circles on my faded quilt, then curls into a ball at her hip. Mere rests her hand on his head. Smiling, I join them on the edge of the bed.

We sit together in comfortable silence.

The breeze carries Mom's laughter floating in through the open window. She and her friend Carla sit on the front porch, drinking sweet tea and talking about whether to order seafood or Mexican for dinner. Two moms hanging out together on a Friday night might not be a big deal in most families, but it's huge at the March house. Mom seems to be squeezing out of her shell and starting to take some time for herself, to be with friends and get out into the world again instead of just focusing on me and Mere and all our troubles. Of course, she's been super busy putting our lives and the business back together, but I think the hurricane changed Mom too. She told me the storm made her realize she needed to stop focusing on what she lost and start appreciating what she did have. We hugged and cried until the tears on our cheeks ran together, but it was a good cry—the kind that left me feeling hopeful for her. For me. For all of us.

"That's Finn," I say when a car rumbles underneath the house.

Mere nods and scratches Jim behind the ears but makes no effort to leave the comfy spot on my bed. Even she has seemed a little happier these days. I've been wondering if Mere just needed a little room to breathe. Mom and I have been so busy putting the barn and house together that there hasn't been time to fuss over her, and honestly, Mere seems the better for it. She's getting her independence back slowly but surely, some-thing we probably should have helped her do long ago.

"Have fun," she says as I stand to leave.

I smile at her again. "I will." I lean down to give her a quick peck on the check before I head out to meet Finn.

When I grab the Sadie Hawkins dance tickets off the fridge, I see where Mom wrote Dad's number on the calendar for us. She and Dad have been texting and talking on the phone. He hasn't been home. None of us are ready for that, but it's good to know where he is, how he's doing, and that if we reach out in an emergency, he'll be there. When she contacted him about my being stranded on the island, he drove down from Virginia and immediately started organizing people to look for me. Thankfully, it hadn't come to that.

"Hey, you look good, Bookworm," Finn says when I step out on the deck.

The ocean breeze brushes my hair and face. The high temperatures finally broke after the storm, and the cool air feels nice on the heat rising on my cheeks. After a long pause, I find my voice. "You too, Finn."

And he does look really good. His black hair is shorter now and perfectly frames his eyes, making their green pop against his tan skin and highlighting the strength of his nose.

Mom and Carla stare at us all starry-eyed, like they're remembering high school dances of their own.

"Have fun," Mom says without standing. "And be careful."

"We will," Finn says, lacing his fingers through mine.

And we will. Finn's still Finn, thank goodness. But it seems like the storm or our time together has affected him as well. For one thing, he keeps his mom's car, which he's been driving since the storm, cleaner than he ever kept his own. For another, he's been trying to eat a little better—at least when we're together.

I lean down to give Mom a kiss too before following him to his car.

"You think Yesenia will be ready?" he asks as he holds the door open for me.

"Probably. She's pretty excited. And Alex was supposed to be at her house an hour ago." But then Yesenia's always pretty excited, especially when she can mark something huge off the bucket list, like inviting dates to the Sadie Hawkins dance.

I smile at recent additions to the front seat. Finn has tucked his duct-taped *Don't Sweat the Small Stuff* book in the compartment holders between the seats and a water bottle instead of a soda in the cup holder.

As he walks around to his side, I inhale deeply and relax against the headrest. The sun sets behind the barn in a kaleidoscope of reds and fuchsias, signaling a beautiful end to the day and hinting at the possibility of tomorrow.

And I remind myself to tell Yesenia about the Tennyson quote I found when I was studying earlier today. I'm surprised she's never used it on me. I wrote it in the notes on my phone and plan to live by it this year—*'Tis not too late to seek a newer world.*

She'll like it. I know I do. Even though I don't know exactly what the future holds, I've learned that I can't control everything. And that's okay. But I've also learned I don't have to compromise my dreams.

As Finn slides into the driver's seat and reaches for my hand, I promise myself I'll continue to chase those dreams, whether that's tonight at this dance, in my relationships with the people I care about, or even at vet school if that's what's meant to be.

An ocean-size smile stretches my face when I realize I'm starting to believe in happily-ever-afters after all.

Acknowledgments

I couldn't write without my patient and supportive family. They love me despite this roller coaster ride of publishing books. Thanks especially to my mom and husband but also to my children, my sister and brother, my stepfather, my in-laws, and all the rest. You know who you are. If you've listened to me talk about writing or come to a book event, I'm talking to you.

Thanks also to Laura Baker, one of the best writing coaches on the face of the planet. Her Discovering Story Magic lessons on character development and emotion always push me out of my comfort zone.

A huge thanks to my student and teacher friends, and especially to my principal, Suzanne Jarrard, who allowed me to teach part-time so I could write and revise all the words, and to Alan Arena, who read for me and talked plot.

Thanks to two of my best friends, who run and walk with me, albeit very slowly. Laurie Brown and Joy Parham have learned more about the business of writing and publishing than I'm sure they ever wanted or intended.

No writer could make it without her tribe, so thanks to my ever-growing circle of writing friends, my 2014 and 2016 Golden Heart Award sisters; my dear friends and critique partners, Holly Bodger and Kim McCarron; and especially Amy DeLuca, my critique partner and kindred spirit.

And of course, thanks to my dream agent, Amanda Leuck, and my dream editor, Jillian Manning. Without their belief in Sophie and her story, this book would not be possible.

Discussion Questions
for Meet the Sky

1. At the beginning of the book, Sophie avoids risks at all costs. Finn confronts them head-on. Which do you think is the healthier way to approach risk-taking? Why?

2. Alfred Lord Tennyson once said, "'Tis better to have loved and lost than never to have loved at all." Do you agree or disagree? Why?

3. As she and Finn experience the worsening storm together, Sophie gradually learns to give up control. When is a time you pushed yourself out of your comfort zone and gave up trying to control a situation? How did it work out for you? If you could, would you change how you handled the situation? Why or why not?

4. Each of the chapters opens with an epigraph—a line of Tennyson poetry. Which line spoke to you the most? Explain.

5. As an English teacher and a reader, I love symbolism. I love looking for hidden messages in the world around me. Did you notice any symbolism or motifs in *Meet*

the Sky? How did they add additional depth to the story?

6. If you didn't notice any symbolism or motifs, think about and discuss what symbols you might have used in *Meet the Sky* or in any story about learning to take risks.

7. All good stories are about dynamic characters that grow and change. What character do you think grows the most? Explain.

8. Obviously, the overriding theme of Sophie's story is one of learning to take risks, but there are several other underlying themes about the human spirit. What other themes did you notice, and how did they apply to you or the world around you?

9. How important do you think the setting of *Meet the Sky* is to Sophie's story? Would she be the same person and learn the same lessons without the Outer Banks and the hurricane? How does when and where you live affect all aspects of your life?

10. How important is Finn to Sophie's story? Would she have grown and learned the same lessons with another person? What sorts of people have you surrounded yourself with, and how do they affect your actions and emotions?

Interview with McCall Hoyle

1) **This is now your second book. How was writing *Meet the Sky* a different experience from writing *The Thing with Feathers*?**

   In *The Thing with Feathers*, most of the conflicts were internal issues that Emilie was struggling to overcome. There was danger, but it was mostly emotional danger. In *Meet the Sky*, Sophie is dealing with internal struggles and conflicts, but she's also got a hurricane to contend with and the whole issue of being stranded with a guy she doesn't like very much. The stories are very different, but I love them both and hope readers will too.

2) **Sophie is a girl who is carrying a lot of burdens in her life—watching over the family business, caring for her sister, and dealing with feelings of rejection after her dad left and Finn stood her up at her dance. And in many ways, she's allowed the past to shape her future. What inspired her character? And what do you hope readers take away from her story?**

   My father died unexpectedly when I was thirty. For several years, I was emotionally paralyzed by grief. I went about the business of living and raising my family and teaching, but I was frozen on the inside. Eventually, I was able to process a lot of my grief through writing. I never would have wanted to lose my dad so unexpectedly, but I learned a lot of important lessons about living every moment to the fullest and about opening my heart to others and taking risks. I want readers to think about how they can live their own lives to the fullest and embrace every day and all its ups and downs.

3) **Throughout *Meet the Sky*, the poetry of Tennyson makes an appearance, and Yesenia's favorite quote, "'Tis better to have loved and lost than never to have loved at all," plays a part in Sophie's decision to take some risks. What drew you to Tennyson's work, and how much did the quotes help shape the book, or vice versa?**

All the Tennyson epigraphs in the book are important, but it was really that one line that started the whole story. As I mentioned earlier, losing my father was the one event that has shaped my life more than any other. My dad was all about taking risks and trying new things. He was not afraid to fail and get back up again. He was brave—a lot like Finn. I think we can learn a lot from people like that, especially if we tend to be a bit reticent and want to try to control everything—pointing to self here. And I think Tennyson's quotation is about more than just taking risks in love. I think it's about taking risks in general.

4) **Like Sophie, you once lived in the Outer Banks of North Carolina. Can you share a little about that experience, and what drew you to use the setting in each of your books so far?**

The Outer Banks is the most ruggedly beautiful place I've ever lived or visited. The narrow strips of land that could have, maybe even should have, been wiped out by hurricanes and Nor' easters always weather the storms. There is something in the resilience of the place and its people that draws me back again and again

5) **Did you ever experience a hurricane or storm while you lived in North Carolina? If so, what was the experience like?**

I lived on the Outer Banks of North Carolina after graduating from college. I was newly married at the time. Mostly, I'm a scaredy cat, so we generally evacuated long before a storm made landfall. e did stay on the island for a Category One torm. The powerful force of nature was both terrifying and awe-inspiring, and that was during a minimal storm. I cannot imagine being on an island in an even more powerful storm.

6) **While he makes a brief appearance, Jim the cat is a very special feline in the book. Can you tell us more about him, and what inspired you to place him in the book?**

I am an animal lover and strongly believe we have much to learn about being better humans from animals. Jim is based on a cat that adopted my family. I often contemplate his amazingness. He is the true definition of a survivor. That little cat with his three-and-a-half legs has been through a lot of trauma. His horrific past could have made him really skittish, but it didn't. He is the most trusting and content creature I've ever met, and he knows how to live in the moment. I think there is a really important lesson in there for most of us.

7) **Now for some fun questions. What things would you write down if you made a bucket list? Are there any items you feel you've already crossed off that list?**

Some things I've always wanted to do but haven't had

the time or the opportunity yet are: hike the Appalachian Trail, see grizzly bears in the wild, visit Alaska, compete with my dog in agility competitions, read the Bible cover-to-cover without skipping around.

Some things I've actually checked off are: finishing a marathon and publishing a book.

8) **If you were stuck inside a closet during a bad storm, what would you grab to keep yourself entertained while you waited out the weather?**

Easy. Books and a book light.

9) **What is your favorite part about being an author?**

Hands down, the best part of being an author is seeing my books in the hands of my own high school and middle school students. A very, very close second is meeting new readers, teachers, and librarians and talking about books and the world.

10) **Finally, what are you working on next?**

I have so many ideas right now. I'm trying to narrow down the list. I feel certain readers can count on an uplifting story about a teenage girl who is either braver or stronger than she originally thinks.

Emilie Day believes in playing it safe: she's homeschooled, her best friend is her seizure dog, and she's probably the only girl on the Outer Banks of North Carolina who can't swim.

Then Emilie's mom enrolls her in public school, and Emilie goes from studying at home in her pj's to halls full of strangers. To make matters worse, Emilie is paired with starting point guard Chatham York for a major research project on Emily Dickinson. She should be ecstatic when Chatham shows interest, but she has a problem. She hasn't told anyone about her epilepsy.

Emilie lives in fear her recently adjusted meds will fail and she'll seize at school. Eventually, the worst happens, and she must decide whether to withdraw to safety or follow a dead poet's advice and "dwell in possibility."

From Golden Heart award-winning author McCall Hoyle comes *The Thing with Feathers*, a story of overcoming fears, forging new friendships, and finding a first love, perfect for fans of Jennifer Niven, Robyn Schneider, and Sharon M. Draper.

Available now wherever books are sold!

BLINK

About the Author

McCall Hoyle writes honest YA novels about friendship, first love, and girls finding the strength to overcome great challenges. She is a high school English teacher. Her own less-than-perfect teenage experiences and those of the girls she teaches inspire many of the struggles in her books. When she's not reading or writing, she's spending time with her family and their odd assortment of pets—a food-obsessed beagle, a grumpy rescue cat, and a three-and-a-half-legged kitten. She has an English degree from Columbia College and a master's degree from Georgia State University. She lives in a cottage in the woods in North Georgia, where she reads and writes every day. Learn more at mcallhoyle.com.